THE OF COUNSEL AGREEMENT

A Guide for Law Firm and Practitioner

Second Edition

HAROLD G. WREN

BEVERLY J. GLASCOCK

Senior Lawyers Division ABA American Bar Association

Cover design by Lauren Manning.

02 01 00 99 98 5 4 3 2 1

Wren, Harold G., 1921–
The of counsel agreement / Harold Wren, Beverly Glascock. —2nd. ed.
p. cm.
Rev. ed. of: The of counsel agreement. c1991.
Includes bibliographical references and index.
ISBN 1-57073-539-5 (pbk.)
1. "Of counsel" relationships (Practice of law)—United States.
I. Glascock, Beverly J. II. Wren, Harold G., 1921– Of counsel agreement. III. Title.
KF310.034W74 1998
3476.73'504—dc21 98-11278
CIP

Discounts are available for books ordered in bulk. Special consideration is given to state bars, CLE programs, and other bar-related organizations. Inquire at ABA Publishing, Book Publishing, American Bar Association, 750 North Lake Shore Drive, Chicago, Illinois 60611.

CONTENTS

Preface to Second Edition xi

Preface to First Edition xiii

CHAPTER I
Of Counsel: A New Status 1
Principal Patterns of Relationships 2
The Part-Time Lawyer 2
The Second Career 4
The Retired Partner 6
The Probationary Partner-to-Be 6
A Permanent Status 7
Other Relationships 8

CHAPTER II
Defining "Of Counsel" 13
The Model Code and ABA Informal Opinions 13
Formal Opinion 330 18
A "Close, Continuing, Personal" Relationship 19
"Not a Partner, Associate, or Outside Consultant" 20
Methods of Compensation 21
Multiple Of Counsel Relationships 22
Law Firms As Of Counsel 23
Advertising the Of Counsel Relationship 24
Summary 25

CHAPTER III
Of Counsel Revisited: Formal Opinion 90-357 27
Designations Governed by Formal Opinion 90-357 28
Permissible Patterns of Relationships 29
Impermissible Patterns of Relationships 30

Core Characteristics of an Of Counsel Relationship **30**
A "Close, Regular, Personal" Relationship **31**
Required Contact with the Firm **32**
Law Firms Of Counsel to One Another **32**
Specialty Counsel **34**
Compensation **35**
Partner or Associate Status Is Not Permissible **37**
Employee Status Is Permissible **37**
Multiple Of Counsel Relationships **38**
Law Firms As Of Counsel **39**
Of Counsel's Name in the Firm's Name **40**
Summary **41**

CHAPTER IV
Particular Of Counsel Relationships after Formal Opinion 90-357 **42**
Specifically Permitted Of Counsel Relationships **43**
The Retired Partner **43**
The Part-Time Practitioner **47**
The Probationary Partner **48**
The Senior Attorney **49**
Specifically Prohibited Of Counsel Relationships **51**
The Lawyer Associated in a Single Case **51**
The Forwarder-Receiver of Legal Business **52**
The Occasional Collaborator **52**
Of Counsel or Outside Consultant? **53**
Other Of Counsel Relationships **56**
The Public Official **56**
The Law Professor **58**
The Out-of-State Of Counsel **58**
Expense-Sharing Arrangements **59**
Liberalized Rules Governing Of Counsel Relationships **60**
The Law Firm As Of Counsel **61**
Multiple Of Counsel Relationships **64**
Of Counsel's Name in the Firm's Name **66**
Summary **68**
Checklist **70**

CHAPTER V
Distinguishing Of Counsel from Other Legal Relationships after Formal Opinion 90-357 **73**
Of Counsel Contrasted with Partner **75**

Avoiding the Appearance of a Partnership 77
Of Counsel Contrasted with Associate 79
Of Counsel As Employee or Independent Contractor 80
Of Counsel and Contractual Liability 82
Of Counsel and Tort Liability 83
Of Counsel and Income Taxation 84
Business Deductions 84
Social Security Taxes 84
Right to Discharge, Right to Terminate 86
Of Counsel Contrasted with Outside Consultant 86
Conflicts of Interest 87
Compensation 87
Summary 89
Checklist 90

CHAPTER VI
Of Counsel and Legal Malpractice 92
Introduction 92
Vicarious Liability in Tort 93
Liability Based on Contractual Arrangements 94
Independent Contractors 94
The Of Counsel Relationship 95
Associated Counsel 103
Express or Implied Partnership 105
Partnership by Estoppel 108
Summary 111
Checklist 112

CHAPTER VII
Of Counsel and Conflicts of Interest 113
The Duties of the Lawyer 114
Common Conflict Problems under the Model Rules 115
Effect of Formal Opinion 90-357 on Conflict Problems 117
Conflicts in Simultaneous Representation 118
Conflicts in Successive Representation 121
Advancing Inconsistent Positions 123
Determining Disqualification of Of Counsel 124
The Peripheral-Representation Exception 124
Summary 126
Checklist 127

CHAPTER VIII
Imputed Disqualification and the Of Counsel Relationship 129
Rules Governing Imputed Disqualification **129**
The Presumption of Shared Confidences **130**
Present Affiliates: Irrebuttable Presumption **130**
Former Affiliates: Rebuttable Presumption **131**
The Chinese Wall **136**
Affiliated Law Firms **138**
Former Government Employees **141**
Imputed Disqualification and the Lawyer As Witness **143**
Summary **145**
Checklist **146**

CHAPTER IX
Advertising the Of Counsel Relationship 147
Lawyer Advertising and Solicitation **148**
History of Lawyer Advertising **149**
The Effect of the First Amendment on Lawyer Advertising **150**
Current Ethics Rules Governing Lawyer Advertising **154**
Current Ethics Rules Governing Solicitation **157**
Advertising and Soliciting the Of Counsel Relationship **159**
Of Counsel's Name in the Firm Name **160**
Listing Out-of-State Of Counsel on Letterhead **162**
Listing Areas of Specialization on Letterhead **163**
Summary **164**
Checklist **165**

CHAPTER X
Uses of the Of Counsel Agreement 166
The Retired Partner **166**
Terms of the Agreement **167**
Independent Contractor v. Employer-Employee Relationship **169**
Tax Advantages of the Independent Contractor Status **169**
Financial Planning and Retirement **172**
Social Security **172**
Medicare **173**
Taxation of Social Security Benefits **174**
Health Care Reform **175**
The Part-Time Lawyer **178**
Of Counsel As a Vehicle for Firm Organization **182**

CHAPTER XI
Planning and Drafting the Of Counsel Agreement 187
Planning the Of Counsel Agreement **188**
Essential Terms of the Of Counsel Agreement **189**
Title and Status **189**
Duties **191**
Compensation **193**
Effect of Pension Plan Payments **195**
Overhead **196**
Fringe Benefits **198**
Right to Terminate **200**
Summary **200**
Checklist **200**

APPENDIX A
Employment Agreement by and between John Q. Lawyer and XYZ, a Partnership [Employee and Partnership Employer] 203

APPENDIX B
Of Counsel Agreement [Independent Contractor and Partnership] 212

APPENDIX C
Of Counsel Agreement [Independent Contractor and Partnership] 215

APPENDIX D
Of Counsel Agreement [Independent Contractor and Professional Service Corporation] 218

APPENDIX E
Of Counsel Agreement [Independent Contractor and Partnership] 223

APPENDIX F
Of Counsel Agreement [Letterhead of Law Firm] 227

APPENDIX G
Of Counsel Agreement [Letterhead of Law Firm] 230

APPENDIX H
Formal Opinion 330 (August 1972) 233

APPENDIX I
Formal Opinion 90-357 (May 10, 1990) 238

Table of Cases 245

Index 249

About the Authors 257

In loving memory of our fathers

PREFACE TO THE SECOND EDITION

In the seven years that have passed since the First Edition of this book, there have been a number of developments in the law affecting the Of Counsel Agreement. Although we have no statistical data, anecdotal evidence indicates the following trends:

- The Of Counsel arrangement is being increasingly used for a variety of purposes other than retirement planning.
- The courts are more concerned than ever about the importance of conflicts and imputed disqualification.
- Legal malpractice suits are becoming far more common, with a corresponding increase in malpractice insurance rates.
- The fiduciary responsibility of lawyers toward their clients is being given greater consideration in legal malpractice cases.
- The possibility of lawyers being held liable to third parties for malpractice, either directly or vicariously, is on the increase.

A well-drafted Of Counsel Agreement becomes essential for any law firm or lawyer who chooses to enter into this arrangement. We have added some newer drafts of possible contracts, which the law firm or Of Counsel may find helpful in drafting its own contract to meet its particular needs.

In addition to those persons mentioned in the Preface to the First Edition, we wish to express our thanks to Leigh B. Middleditch, Jr., Chair of the Senior Lawyers Division of the American Bar Association; John H. Pickering, Immediate Past Chair of the Division; and George H. Cain, Chair, Book Committee. We do appreciate all the efforts of Richard G. Paszkiet, Executive Editor, Book Publishing, ABA Publishing, and his staff, for their assistance in the production of this Second Edition. We would also like to express our deep appreciation to John R. Glascock, Jr., Amy M.

Thorpe, and Francis J. Mellen, Jr., who encouraged us in this second endeavor. Finally, thanks to all those readers of the First Edition who gave us encouragement and many helpful ideas.

Harold G. Wren
Beverly J. Glascock

PREFACE TO THE FIRST EDITION

In the not too distant past, it was common for law firms to list certain distinguished members of the community on their letterheads as being "Of Counsel." One of the authors remembers how puzzled he was by this nomenclature when he was a young lawyer associated with what was then considered a fairly large firm. The firm listed a former governor of the state as being "Of Counsel." He never saw this particular gentleman around the office, and he wondered just what his role would be. Someone suggested that he was the firm's lawyer. For example, if the firm ever needed representation in court, then this very distinguished gentleman would serve as its lawyer. This made little sense to him, since he felt that the firm would certainly be able to represent itself if such a situation should arise. More recently, he has asked a retired state supreme court justice what he thought the phrase meant, and the judge replied that this was a designation that a law firm commonly used for persons whom it might occasionally ask to do things for the firm for no compensation. Whatever the phrase means, it is highly ambiguous, and it may well mean a variety of things depending upon the manner in which it is used.

Today, we doubt that many law firms use the designation "Of Counsel" as a way of decorating their letterheads. But the legal profession has found a number of new uses of the designation that are consonant with both a word and a profession that are rapidly changing. As a result, the Senior Lawyers Division of the American Bar Association was called upon by lawyers all over the country for guidance and advice in establishing an Of Counsel relationship.

Most of their recommendations were based upon Formal Opinion 330—issued in 1972 by the Standing Committee on Ethics and Professional Responsibility of the American Bar Association—the first formal opinion to define what the relationship entails. That opinion remained unchanged until May 10, 1990, when the committee issued Formal Opinion 90-357. Formal Opinion 90-357 expressly superseded Formal Opinion 330 and a number of informal opinions upon which 330 was based. The principal effect of 90-357 was to give the legal profession freedom to contract for an Of Counsel relationship in a variety of different situations, without being forced onto a procrustean bed that neither side desired.

The purpose of this book is to guide lawyers and law firms that are contemplating entry into an Of Counsel relationship. We have sought to describe the fact situations that make this arrangement particularly desirable and the legal doctrines that may impose some limitations on the parties' complete freedom to contract as they desire.

For purposes of readability, where the term "Of Counsel" appears, we have chosen to capitalize the initial letters of the two words and to use neither a hyphen nor quotation marks. We have also chosen to use the masculine gender when singular personal pronouns are in order. We have made these choices solely for purposes of style and readability, and it is our fervent hope that no reader will be offended.

We would like to express our deep appreciation to Robert M. Ervin, Esq., Don M. Jackson, Esq., John W. Storer, Jr., Esq., E. Charles Eichenbaum, Esq., and F. William McCalpin, Esq., officers of the Senior Lawyers Division of the American Bar Association, who encouraged us in this endeavor; to Victor Futter, Esq., Chair, Publications Committee, Senior Lawyers Division of the American Bar Association, who read the manuscript with great care; to Susan Yessne and Joseph Weintraub of the ABA Press; and to Rina Moore, our resident word processor expert. Finally, we wish to thank those members of the bar who shared with us their experiences with the Of Counsel relationship.

CHAPTER I

Of Counsel: A New Status

At one time, the Of Counsel designation was used to show that a law firm had powerful friends in high places. The listing of a senator, congressional representative, or former judge available to talk to the partners of the firm if needed was perhaps the most important use of the phrase.[1] This use of the designation is now all but obsolete. In today's world, few clients, particularly large corporate ones, are impressed by the names that a law firm might place on its letterhead; few law firms would even find it necessary or desirable to do this. Yet the *New Jersey Law Journal* reported, "Firms are even signing on of counsel as a marketing tool, in much the same way that corporations seek out famous names for their boards of directors."[2]

Aside from decorating a firm's letterhead, the phrase "Of Counsel" has been most commonly used for those partially or fully

1. A writer in the *Maryland Bar Journal* describes this type of Of Counsel as follows:

> They were the elder statesmen, the distinguished gentlemen of the old school, who functioned primarily as firms' goodwill ambassadors. They lent legitimacy and prestige to a firm, and in return they were given the benefits of firm membership without the pressure to perform and make a serious time commitment.

2. Adler, *Of Counsel: A New Breed*, 122 N.J.L.J. 1 (Dec. 29, 1988), hereinafter cited as "Adler."

retired from the practice of law. A retired partner would use the designation to describe an honorary status with the firm whether or not the retired partner actually maintained a professional working relationship with it.

Using the designation in these limited settings is no longer the case. The Of Counsel designation is now used in so many different contexts that one cannot assign a single meaning to it. Contracting parties use it in several different ways depending upon what they wish to accomplish. For example, the term might be used to describe a relationship between a law firm and a lawyer who works part-time for the firm and devotes the balance to an otherwise solo law practice, law teaching, or a totally unrelated business endeavor. Or, it might be used to describe the relationship between a law firm and an expert in an area of law in which the firm does not think of itself as being particularly well qualified. In short, the precise meaning of "Of Counsel," a vague term that for years was never formally defined, has become even more ambiguous. This book seeks to add a measure of definition and precision to it.

Principal Patterns of Relationships

Each Of Counsel arrangement is unique, yet distinct patterns can be identified. In practice, Of Counsel relationships have followed four principal patterns: (1) part-time lawyers, including those who have recently changed careers; (2) retired partners who do not actively practice law on a full- or part-time basis but occasionally consult with their former firm; (3) probationary partners-to-be, who view the Of Counsel status as a stepping-stone to full partner status; and (4) lawyers who have attained a permanent status within a firm but do not expect to attain full partner status.

The Part-Time Lawyer

For a variety of reasons, some lawyers are not interested in practicing law on a full-time basis, yet desire to have a relationship with a law firm that enables them to receive complete logistical support (secretarial service, telephone, computer services, law library, and so on), which would not be justified economically for someone practicing on a part-time basis. From the standpoint of the law firm, the partners and associates receive the benefit of such a lawyer's expertise or the special personal relationships the lawyer who is Of Counsel may have developed.

There are innumerable situations in which a lawyer might wish to practice law on a part-time basis only. For instance, a senior lawyer may choose an Of Counsel arrangement with the former firm as an alternative to retirement.[3] A younger lawyer may enter a part-time Of Counsel arrangement as a way of becoming affiliated with a firm. Part-time Of Counsel arrangements are ideal for lawyers who want to devote a fixed number of hours per week to the practice and be free to do other things the rest of the week. The arrangement can be particularly attractive to the young lawyer familiar with modern technology (including LEXIS, WESTLAW, photocopying, word processing, e-mail, Internet, fax, and modems, as well as telephone answering, call-waiting, and call-forwarding systems) to carry on a highly effective law practice at home.

Mimi Azrael, a lawyer in Maryland, likes being Of Counsel because it gives her greater autonomy and control of her time than she would have as a partner. As a litigator, she can be selective about the kinds of cases she works on, and pursue more pro bono work that reflects well on her firm. Ms. Azrael has said:

> There is a great synergy in the arrangement. It serves me, the firm, and ultimately, the client, well. Clients get both the security of a general practice firm and the services of a specialist. Everyone is satisfied.[4]

Fay Hartog, Of Counsel to the large Chicago firm Seyfarth, Shaw, Fairweather & Geraldson, is typical of the young mother who prefers Of Counsel status over the traditional associate-to-partner promotion track. After the birth of her second child, Hartog left the firm to accept a less demanding and more flexible position as in-house counsel with a suburban school district. The firm invited her to "drop in occasionally as an Of Counsel." She ended up working two jobs fifty to sixty hours a week.

After going through a divorce in 1987, and eventually remarrying, she became Of Counsel formally with the firm, and is now compensated according to her billings. She says:

> I direct my own activities and don't have to let anyone know. I also don't have to sit on committees, deal with promotional activities, or go to the firm retreats. I'm also not an economic

---

3. Some firms use Of Counsel as a form of "disguised retirement, wherein older attorneys cut back their hours and responsibilities. They could be eased into receiving smaller draws or just earning a salary, instead of having to leave cold turkey." Buchholz, *Of Counsel: It's not just for retiring anymore*, 81 A.B.A.J. 70 (Oct. 1995), hereinafter cited as "Buchholz."

4. Quoted in the *Maryland Bar Journal*. See also Buchholz, *supra* note 3.

> burden on the firm. The most important thing I have is control over my life, which puts me in charge of the benefits and the risks.[5]

From the standpoint of the law firm, such a lawyer must be able to offer something the firm needs, whether this be expertise, contacts, or the answer to some other special need, before the parties will be able to reach a mutually satisfactory agreement.

Jeff Kolton's situation in Washington, D.C., provides another illustration of a synergistic relationship wherein both Of Counsel and the firm profit from their relationship. In 1989, Kolton founded FranData Corp. to provide franchise market research information. Kolton became Of Counsel to Lewis & Trattner, a law firm specializing in franchising and licensing. Warren L. Lewis, partner, points out the advantages of the arrangement with Kolton:

> Jeff has a lot of exposure in the [franchising] industry. He's well-known and respected, and we get to do the primary serving for his clients. We tend to meet several times a week, and have lunch every other week to stay in touch.[6]

FranData's office is within walking distance of the firm's office, and the two offices are linked by computer. FranData's staff consists of seven full-time and five part-time employees. Lewis & Trattner pays for Kolton's malpractice insurance, bar memberships, and marketing costs, but not his health insurance. Kolton says: "I'm bringing in more clients and am very comfortable with the style of the attorneys at the firm."[7]

The Second Career

George M. Cain of the Senior Lawyers Division has written an excellent book, *Turning Points*,[8] outlining a variety of situations in which, for one reason or another, lawyers have chosen a new direction in their lives. In some cases, these are younger people who have chosen a completely new career. In other instances, they involve older lawyers who are leaving the academic world, corporate

---

5. Quoted in Buchholz, *supra* note 3.
6. Quoted in Buchholz, *supra* note 3.
7. *Id.*
8. GEORGE M. CAIN, TURNING POINTS (ABA Publishing 1994).

counsel positions, public office, the legislature, or the judiciary.[9] Whatever their background, such persons bring a high degree of expertise and wisdom to any law firm to which they might become Of Counsel.

Lawyers who have been active in these roles find the Of Counsel arrangement well suited to their particular needs. Experienced professionals can act in a supervisory role by reviewing briefs of partners and associates, helping where a high degree of expertise is required, and serving the firm in other useful ways.

Harry Blumenthal, now a partner in his own Maryland firm, was Of Counsel from 1983 to 1996. During this period, he ran his own insurance company and maintained a practice in Florida, and was still able to work a four-day week as Of Counsel to the firm in Maryland.

The Of Counsel arrangement is unique in that it allows a measure of independence for a lawyer to develop his own clients while continuing to work in conjunction with the firm on firm matters. Needless to say, the lawyer and the law firm must both pay close attention to potential conflicts of interest.[10]

A recent situation in New York illustrates a typical conflict. David Boies, Jr., a prominent litigator and partner in the prestigious firm of Cravath Swaine & Moore, chose to represent George M. Steinbrenner, Jr., in a suit against Major League Baseball. When the managing partner discovered that there was a conflict because of the firm's representation of Time Warner, Inc., owner of the Atlanta Braves, Boies left the firm. Steven Brill, publisher of the *American Lawyer* and founder of Court TV, described Cravath's loss: "[I]t's like it's 1956, and Mickey Mantle is suddenly a free agent."[11]

Had Boies been Of Counsel to the firm, rather than partner, his situation would have been no different. In representing Steinbrenner, he would still be faced with a potential conflict. Whether or not Major League Baseball will seek to disqualify him by reason of his prior association with Cravath remains to be seen.

---

9. Adler, *supra* note 2. Some state constitutions have mandatory retirement for judges, typically at age seventy. Through December 31, 1993, institutions of higher education were free to impose mandatory retirement on tenured law professors at age seventy. *See* 29 U.S.C. § 631(d), as amended by Pub. L. No. 99-592, § 6(a), as repealed effective Dec. 31, 1993, by Pub. L. No. 99-592, § 6(b).

10. *See* Chapters 7 and 8.

11. *See* Buchholz, *supra* note 3.

The Retired Partner

Many Of Counsel arrangements are based on a common fact pattern: After retirement from a firm, the former partner continues to consult and advise the firm on an occasional basis. While this arrangement is sometimes deemed a form of disguised retirement,[12] it remains a useful device in structuring a law firm. It provides the lawyer with a transition period without responsibility for the day-to-day problems of law practice. Rather than worry about deadlines, bottom lines, and productivity, the retiree may practice or not, and still have time to devote to other interests.

From the firm's standpoint, the retired partner can be called on to help solve other problems that arise within the firm. The retiree can represent the firm at bar association and other professional meetings, make speeches before laypersons, or train new lawyers of the firm in the practice of law. Most important, the firm can rely on the retired partner to contribute the wisdom essential to any successful practice. Some retired partners who become Of Counsel to their former firm may continue to draw a salary. While not determinative, this could be an indication that Of Counsel was an employee, and not an independent contractor. Others lend their expertise for no compensation at all. In either situation, the retired partner may or may not be receiving payments from the firm's pension or other retirement plan. Whatever the retired partner may receive as pension from the firm must be carefully coordinated with any other monetary arrangements made with the firm by reason of being Of Counsel.[13]

The Probationary Partner-to-Be

The concept of Of Counsel is often used where a law firm desires to bring in a highly talented or experienced lawyer but is reluctant to make such a person a partner. This arrangement is advantageous both to the firm and the lawyer involved. Corporate counsel who have had extensive experience in the business world, labor lawyers who have worked in industrial relations, younger lawyers with specific professional skills, former partners of law firms that have been dissolved—all welcome a tryout relationship before it becomes permanent.

---

12. *See* Buchholz, *supra* note 3.

13. *See* discussion of problems of Of Counsel and retirement, *infra* Chapter 10.

Howard Kaplan, a partner with Horn, Kaplan, Goldberg, Gorny & Daniels, of Atlantic City, says, "We have hired as of counsel younger guys who wanted to come in as partner; we didn't want to become married until we were engaged."[14] The probationary partner-to-be has too much experience and/or expertise to come into the firm as an associate, but not enough to warrant his becoming a partner of the firm. For example:

> William W. Weisner's move to of counsel at the large New York City firm of Patterson, Belknap, Webb & Tyler was spurred by slightly different considerations. Although a partner at Graham and James' New York office, which is based in San Francisco, he wanted to be associated with a headquarters office rather than a branch. He also wished to remain in New York.
>
> Finally, Weisner, 36, wanted to be part of a firm that was interested in expanding its real estate practice, yet one in which he could play an important role rather than just be "another cog in the wheel. . . . This isn't a 40-person department, but one with eight attorneys."
>
> While Weisner brought real estate clients to his new firm, neither he nor Patterson, Belknap could value the amount of billings and decided for a look-see period. Thus the of counsel title offers firms an easier way to bring in experienced lawyers than through hiring lateral partners.[15]

A Permanent Status

While the Of Counsel arrangement is often useful as a steppingstone to full partner status, the term is also used to designate a permanent status, ranking between those of partner and associate. Although various terms are used to describe this post ("senior attorney,"[16] "resident counsel," "principal attorney," and the like), all have one unifying characteristic: Neither the law firm nor the lawyer has any expectation that the one so designated will be promoted to partner status. The advantage of this arrangement is that

---

14. *See* Adler, *supra* note 2, at 4.

15. Buchholz, *supra* note 3 at 71, quoting Weisner.

16. Barbara Buchholz reports that the use of this term is now passe. *See* Buchholz, *supra* note 3. Since Formal Opinion 90-357, the other terms mentioned in the text are also passing out of use. The term "Of Counsel" will be used in place of the various terms mentioned in the text as it acquires a word-of-art meaning.

the lawyer's status has a quality of tenure coupled with a measure of independence.

Avory Aisenstark, a full-time Associate Baltimore City Solicitor, is also Of Counsel to Adelberg, Rudow, Dorf, Hendler & Sameth, L.L.C. He works with the law firm in the areas of appellate litigation and administrative law. Aisenstark says:

> I didn't want to practice law on my own; I wanted an arrangement with an established firm, and I wanted to work among other lawyers and to have support services. Being an Of Counsel means only that I am other than a formal employee.

There are any number of situations in which the Of Counsel arrangement will be used to satisfy some special need of the firm or Of Counsel.

In one case, a large law firm notified an associate that it was unlikely that he would "make partner," despite his excellent record. He had devoted his energies to one corporate client, who was completely satisfied and delighted with his services. Rather than run the risk of losing the client, or having the lawyer leave the firm, it offered him a permanent Of Counsel position with a high salary and excellent benefits. When the lawyer accepted, all parties were satisfied: The firm kept its client; the lawyer continued the work that he enjoyed, with complete financial security; and the client was happy that he would continue to represent it without having to retain additional counsel.

Other Relationships

Sometimes two or more law firms in different localities may enter into an Of Counsel relationship with each other. Law Firm A will become Of Counsel to Law Firm B, and vice versa. While these arrangements are perfectly appropriate,[17] they must be carefully drafted if the parties are to avoid problems of conflicts, imputed disqualification, and malpractice.[18]

There are obvious risks in this arrangement. It may be impractical to list on their respective business cards, letterheads, and so forth the nature of the precise relationship. Arguably, one firm might be deemed to be an independent contractor in relation to the other and avoid vicarious liability for each other's torts; but most courts would probably be unwilling to adopt this view.

---

17. ABA Formal Op. 90-357; *see* discussion *infra* Chapter 4, at pp. 66 *et seq*.
18. *See infra* Chapters 6, 7, and 8.

The merger of two or more law firms, often in two or more jurisdictions, is no longer an unusual event. When this occurs, the new firm must examine the client lists of the former firms, and avoid any representations that might result in conflicts or imputed disqualification.

When a lawyer moves from one partnership to another and brings a client along, the second firm and its lawyers may know little or nothing about the new lawyer's client, and yet risk exposure to potential malpractice liability.[19]

In 1985, Monon Corporation retained Henry Price, then with Barnes & Thornburg in Indianapolis, to represent it in a lawsuit against Wabash National Corporation and its employees, for patent infringement. Monon specifically instructed Price that in any formal agreement between the parties, he should not release Wabash from any patent infringement claims related to a specific patent application filed by Monon in 1985. Despite this instruction, Price released Wabash. When the patent was later issued in 1990, and Monon sued to enjoin Wabash for patent infringement and for damages, the release operated to bar Monon from relief.

Monon then brought suit against Price and the law firm, Townsend, Yosha, Cline & Price, with whom Price was connected at the time of the release. His precise role in the firm, his relationship with the other lawyers, and their relationships with one another were not clearly defined. One of the lawyers, Yosha, practiced law as Louis Buddy Yosha, Professional Corporation (LBYPC). Even within the firm, the principals were unsure of their relationships with one another: Townsend claimed that he never heard of LBYPC until Monon filed its lawsuit; Yosha testified:

> Q . . . [I]s it fair to describe Townsend, Yosha, Cline & Price as an association of lawyers?
>
> A I don't know what I would put on it. No, I said I told you before I can't tell you the label. I can tell you what it's not. If you say: Is it fair to say it? Yeah, that doesn't bother me. An association of lawyers, I don't know. I couldn't dispute that and say, no, we weren't an association of lawyers.[20]

Cline was unaware of Price's role in the firm, at least so far as Monon was concerned:

---

19. *See*, generally, Chapter 6, *infra*.

20. Monon Corporation v. Townsend, Yosha, Cline & Price, et al., Case No. 49A02-9511-CV-675, 686 N.E.2d __ (Ind. App. 1997).

> Nobody . . . other than Price interacted with this client or his case at all. . . . Henry really had his own operation within our firm. I didn't even know about this case or this client, and I ended up getting sued.
>
> I just think they took their shotgun out and decided to shoot everything in sight with their lawsuit.[21]

In the trial court, the lawyers moved for summary judgment, contending that they were employees of LBYPC,[22] and were not liable for Price's tort. In reversing the lower court's decision in their favor, the Indiana Court of Appeals ruled:

> [T]he record contains sufficient evidence and inferences from which the trier of fact could conclude that the firm of Townsend, Yosha, Cline & Price was a partnership. The firm here used the name of Townsend, Yosha, Cline & Price on its letterhead, cards, listings, pleadings, and agreements, without any language of limitation. Some of the attorneys referred to each other as partners, or may have done so, and signed documents as partners. . . . Further, the Attorneys would take "draws" and "bonuses" based upon the fees which came into the firm.[23]
>
> . . . [T]he evidence supports the view that they carried on as co-owners of a business for profit. . . . [A] genuine issue of

21. *See* Swiatek, *Ruling on Rule 27,* THE INDIANA LAWYER, v. 8, no. 1, at 1, 29.

22. It would be possible to organize a law firm so that lawyers in the firm would all be Of Counsel to the firm leader, whether the leader was a wholly owned professional corporation, or simply an individual. Each lawyer, other than the firm leader, would be an independent contractor vis-à-vis the leader or the corporation. Such a form of business organization would not necessarily relieve the leader or the corporation from liability for the torts of the lawyers, but it would insulate each lawyer from liability for the torts of fellow lawyers. See discussion *infra,* Chapter X, at pp. 183–84. The Indiana State Bar Association and the Indiana Supreme Court have suggested that Indiana Admission and Discipline Rule 27 be modified to allow lawyers to join other professionals in forming limited liability entities (LLEs). Attorneys forming an LLE would not be personally liable for each other's conduct, but would be required to carry legal malpractice insurance.

23. Monon Corporation, *supra* note 20, at 8. Monon sued not only the lawyers and the firm, but also any successor partnerships, such as those that Yosha and Cline created after the malpractice incident.

fact exists about whether the firm really was a partnership for the purposes of vicarious liability.[24]

Monon dramatizes the importance of using care in drafting Of Counsel and partnership agreements. One of Monon's lawyers has commented:

> [Y]osha and those who claim to be employees thought they could shield themselves from liability, yet represent themselves to the public as partners. . . . This case holds now that you have to be very careful when you're representing to others whom you have an affiliation with.[25]

Had Price joined the Townsend firm as Of Counsel in an independent contractor status, with careful drafting of the Of Counsel agreement, much of the vicarious liability might have been avoided.

A number of important principles are illustrated by *Monon*:

- In the usual partnership, each partner is an agent and principal of the other, and each is vicariously liable for the other's torts.
- Under Indiana's Professional Corporation Act of 1983, the vicarious liability for legal malpractice is the same as would be the case if the firm were a partnership engaged in the practice of law.
- LBYPC was one of the partners of the Townsend, Yosha, Cline & Price partnership. The other partners were not "employees" of the professional corporation, as the lawyers contended.
- Even if the firm were not considered an actual partnership, the court might well find the lawyers to be a partnership by estoppel, since "the Attorneys held themselves out as a partnership and . . . Monon relied on their representations to its detriment."
- Monon was free to amend its complaint, adding LBYPC and various later partnerships in which the lawyers practiced as parties defendant.

Although *Monon* does not involve the Of Counsel–law firm relationship, it illustrates how liability might be attributed to a law

---

24. *Id.*
25. Swiatek, *supra* note 21.

firm because of Of Counsel's torts. While a law firm may not be able to insulate itself from liability for Of Counsel's torts, the independent contractor status of Of Counsel may well protect the lawyer from liability for the torts of the firm or its members.

The Of Counsel designation can be affixed to an infinite number of relationships. Sometimes "Of Counsel" is used to denote a reciprocal relationship between a law firm and an individual lawyer in another firm, a relationship that might be formed in an effort to expand the areas of specialty that the firm offers its clients. Or the relationship may be formed between out-of-state or foreign law firms in an effort to extend both firms' geographical reach in the market.

Because there are so many variations, the term resists a singular meaning. As the *California Lawyer* explained:

> "Of counsel" is coming to mean a general kind of independent contractor, and it's a much more free-floating, entrepreneurial thing than it was 15 or even 10 years ago.[26]

Not all of these variants can in fact be designated Of Counsel relationships. Currently, Formal Opinion 90-357 governs proper use of the designation. Before establishing an Of Counsel relationship, the parties should familiarize themselves with this ABA Formal Opinion, other formal and informal opinions of the American Bar Association, and the rulings of state bars to determine whether the parties' arrangement comes within the definitions set out in those opinions.

Formal Opinion 90-357, issued in May 1990, has superseded Formal Opinion 330 and six of the eight informal opinions of the American Bar Association that have dealt with this subject. These opinions have now been withdrawn. Two other informal opinions, issued after 330, have not. Despite these withdrawals, 90-357 relies on this background in articulating the rules with respect to Of Counsel. The next chapter considers this earlier background to lay a foundation for understanding the current status of the law with respect to Of Counsel.

---

26. Wagner, *Variations on the "Of Counsel" Theme*. 6 CAL. LAW. 59 (July 1986) (quoting Robert G. Gordon, law professor and legal historian at Stanford University Law School).

CHAPTER II

Defining "Of Counsel"

Despite its long history, "Of Counsel" was not formally defined until 1972, when the ABA Standing Committee on Legal Ethics and Professional Responsibility issued Formal Opinion 330.[1] Through that opinion, the ABA, relying on the ABA Model Code and prior published informal opinions on the subject, adopted a restricted meaning of the phrase. Widespread disregard of Formal Opinion 330 led the ethics committee to issue subsequent informal opinions and to reconsider the subject formally in Formal Opinion 90-357.[2] This chapter explores the background of Formal Opinion 330 and determines the extent to which this body of law has been superseded by Formal Opinion 90-357.

The Model Code and ABA Informal Opinions

Most of the guidelines regarding the ethics committee's definition of "Of Counsel" are based on a single passage contained in the ABA's Model Code of Professional Responsibility:

> A lawyer may be designated "Of Counsel" on a letterhead if he [or she] has a *continuing relationship* with a lawyer or law

1. See ABA Comm. on Professional Ethics and Responsibility, Formal Op. 330 (Aug. 1972), *reprinted in* Appendix H.

2. ABA Comm. on Ethics and Professional Responsibility, Formal Op. 90-357 (May 10, 1990), *reprinted in* Appendix I.

> firm, other than as a partner or associate.[3] (Emphasis supplied.)

The Model Code emphasized that lawyers must be scrupulous in representing their professional relationships to the public.[4] Yet, despite ethical mandates that the relationship be "continuing," the Model Code failed to define precisely the *nature* of the relationship. That task was left to the Standing Committee on Ethics and Professional Responsibility, which issued several informal opinions in response to individual inquiries about proper use of the designation.[5]

In the first of these, Informal Opinion 678 (1963), the committee considered the propriety of using the Of Counsel designation to describe a prolonged relationship between a District of Columbia lawyer and a Washington State law firm for the purpose of only one case. In the opinion, the committee defined "Of Counsel" as the term had been customarily used:

> [The] term, "of counsel," shown on a firm's letterhead or shingle, is customarily used to indicate a former partner who is on a retirement or semi-retirement basis, or one who has retired from another partnership or the general private practice or from some public position, who remains or becomes available to the firm for consultation and advice, either generally or in a particular field.[6]

The committee concluded that using the phrase to describe the relationship in question would be misleading, since the relationship was only temporary, even though it might exist over an extended period of time.[7]

By the mid-1960s, another common use of the phrase was to describe an ongoing relationship between a law firm and an inac-

---

3. Model Code of Professional Responsibility DR 2-102(A)(4) (1969, amended 1980).

4. Model Code of Professional Responsibility EC 2-13 (1969, amended 1980).

5. ABA Comm. on Professional Ethics, Informal Ops. 678 (1963), 710 (1964), 1134 (1969), 1173 (1971), and 1189 (1971).

6. ABA Informal Op. 678 (1963).

7. *Id.*

tive or retired public official, such as a retired judge. Informal Opinion 710 (1964) reflected the committee's approval of the use of the designation in such a situation. A retired judge had asked the committee whether the phrase could be used to describe his relationship with a firm that included his son. The committee approved the judge's use of the phrase, stating:

> [Y]ou are clearly within the area which with propriety would permit the firm to include your name "of counsel," inasmuch as you were a former partner of your son; you are on retirement from a public position and in semi-retirement from the general practice; and it is assumed that you would be available to the firm for consultation and advice either generally or in a particular field.[8]

There soon was a growing desire in law practice to expand the use of "Of Counsel" to describe more unconventional legal relationships. A series of opinions issued by the committee reflected this desire. For example, in Informal Opinion 1134 (1969), the committee considered whether the phrase could be used to describe a relationship between a law firm and a lawyer who was a current, rather than inactive, public official.[9] The inquiring law firm desired to list a U.S. senator as Of Counsel. Although the senator had never been a member of the firm, a continuing relationship between the senator and the firm had existed for years before he was elected to office. Even after he became a senator, he occasionally continued to perform legal services for the firm and its clients. The committee permitted the senator to use the designation, provided he was actively and regularly practicing law in the offices of the firm and rendering legal advice to the clients of the firm. In reaching this conclusion, the committee relied on the implications of DR 2-102(B), which states:

> A lawyer who assumes a judicial, legislative, or public executive or administrative post or office shall not permit his [or her] name to remain in the name of a law firm or to be used in professional notices of the firm during any significant period in which he [or she] is not actively and regularly practicing

8. ABA Informal Op. 710 (1964).
9. ABA Informal Op. 1134 (1969).

> law as a member of the firm, and during such period other members of the firm shall not use [the lawyer's] name on the firm name or in professional notices of the firm.[10]

In allowing the senator to be designated Of Counsel, the committee for the first time acknowledged that a continuing relationship could exist between a law firm and an individual lawyer other than a retired partner or an inactive public official.

With this newly expanded concept, practitioners began to question whether the designation could be further expanded to include other nontraditional relationships. The committee was first asked whether a *law firm,* as distinct from an individual lawyer, could be designated as Of Counsel to another law firm or individual lawyer. Relying on the literal language of DR 2-102(A)(4), the committee wrote:

> The Code, in our opinion, precludes the use by a law firm of such designation "Of Counsel" by the very omission of the words "law firm" in such privileged designation.[11]

The committee was then asked whether an Of Counsel relationship could exist simultaneously with more than one lawyer or law firm. Relying again on the language of DR 2-102(A)(4), the committee concluded that the Model Code prohibited multiple simultaneous Of Counsel relationships. In so doing, the committee added a new requirement to the designation:

> [I]t is not proper, in our opinion, for any lawyer or law firm to be designated "Of Counsel" to more than one lawyer or law firm . . . because the continuing relationship referred to in DR 2-102(A)(4) connotes a *close, daily, in-house association,* free and clear of problems of conflict.[12] (Emphasis supplied.)

In explaining why multiple Of Counsel relationships were impermissible, the committee, for the first time, stated that all Of Counsel relationships must encompass a "close, daily, in-house association." It soon became apparent that this added requirement

---

10. MODEL CODE OF PROFESSIONAL RESPONSIBILITY DR 2-102(B) (1969, amended 1980).

11. ABA Informal Op. 1173 (1971).

12. *Id.*

was causing confusion in the practice, since a literal reading precluded even retired partners and inactive public officials from using the designation. The committee attempted to correct this result in a later informal opinion by carving out an exception for retired partners:

> It is our opinion that the continuing relationship necessary for the designation "Of Counsel" referred to in DR 2-102(A)(4) which we have defined as close, daily, in-house association is susceptible to one exception which permits such classification to the designee if he had a previous continuing relationship with such other lawyer or law firm and during such relationship was physically present in the same office and/or suite with such other lawyer or law firm but which association of many years has been interrupted by the designee's inability to come to the office or his removal from the city or geographical area of his prior practice providing he is not associated with or holding himself out as being associated with any other lawyer or law firm.[13]

Although this exception attempted to restore the flexible nature of the Of Counsel relationship as it pertained to retired partners, it was so specific that few of them fell within it. An Of Counsel relationship had to be one in which there was a "close, daily, in-house association" or a "previous continuing relationship." A "previous continuing relationship" was in turn defined as one in which the lawyer had been *physically present* in the office of the lawyer or law firm but was now unable to go to the office because of some sort of "inability" or because the lawyer no longer resided in the area.

As a corollary, the committee, in the same opinion, considered whether firms should be allowed to list in legal directories the names of lawyers from other cities or states who were occasionally or regularly associated with the firm. The committee disallowed the Of Counsel designation to describe these relationships. Instead, it directed that nonresident counsel be designated only by terms such as "New York Counsel," "Correspondent," "European Counsel," or the like.[14]

---

13. ABA Informal Op. 1189 (1971).
14. *Id.*

Less than one year after these two informal opinions were issued, a professional corporation wrote the committee and asked whether it could be designated as "Of Counsel" or "In Association with" another firm, lawyer, or professional corporation. The committee determined that a formal opinion would be helpful in clarifying the many questions that had arisen in using the phrase "Of Counsel." The result was Formal Opinion 330.

Formal Opinion 330

From 1972 to 1990, Formal Opinion 330 represented the American Bar Association's official view of the Of Counsel relationship. This has now been superseded by Formal Opinion 90-357, but a knowledge of Formal Opinion 330 is essential to understanding the current view of the ABA committee, as well as the current views of many state ethics committees.

In Formal Opinion 330, the committee reexamined the nature of the Of Counsel relationship as it had come to be defined in previous informal opinions. The controlling guidelines for using the term "Of Counsel" appeared in the headnote of Formal Opinion 330:

> The relationship indicated by the term "Of Counsel" is a close, continuing, personal relationship between an individual lawyer and a law firm or lawyer, and the relationship is one that is not that of a partner, associate, or outside consultant. A law firm may not be "Of Counsel" to another lawyer or law firm. While a lawyer conceivably could be "Of Counsel" to two law firms or lawyers, one cannot simultaneously have more than a maximum of two "Of Counsel" relationships. The term "Of Counsel" may be used, if it correctly describes the existing relationship, on letterheads and professional announcement cards and in law lists and directories.[15]

Under Formal Opinion 330, the concept of Of Counsel had two basic aspects: First, there had to be a "close, continuing, personal relationship" between the parties, and second, the relationship could not be one of partner, associate, or outside consultant.[16] A copy of the full text of Formal Opinion 330 appears in Appendix H.

---

15. ABA Formal Op. 330 (1972).
16. *Id.*

A "Close, Continuing, Personal" Relationship

The Model Code stated that the Of Counsel relationship must be a "continuing" one.[17] Formal Opinion 330 added that the relationship had to be "close, continuing, and personal":

> Generally speaking, the close, personal relationship indicated by the term "Of Counsel" contemplates either that the lawyer practice in the offices of the lawyer or law firm to which he is "Of Counsel" or that his relationship, for example by virtue of past partnership of a retired partner that has led to continuing close association, be so close that he is in regular and frequent, if not daily, contact with the office of the lawyer or firm.[18]

The committee defined a close, continuing, and personal relationship by giving specific examples found in permissible Of Counsel relationships. Most of these examples involved the traditional Of Counsel relationship, *viz.*, one involving a retired partner or public official. A "close, continuing, personal" relationship could exist, the committee wrote, between a firm and a retired or semiretired former partner who remains available to the firm for consultation and advice.[19] It might also exist between a firm and a retired public official who regularly and locally is available to the firm for consultation and advice.[20] The committee listed one type of arrangement to which the phrase could never apply: a relationship better described as a forwarder-receiver of legal business.[21]

Formal Opinion 330's definition of a "close, continuing, personal" relationship differed significantly from the "continuing relationship" as defined in prior informal opinions. A "continuing relationship" required a "close, daily, in-house association between the lawyer and other lawyer or law firm." Prior informal opinions permitted an exception to exist under certain circumstances.[22] The exception was permitted where (1) the designated lawyer and

17. Model Code of Professional Responsibility DR 2-102(A) (4) (1969, amended 1980) ("A lawyer may be designated 'Of Counsel' on a letterhead if he has a continuing relationship with a lawyer or law firm, other than as partner or associate").

18. ABA Formal Op. 330 at 69 (1972).

19. *Id.*

20. *Id.*

21. *Id.*

22. ABA Informal Op. 1189 (1971).

other lawyer or firm had a previous continuing relationship, (2) during which the lawyer was physically present in the offices of the firm or other lawyer and (3) the lawyer was now unable to come to the office or had moved from the city or state where the office was located, providing the lawyer was not associated with another law firm. Under this exception, a former partner who was not in daily contact with the firm could still use the designation if all of the above requirements were satisfied. By contrast, Formal Opinion 330 required "regular, frequent, if not daily, contact" with the firm even in the case of the retired partner.[23] There were no exceptions to this requirement.

"Not a Partner, Associate, or Outside Consultant"

DR 2-102(A)(4) states:

> A lawyer may be designated "Of Counsel" on a letterhead if he or she has a continuing relationship with a lawyer or law firm, other than as a partner or associate.[24]

This provision is based upon language found in ethical principles that require a lawyer to represent his or her professional status so as not to mislead third persons.[25] A lawyer's designated status as Of Counsel would mislead third persons if, in fact, the lawyer was a partner or an employee of the firm, such as an associate.

One of the many incongruities of Formal Opinion 330 was the inconsistent use of terms in the text of the opinion and the headnote. For instance, the *headnote* stated that Of Counsel must not be like a "partner, associate, or outside consultant."[26] But the *text* of the opinion did not specifically state the same requirement. The text stated that the relationship must be one that is not that of a partner or an *employee*:

> [T]he individual lawyer who properly may be shown to be "Of Counsel" to a lawyer or law firm is a member or component

23. *See* ABA Formal Op. 330 (1972).

24. Model Code of Professional Responsibility DR 2-102(A)(4) (1969, amended 1980).

25. Model Code of Professional Responsibility EC 2-13 (1969, amended 1980).

26. ABA Formal Op. 330 at 69 (1972).

part of that law office, but his status is not that of a *partner or an employee* (nor that of a controlling member of a professional legal corporation).[27] (Emphasis supplied.)

There was no explanation why the committee used the term "employee" in the text but "associate" in the headnote.[28] This inconsistency became particularly cogent when one considered the differences between an employee and an associate.

The term "employee" has come to mean one who works under the control of another. Employees of the lawyer might be nonlawyers (secretaries, legal administrators, paralegals, and the like) or other lawyers. While the typical lawyer-employee has come to be regarded as an associate,[29] the presence of new categories of lawyers in practice today signifies that the term "employee" can include many types of lawyer-employees besides "associates."

The term "associate" may have been used in the headnote in keeping with the literal language of the Model Code. It might also be that the committee felt the two terms were synonymous, even though they are not.

The inconsistent use of these two terms in Formal Opinion 330 caused particularly troublesome questions for practitioners setting up the Of Counsel relationship. It was at least clear that the relationship should not be like that of an associate. But did it preclude any kind of employee relationship between Of Counsel and the other lawyer or firm?

Methods of Compensation

The method of compensation is an important part of any working relationship. In Formal Opinion 330, the committee felt that it should address the problem of how Of Counsel should be compensated. Formal Opinion 330 provided:

---

27. *Id.* at 69-70.

28. The committee also used the phrase "outside consultant" in the headnote. The text, however, mentions that phrase only as an example of impermissible forms of compensation: "He is compensated as a *sui generis* member of that law office, however, and not as an outside consultant." It is also noted that "outside consultant" is not defined in the opinion or the Model Code. This issue is taken up in further detail in Chapter 4.

29. ABA Formal Op. 330 at 68 (relying on ABA Comm. on Ethics and Professional Responsibility, Formal Op. 310 (1963)).

> While it would be misleading to refer to a lawyer who shares in the profits and losses and general responsibility of a firm as being "Of Counsel," the lawyer who is "Of Counsel" may be compensated either on a basis of division of fees in particular cases or on a basis of consultation fees. [The lawyer] is compensated as a *sui generis* member of that law office, however, and not as an outside consultant.[30] (Citations omitted.)

Formal Opinion 330 precluded Of Counsel from sharing in the gross profits of the firm. A literal reading of the opinion required that the method of compensation be directly related to the work performed. But it was not clear whether the opinion also precluded Of Counsel from being compensated on a regular salary basis, whether weekly, monthly, or yearly.

Despite this lack of clarity, many Of Counsel continue to be compensated on an hourly basis, with a percentage of the hourly rate charged for the actual work performed by Of Counsel. Others are compensated on a flat annualized rate without regard to work done, or on a flat salary or draw plus a percentage of the fees on work brought in.

In still other arrangements, Of Counsel opt for little or no compensation for the legal work they perform. In these arrangements, they may already be receiving income from the firm in the form of a pension or other retirement benefit for their past services. Formal Opinion 330 could be read as limiting use of the designation in these arrangements.

Multiple Of Counsel Relationships

Formal Opinion 330 limited to two the number of firms with which a lawyer might have an Of Counsel relationship. This limit appeared in the headnote as follows:

> While a lawyer conceivably could be "Of Counsel" to two law firms or lawyers, one cannot simultaneously have more than a maximum of two "Of Counsel" relationships.[31]

The actual text of the opinion varied somewhat from this summary. In describing the number of Of Counsel relationships that a lawyer might simultaneously maintain, the committee recognized that "there is no per se prohibition against one's being "Of Coun-

---

30. ABA Formal Op. 330 at 69 (1972).
31. *Id.* at 67.

sel" to two law firms."[32] The committee noted that a lawyer might possibly be able to establish the requisite relationships with two lawyers or law firms simultaneously:

> Given this view of the relationship indicated by the term "Of Counsel," it follows that one lawyer possibly could have the requisite relationship with two firms simultaneously, for example, one with which he practiced many years before his retirement and another at a location to which he has moved after his retirement.[33]

But the committee was not willing to state the point at which the number of relationships would be too great to satisfy the necessary qualities of closeness and continuity:

> To the extent that one lawyer does in fact have the requisite relationships properly to be designated "Of Counsel" to more than one lawyer or law firm simultaneously, Informal Opinion 1189 is modified.[34]

Law Firms As Of Counsel

Formal Opinion 330 affirmed the view expressed in prior informal opinions that a *law firm* cannot be listed as Of Counsel to another lawyer or law firm:

> Without necessarily adopting the descriptive language in Informal Opinion 678, we recognize that DR 2-102(A)(4) uses "Of Counsel" in a manner not inconsistent with earlier usage and that the term relates to an individual lawyer. Thus the term cannot be used with regard to a law firm, whether it be a partnership or professional legal corporation.[35]

The reasoning here was that the literal language of the Model Code connoted an *individual* lawyer. Prior informal opinions had concluded that a law firm could not be Of Counsel because "the practice of law is personal in nature and a law firm as such is never admitted to practice in any state."[36]

---

32. *Id.* at 70.
33. *Id.*
34. *Id.*
35. *Id.* at 69.
36. *See* ABA Informal Op. 1173 (1971); *see also* ABA Informal Op. 1189 (1971).

Yet the committee, in a later opinion, approved of arrangements between law firms that closely resembled Of Counsel relationships, although it prohibited the firms from describing their relationship as anything other than "affiliated" or "associated."[37] In one instance, the committee permitted an arrangement between law firms located in different cities whereby the firms effectively became Of Counsel to each other.[38] The arrangement provided for a partner in one firm to be Of Counsel to another law firm in another city, while a partner in the second firm was simultaneously Of Counsel to the first firm.

Advertising the Of Counsel Relationship

The final consideration of Formal Opinion 330 was the ethical consequence implied by using the term "Of Counsel" in firm announcements and other public communications. As noted previously, DR 2-102(A)(4) permits the designation "Of Counsel" to be used in connection with letterheads, as long as the requisite relationship exists. In Formal Opinion 330, the committee considered whether the designation could ethically be used in connection with announcement cards, shingles, law lists, and directories. The text of the opinion stated:

> Where a relationship exists which may be described accurately as an "Of Counsel" relationship, we hold that the relationship may be designated on a professional announcement card, on a shingle, and in a law list or legal directory.[39]

But the opinion failed to consider other significant ethical considerations that arise by virtue of announcing the relationship in professional communications. Could the name of the lawyer who is Of Counsel be included in the firm name? Should Of Counsel's jurisdictional limitations be listed on professional announcement cards, letterheads, directories, and law lists?

---

37. These designations are allowed if the firms are "closely associated or connected with the other lawyer or firm in an ongoing and regular relationship." ABA Comm. on Ethics and Professional Responsibility, Formal Op. 84-351 at 4 (1984).

38. ABA Comm. on Ethics and Professional Responsibility, Informal Op. 1315 (1975).

39. ABA Formal Op. 330 (1972).

Summary

The guidelines controlling the Of Counsel relationship were originally set out in ABA Formal Opinion 330, under which the relationship had to satisfy two basic requirements: First, it had to be "close, continuing, personal." Second, it could not be like that of a partner, associate, or outside consultant.

A "close, continuing, personal" relationship differed significantly from a "continuing relationship" as it was described in prior informal opinions. A "continuing relationship" seemed to require nearly a "daily, in-house association" between Of Counsel and the other lawyer or firm. But there was an exception to this requirement if there had been a previous relationship in which Of Counsel had been physically present in the offices of the lawyer or firm but was now precluded from going to the office. Under Formal Opinion 330, Of Counsel had to have frequent, "if not daily," contact with the office of the lawyer or firm. This requirement posed unusual difficulties for many Of Counsel, particularly retired partners. Little justification was offered for it. It did not reflect the reality of present-day affairs, nor was it consonant with the purpose and intent of the traditional concept of Of Counsel.

Formal Opinion 330 also required that Of Counsel could not be a partner, associate, or outside consultant. But the text of the opinion stated that the relationship must not be that of partner or employee. We do not know why the committee chose to use the word "associate" in the headnote and "employee" in the text. Perhaps it felt that these terms were synonymous. The inconsistency raised many questions. Could a lawyer and a law firm set up the Of Counsel arrangement as an employer-employee relationship if they so desired? Formal Opinion 330 seemed to forbid such an arrangement.

By permitting Of Counsel to be compensated on a basis of division of fees in particular cases or on a basis of consultation fees, Opinion 330 implied that Of Counsel could only be compensated for work actually performed. This was read by some as restricting a retired partner from using the designation if his sole income was the firm's pension or other retirement benefits.

Formal Opinion 330 reaffirmed the view that a law firm could not be designated Of Counsel. This view was based on the literal language of the Model Code. But the policy underlying this view was not clearly expressed.

In short, the ABA concept of the Of Counsel relationship, as evidenced by Formal Opinion 330, was unduly restrictive. And although the ABA concept seemed lucid, it was far from definitive. In practice, there was often diverse interpretation that seemed contrary to the existing definition. More important, the opinion contained no discussion of the essential nature of the contractual relationship that opens the door to a variety of arrangements. Under the circumstances, the ethics committee correctly felt that it was time to issue a new formal opinion to eliminate this unnecessary confusion. The next chapter analyzes Formal Opinion 90-357, the vehicle chosen by the committee to accomplish this task.

CHAPTER III

Of Counsel Revisited: Formal Opinion 90-357

For eighteen years, formal Opinion 330 remained the view of the American Bar Association with reference to Of Counsel. By 1990, the Committee on Ethics and Professional Responsibility recognized that there had been so many changes in the profession that it was time to review and restate its opinion.

In Formal Opinion 90-357, it reconsidered the subject for several reasons: First, there had been a proliferation of variants of the term and of arrangements designated by the term or one of these variants. Second, some of the committee's prior opinions had been unnecessarily restrictive on certain relationships commonly designated as "Of Counsel." Third, the replacement of the ABA Model Code of Professional Responsibility by the ABA Model Rules of Professional Conduct presented an opportune moment for such a review.

The committee addressed this last situation first and concluded that there was no substantive difference between the Model Code and the Model Rules:

> [T]he textual basis in both the Model Rules and the Model Code for determining whether particular uses of the title are or are not ethically permissible is in substance the same—a prohibition against misleading representations—although the particular provisions embodying this prohibition are different in form. . . . The essence of the ethical requirement under both the Model Rules and the Model Code is avoidance of misrep-

resentations as to the lawyer's status, and the relationship between lawyer and firm.[1]

Designations Governed by Formal Opinion 90-357

Formal Opinion 90-357 governs the designation "Of Counsel" and all variant titles that use the word "counsel," such as "special counsel," "tax [or other specialty] counsel," and "senior counsel." The opinion does not cover terms that do not employ the word "counsel," such as "consultant," "consulting attorney," or "corresponding attorney."[2]

Even though there are slight differences between the variant titles that employ the word "counsel," the committee views these as sharing similar characteristics so that they should all be governed by the opinion.

The term "Of Counsel" is used in a wide variety of situations. For example, the Of Counsel agreement may be used to accomplish certain ends not otherwise obtainable under more traditional arrangements, as illustrated below:

A Law Firm, F, and two independent lawyers, L and M, wished to practice law, using the following letterhead:

[FIRM F, or L, or M]
A member Firm of the Law Offices at X Square

In addition, they proposed to describe themselves in advertisements as follows:

The Law Offices at X Square
An Association of Independent Lawyers
and Law Partnerships

Both the proposed letterhead and the proposed advertisement violate the rule against the use of trade names, including locational trade names. However, an alternative possible approach for law firm F and lawyers L and M, depending on the precise nature of their relationship, might be to enter into mutual Of Counsel relationships that are expressly named as such. Firm F may become Of Counsel to lawyers L and M and lawyers L and M may become Of Counsel to firm F, as long as the parties maintain the requisite

---

1. ABA Comm. on Ethics and Professional Responsibility, Formal Op. 90-357 at 2 (1990), *reprinted in* Appendix I.

2. *Id.* at 3.

ties to support the Of Counsel relationship. Such an arrangement would permit the group to advertise their affiliation with the requisite degree of specificity, and to list each other on their individual stationery while using a label with a known and therefore acceptable clear meaning.[3]

If Firm F becomes Of Counsel to L and M and vice versa, and the group maintains the requisite relationship to support that designation, the three entities will be able to advertise jointly and indicate an Of Counsel affiliation with each other [and also] identify themselves as "associated" or "affiliated" with each other, provided that the requisites for an Of Counsel relationship are met.[4]

Permissible Patterns of Relationships

Formal Opinion 90-357 suggests four permissible patterns of relationships in the use of the term "Of Counsel":

1. *The Part-Time Practitioner*—A part-time practitioner is one who practices law in association with a firm or other lawyer, but out of the mainstream of the other lawyers of the firm. This person's part-time practice might originate from a change from full-time practice to part-time practice, or a change from a salaried position, such as a government official, law professor, retired judge, or corporate lawyer, to the practice of law.[5]
2. *The Retired Partner*—The retired partner is one who is not actively practicing law but remains associated with the firm and is available for occasional consultation.
3. *The Probationary Partner*—The probationary partner-to-be is one who is hired into the firm with the expectation of becoming a partner within a relatively short period of time.
4. *The Permanent Senior Attorney*—Although a variety of terms[6] have been used to describe this particular lawyer, the common characteristic is that he does not expect to at-

---

3. New York City Ethical Opinion 1995-8, 1995 WL 875457 (N.Y.C. Ass'n of the Bar Comm. Prof'l Ethics 1995), modifying New York City Opinions 891, 81-3, 81-71, 81-102, 82-28.

4. *Id.* at 6.

5. There is an infinite variety of personal situations in which the Of Counsel paradigm is appropriate. *See* Chapter 1, *supra*, at pp. 3 *et seq*.

6. For example, "senior attorney," "senior counsel," "special counsel," "senior associate," "counsel."

> tain full partner status but has a permanent tenure-like status between partner and associate.[7]

In the committee's view, all of these relationships are proper Of Counsel relationships, even though prior informal and formal opinions may have concluded that they were not. They all contain "core characteristics" necessary for the requisite relationship.[8]

Impermissible Patterns of Relationships

Formal Opinion 90-357 cites four relationships that always fall outside the ambit of the Of Counsel relationship. These are:

1. A single case.[9]
2. The forwarding or receiving of legal business.[10]
3. Collaborative efforts among otherwise unrelated lawyers or firms.[11]
4. Outside consultants.[12]

Core Characteristics of an Of Counsel Relationship

Relationships that do not fall within one of these four inclusive or four exclusive categories must contain the "core characteristics" of an Of Counsel relationship before they can properly use the designation. The committee in 90-357 defines that characteristic just as it had previously defined a permissible Of Counsel relationship in Formal Opinion 330:

> That core characteristic properly denoted by the title "counsel" is, as stated in Formal Opinion 330, a "close, regular, per-

---

7. State and local bar associations have followed this four-part categorization, or something similar. *See, e.g.*, Ohio Adv. Op. 97-2, 1997 WL 188916 (Ohio Bd. Comm. Grievance Disputes 1997). New Jersey creates an additional category by differentiating the "permanent senior associate who is not on a partnership track" from the "'special' counsel who has developed an expertise in a particular field of law." *Cf.* New Jersey Atty. Advisory Op. 21, 147 N.J.L.J. 979, 6 N.J.L. 475, 1997 WL 104570 (N.J. Advisory Comm. Prof'l Ethics 1997).

8. *See* core characteristics listed below.

9. *See* Chapter 4.

10. *See* Illinois Adv. Op. 776, 1982 WL 198379 (Ill.St.Bar.Assn.), *infra* p. 36; *see also* Chapter 4.

11. *See* Chapter 4.

12. *See* Chapter 4.

sonal relationship"; but a relationship which is neither that of a partner (or its equivalent, a principal of a professional corporation), with the shared liability and/or managerial responsibility implied by that term; nor, on the other hand, the status ordinarily conveyed by the term "associate," which is to say a junior non-partner lawyer, regularly employed by the firm.[13]

A "core characteristic" can be separated into two distinct components. The first is the "close, regular, personal" relationship. The second is the requirement that the relationship not be like that of partner or associate.

A "Close, Regular, Personal" Relationship

Formal Opinion 330's interpretation of a "close, continuing, personal" relationship limited the kinds of permissible Of Counsel relationships.[14] Under the guidelines of 330, the lawyer had to practice "in the office" of the firm or other lawyer or had to be "regularly and locally" available for consultation and in "daily contact" with the firm.

Formal Opinion 330 was unduly restrictive even in the most common Of Counsel situation, *viz.*, the relationship between a retired partner and his or her firm.[15] Like 330, Formal Opinion 90-357 requires a "close, regular, personal"[16] relationship between the parties, but the committee allows for more flexibility in meeting this requirement.[17] The sections that follow consider how Formal Opinion 90-357 has relaxed these restrictions.

---

13. ABA Formal Op. 90-357 at 3 (1990).

14. *See* Chapter 2.

15. *See* Chapter 2.

16. The committee in Formal Opinion 90-357 uses the language as it is found in the test of Formal Opinion 330 in describing this aspect of the relationship. The headnote of Formal Opinion 330 used the language "close, continuing, personal" in describing this same aspect.

17. The ethics committee of the New York City Bar has noted that Formal Opinion 90-357 relies on Formal Opinion 330 for the definition of Of Counsel (New York City Ethical Opinion 1995-8, 1995 WL 875457 (N.Y.C. Ass'n of the Bar Comm. Prof'l Ethics 1995)), citing New York City Ethical Opinion 81-3 (1982) for the same test ("close, continuing, regular and personal relationship [or a] present day-to-day working familiarity with the affairs of the law firm in question").

REQUIRED CONTACT WITH THE FIRM

One welcome change contained in Formal Opinion 90-357 was the elimination of any possible suggestion that Of Counsel had to be in daily contact with the firm or other lawyer. Formal Opinion 90-357 states:

> [I]nsofar as Formal Opinion 330 carries any implication that the contact must be so frequent as to verge on *daily*, the Committee now disavows it.[18]

The committee's current view has important ramifications for many relationships that previously failed to satisfy this requirement. A lawyer may now maintain multiple relationships with several law firms without jeopardizing the Of Counsel status with any one firm or other lawyer.[19] But there remains the very practical limitation that multiple relationships may cause an increased risk of conflicts of interest with resulting instances of imputed disqualification.[20] Some states, such as California and Ohio, have specifically warned against the increase in the potential for imputed disqualification due to an increased number of relationships.[21]

Even though daily contact is no longer required, "frequent and continuing contact" is. But the committee failed to define this requirement affirmatively. At the minimum, it requires more than "merely an availability for occasional consultations.[22]

LAW FIRMS OF COUNSEL TO ONE ANOTHER

Formal Opinion 90-357 made it clear that law firms, as well as individuals, could be Of Counsel to one another. In 1994, the Ethics

---

18. ABA Formal Op. 90-357 at 4 (1990) (emphasis supplied).

19. State and local bar associations have taken different views about the propriety of multiple Of Counsel relationships. Iowa allows only one. *See* Iowa State Bar Ass'n, Opinions 87-9 (1987) and 82-19 (1982). Texas permits two. *See* State Bar of Texas, Opinion 402 (1982). Other states do not limit the number. *See* California Ethical Opinion 1993-129 (1993); Connecticut Bar Ass'n, Opinion 88-13 (1988); Bar Ass'n of Nassau County (N.Y.), Opinion 88-46 (1988); Ass'n of the Bar of the City of New York, Opinion 80-22 (undated); Ohio Adv. Op. 97-2 (1997); Philadelphia Bar Ass'n, Opinion 86-54 (1986) and 86-143 (1986).

20. *See infra* Chapter 7 (conflicts of interest) and Chapter 8 (imputed disqualification).

21. *See* California Ethical Opinion 1993-129 (1993) and Ohio Adv. Op. 97-2, *supra* note 19.

22. ABA Formal Op. 90-357 at 5 (1990).

Committee became concerned about the proliferation of a wide variety of business arrangements within the legal profession because of the potential of misleading the public by the use of such words as "affiliated," "associated," "correspondent," or "network," without a "meaningful description of the nature of the relationship."[23]

The resulting Formal Opinion 94-388 emphasized the necessity of full disclosure of two fundamentals:

> The first [precept] is the obligation not to misstate what a law firm has to offer. The second is to assure that a client of one firm is aware of the relationship between that firm and any other firms with which it is involved insofar as the relationship may give rise to conflicts of interest, the sharing of fees, or certain other instructions that implicate the Model Rules of Professional Conduct. This opinion presumes that the actual formation of relationships between law firms will have occurred only where the law firms were able to comply with their obligations to existing clients with respect to all such matters.[24]

Formal Opinion 94-388 noted that the relationships between law firms ranged "from something very close to an actual partnership to one involving occasional referrals."[25] Because of the possibility of misleading the general public, the Ethics Committee noted that where a law firm is described as being a "member of a 'network,' in an 'association' or is a 'correspondent' of another firm," clients and prospects should be provided with more detailed information.[26]

The Opinion emphasized that a client is "entitled to know of conflicting commitments where . . . the relationship between the firms is 'close, regular, continuing and semi-permanent, and not merely that of forwarder-receiver of legal business.'" It then added:

---

23. ABA Comm. on Ethics and Professional Responsibility, Formal Op. 94-388 (1994), *relationships among law firms* at 1.

24. *Id.*

25. ABA Formal Op. 94-388 at 2 (1994).

26. ABA Formal Op. 94-388 at 2 (1994). The committee listed five major points that should be disclosed: (1) participation of "professional personnel" from the other firm(s); (2) whether the client's fee would be shared; (3) whether there was a sharing of profits; (4) whether there were "common training programs and/or strategies and/or expertise; and (5) whether the firms "conduct any other common operations, or by contrast, the relationship is simply a marketing device." *Id.*

> [L]awyers of the "affiliated" or "associated" firm will not simultaneously represent persons whose interests conflict with the client's interests, just as would be true of lawyers who occupy an "Of Counsel" relationship with the firm. The same expectation necessarily exists when two firms are "Of Counsel" to each other. . . . In each case, of course, if the lawyer believes the representation will not be adversely affected, the client can be asked to consent to the representation.[27]

SPECIALTY COUNSEL

Prior informal opinions indicated that a permissible Of Counsel relationship could exist even though Of Counsel activities were limited to consultation in a particular area of law. Several variant terms can be used to designate an Of Counsel relationship in which the lawyer has a special expertise. A consultant specializing in tax, patent and trademark, or antitrust could be designated as "tax counsel," "patent and trademark counsel," or "antitrust counsel" respectively, provided the consultant maintained a close and continuing relationship with the law firm or other lawyer. Formal Opinion 90-357 confirmed this view:

> Such terms, although in the Committee's view as permissible as other variants of the term "counsel," must like them be confined to relationships that in fact involved frequent and continuing contacts, and not merely an availability for occasional consultations.[28]

But the committee did not follow the position of several state bars that held the designation should contain more descriptive language to indicate the limitations reflected by the variant terms.[29] The committee expressed its view that the variant term itself connotes the true nature of the relationship:

> There is, moreover, in the term designating a specialty, a clear representation that the of counsel lawyer in fact has a special expertise in the designated area; and, for the firm, that it also

---

27. ABA Formal Op. 94-388 at 4 (1994), quoting (first sentence) Formal Op. 84-351, and citing Formal Op. 90-357 and Informal Op. 1315 (1975). *See infra* Chapter 7 (conflicts of interest) and Chapter 8 (imputed disqualification).

28. ABA Formal Op. 90-357 at 4-5 (1990).

29. *E.g.*, Arizona State Bar Ethics Opinion 87-24 (1987).

has, by reason of the of counsel relationship, that special expertise.[30]

COMPENSATION

Where Formal Opinion 330 seemed to limit the methods of compensating Of Counsel, Formal Opinion 90-357 wisely handled the issue by making it clear that compensation arrangements are not relevant to the determination of a permissible Of Counsel relationship:

> It is the Committee's view that, the other conditions just described having been met, it is not relevant to the permissibility of use of "of counsel" what the compensation arrangements are.[31]

The committee recognized that many Of Counsel are retired partners who have a pension or other retirement benefit or who share in the firm's profits. By the earlier Formal Opinion, such persons could not be designated as being Of Counsel. Under 90-357, such considerations are simply inapplicable.

In dealing with various compensation arrangements, the ABA Ethics Committee and state and local bar associations have distinguished a wide variety of arrangements for the division of fees,[32] office sharing, and/or referrals of legal business from the typical compensation arrangements that characterize the Of Counsel relationship. For example, where two lawyers acted more like for-

30. ABA Formal Op. 90-357 at 5 (1990).

31. *Id.* at 4.

32. *Cf.* ABA Formal Op. 93-374 (allowing the sharing of court-awarded fees between a lawyer and a non-profit organization that sponsors pro bono litigation); Florida Ethical Opinion 94-7, 1995 WL 815246 (Florida State Bar Association) (Of Counsel considered to be a member of the firm for purposes of the fee division rules only if practicing exclusively through that firm); Michigan Ethical Opinion RI-216, 1994 WL 423011 (Michigan Professional and Judicial Ethics Committee) (heirs and estate of deceased lawyer may make agreement with law firm wherein the valuation and payment for lawyer's interest could be based on pro rata portion of the future receipt by the firm of contingent fees to be paid by another law firm for referrals during decedent's life); Michigan Ethical Opinion RI-133, 1992 WL 510804 (Michigan Professional and Judicial Ethics Committee) (lawyer may rent office space from lawyer/landlord based on a calculation of gross income from the lawyer/tenant's law practice, so long as client confidences are not violated in determining the amount of rent due).

warders and receivers of legal business, they could not properly hold themselves out as Of Counsel:

> The "Of Counsel" lawyers maintained separate offices and appear to be the receivers of legal business forwarded by the firm. The method used to compensate the "Of Counsel" lawyers is more in the nature of paying an outside consultant rather than as a sui generis member of the firm. We are of the opinion that an "Of Counsel" relationship does not exist and that it is not proper for the firm to show the two lawyers as "Of Counsel" on their letterhead, exterior door listing or elsewhere.[33]

Any compensation between Of Counsel and a law firm or other lawyer must be arranged so that there is no implication that Of Counsel is a partner. An arrangement that involves a sharing in the firm's general profits or other indicia that might imply, or even make, one a partner would be inappropriate. If the drafter of an Of Counsel agreement wishes to use percentages of gross or net profits, for example, he should relate the percentage to the services to be performed by Of Counsel.

Issues of compensation are not limited to salary arrangements. More often than not, employee fringe benefits, such as medical insurance, life insurance, accident and disability insurance, eligibility in the firm's pension or profit-sharing plan, and coverage under the firm's professional liability plan, are equally important to a lawyer contemplating joining a firm as Of Counsel.

In the past, it might not have been desirable for persons in the position of Of Counsel to participate in the various benefit programs and other fringe benefits offered by the firm. The reasoning was twofold: First, Formal Opinion 330 precluded use of the term where the relationship resembled that of an associate or employee. Receipt of these benefits as part of a compensation package tended to make the relationship resemble that of an employer-employee, rather than independent contractor. Second, and perhaps more important, receipt of these benefits by Of Counsel could be an important indication of an employer-employee relationship in a malpractice claim against the firm.

Since Formal Opinion 90-357 expressed the committee's view that the compensation arrangement is irrelevant to the issue of

---

33. Illinois Advisory Opinion 776, 1982 WL 198379 (Illinois State Bar Ass'n).

using the designation, the Of Counsel's receipt of these fringe benefits should not affect an ability to use the designation. But the committee did not address whether such arrangements expose the parties to vicarious liability for malpractice of another.[34]

Partner or Associate Status Is Not Permissible

The second aspect of the core characteristic described in Formal Opinion 90-357 is that the Of Counsel relationship must not resemble that of partner or associate. The ethical considerations that form the basis of this requirement are found in EC 2-13, which essentially provides that a lawyer should be scrupulous in representing an accurate professional status and should avoid any misrepresentations concerning it.

The headnote of Formal Opinion 330 precluded use of "Of Counsel" where the relationship was like that of "partner, associate or outside consultant." Formal Opinion 330 concluded that the term "associates" describes those who are "lawyer-employees" of the firm who "are not partners and do not generally share in the responsibility and liability for the acts of the firm."[35] Changes in the practice of law since this opinion was issued made this definition obsolete.

Formal Opinion 90-357 clears up much of this confusion. The committee precludes using the Of Counsel designation where the relationship is like that of partner or associate, and it affirmatively defines "associate" as "a junior non-partner lawyer, regularly employed by the firm."[36] This substantial improvement over the language used in Formal Opinion 330 makes it possible for senior lawyers to be Of Counsel without being characterized as associates.

Employee Status Is Permissible

One of the many problems of Formal Opinion 330 was its inconsistent use of the term "employee." A strict interpretation of the text of 330 precluded Of Counsel from being like an employee or the Of Counsel arrangement from resembling an employer-employee relationship in any way. Thus, Of Counsel could not be compensated

---

34. *See* Chapters 5 and 6.
35. *See* Chapter 2.
36. ABA Formal Op. 90-357 at 3 (1990).

with a fixed salary and could not participate in any of the firm's benefit programs. This restriction precluded use of the term by lawyers brought into the firm laterally with the expectation of becoming partner within a relatively short time. It also limited use of the term to describe lawyers who were in a permanent status between partner and associate and senior lawyers whose compensation arrangements included some or all of the profits of their work product.

Formal Opinion 90-357 alleviated this problem by explicitly permitting the designation to be used in the two arrangements described above in which employee status was presumed:

> Insofar as Formal Opinion 330 may be read to conclude that either the probationary partner model or the permanent between-partner-and-associate model are not permissibly designated of counsel, that conclusion is disavowed.[37]

There may be other relationships that could be identified as Of Counsel relationships but for the fact that the parties assume an employer-employee arrangement. The committee did not express an opinion on the propriety of these arrangements. For the most part, Formal Opinion 90-357 deals with independent-contractor situations. The retired partner, the part-time practitioner, and the lawyer entering a second career typically conform to this model.

By contrast, 90-357 bases the "probationary partner-to-be" or the "permanent between-partner-and-associate model" on the employer-employee relationship. When drafting the Of Counsel agreement, the drafter should select one or the other—independent contractor or employer-employee relationship—for the bulk of the agreement, and make specific exceptions in those areas in which the alternate approach may be desired.[38]

Multiple Of Counsel Relationships

The committee's initial view was that a lawyer could not be Of Counsel to more than one law firm. This view was modified in Formal Opinion 330, which set a limit of two firms. Formal Opinion 90-357 has removed any limitation on the number of firms with

---

37. *Id.* at 4.

38. *See* Chapter 11 for discussion of problems of drafting.

which a lawyer may have an Of Counsel relationship. The committee expressed its new position as follows:

> The proposition that it is not possible for a lawyer to have a "close, regular, personal relationship" with more than two lawyers or law firms is not a self-evident one. A lawyer can surely have a close, regular, personal relationship with more than two clients; and the Committee sees no reason why the same cannot be true with more than two law firms.[39]

The controlling criterion is "close, regular, personal" relationships. If the lawyer can maintain multiple close and regular relationships simultaneously, the designation is proper for each.[40] As a practical matter this may not be possible, since multiple Of Counsel relationships affect conflict-of-interest issues and attributions between the lawyer and firm or other lawyer. For purposes of conflicts of interest, Of Counsel are "associated" with the firm.[41] For purposes of imputed disqualifications, if two or more firms share the same Of Counsel, the two firms and Of Counsel all effectively become a single firm.[42]

Law Firms As Of Counsel

Prior views of the committee held that a law firm could not be held out as being Of Counsel to another firm or lawyer. Formal Opinion 90-357 reversed these views and expressed its new opinion as follows:

> [T]he Committee's prior opinions do not suggest, and the Committee does not now perceive, any reason of policy why a firm should not be of counsel to another firm.[43]

As with multiple Of Counsel relationships, the committee cautioned that relationships created between firms would "entail complete reciprocal attribution of the disqualifications of all lawyers in

39. ABA Formal Op. 90-357 at 5 (1990).
40. *See* Chapter 4.
41. *See* Chapter 7.
42. *See* Chapter 8.
43. ABA Formal Op. 90-357 at 6 (1990).

each firm."[44] Before entering into such relationships, a law firm would also have to consider very carefully the potential increase in liability for the errors and omissions of the other firm.

Of Counsel's Name in the Firm's Name

In Formal Opinion 90-357, the committee, for the first time, authorized use of Of Counsel's name in the firm's name—but only if the lawyer was a retired name partner and "the firm is long-established and well-recognized."[45] If Of Counsel has recently joined the firm, his name cannot be included in the firm's name because it might give a misleading impression of the extent of this person's responsibility and potential liability. The committee stated:

> [We believe] that in the case of a new or recent firm affiliation there is no escaping an implication that a name in the new firm name implies that the lawyer is a partner in the firm, with fully shared responsibility for its work. On the other hand, the Committee also believes that there is not a similar misleading implication in the use of a retired partner's name in the firm name, while the same partner is of counsel, where the firm name is long-established and well-recognized.[46]

Even though the committee approved including Of Counsel's name in the firm's name in these limited situations, no view was expressed concerning Of Counsel's potential malpractice liability:

> The Committee does not express a view as to whether, when the retired partner's name remains included in the firm name, the retired partner may on that account be exposed to malpractice liability as if he or she were still a general partner.[47]

---

44. *See id.* and Chapter 4, *infra*, at 61. In 1994, the ABA Committee on Ethics and Professional Responsibility stated that it was entirely proper for law firms to be Of Counsel to one another or to be associated or affiliated with one another. For purposes of conflicts of interest and imputed disqualification, a law firm must make a full disclosure of the resources that such an arrangement makes available to clients and of the precise relationship between the firms. ABA Formal Op. 94-388 (1994). *See* Chapters 7 and 8.

45. ABA Formal Op. 90-357 at 6 (1990).

46. *Id.*

47. *Id.* note 11 at 6.

Summary

Many of the restrictions that the earlier Formal Opinion 330 placed upon parties entering into Of Counsel relationships have been relaxed under Formal Opinion 90-357. This is a welcome change and will enhance the ability of the parties to tailor the arrangement to suit their own needs. Under the recent view of the committee, the designation can be used whether the parties anticipate the relationship to be temporary or permanent. A retired partner who will only be available for occasional consultation can still be listed as Of Counsel. The term can also be used to describe the relationship between a part-time practitioner and a law firm. Lawyers can maintain multiple Of Counsel relationships. But perhaps the single most important change from the prior opinion is the ability of firms to list one another as Of Counsel. The use of the term to describe relationships between foreign law firms and transcontinental law firms will undoubtedly become more common in the near future.

CHAPTER IV

Particular Of Counsel Relationships after Formal Opinion 90-357

In Formal Opinion 90-357, the ABA's Standing Committee on Ethics and Professional Responsibility issued guidelines to follow when using the Of Counsel designation. While the committee was more liberal on this subject than in its prior Formal Opinion 330, it retained some restrictions on the use of the term and did not address a number of areas important to the practicing bar. The committee officially withdrew Formal Opinion 330 and the informal opinions that preceded it, but it continued to cite these opinions, pointing out those instances where it disavowed what it had said in earlier opinions.

In Formal Opinion 330, the committee defined an Of Counsel relationship by focusing on the closeness and continuity of the relationship. The committee distinguished two common Of Counsel relationships: (1) where the lawyer practices or continues to practice in the offices of the lawyer or law firm and (2) where the lawyer does not practice in the office of the lawyer or firm but is in regular and frequent contact with the firm.

Although the committee made a number of significant changes regarding the details of the Of Counsel arrangement in 90-357, it retained the fundamental characteristic that the relationship must be a *close and continuing* one:

> That core characteristic properly denoted by the title "counsel" is, as stated in Formal Opinion 330, a "close, regular, personal" relationship; . . .[1]

1. ABA Comm. on Ethics and Professional Responsibility, Formal Op. 90-357 at 3 (1990), *reprinted in* Appendix I.

The phrase "Of Counsel" has come to mean many different things. There are so many variant uses of the phrase that the only thing common to these relationships is that they do not fit neatly into one category. Both 90-357 and 330 considered some of these variants. This chapter considers these as well as other arrangements commonly designated as Of Counsel to determine whether they comport with the most recent pronouncement of 90-357. We shall also consider how these arrangements are treated by various states.

Specifically Permitted Of Counsel Relationships

In Formal Opinion 90-357, the ethics committee outlined four major instances wherein the Of Counsel designation could be properly used: part-time practitioners, retired partners, probationary partners, and senior attorneys. The part-time practitioner category was broken down into two subcategories: (1) lawyers who changed from a full-time to a part-time practice and (2) those who changed their careers.

Although the permitted categories may not conform precisely to the variety of situations confronting lawyers in practice, it provides a useful guide for those entering into Of Counsel contractual relationships. To the extent that the parties can draft an Of Counsel agreement that fits within one or more of these categories, they will be certain to satisfy the ethical standards of the profession.

The Retired Partner

In 1963, the ABA Standing Committee on Ethics and Professional Responsibility issued its first opinion relating to the Of Counsel relationship. In that opinion, the committee recognized that many Of Counsel are retired partners of a law firm. The committee stated:

> It is the *impression* of the members of this Committee that the term, "of counsel," . . . is customarily used to indicate a former partner who is on a retirement or semi-retirement basis, or one who has retired from another partnership or the general private practice or from some public position, who remains or becomes available to the firm for consultation and advice, either generally or in a particular field. (Emphasis supplied.)[2]

2. ABA Comm. on Professional Ethics, Informal Op. 678 (1963).

In 1972, when the committee first formally defined the Of Counsel relationship in Formal Opinion 330, it did not exempt retired partners from the "close, continuing, personal" requirement. But it did conclude that an Of Counsel who is a retired partner of the firm will be deemed to have already developed a *close* association with the firm. Consequently, this lawyer would not be required to practice in the offices of the lawyer or firm to have Of Counsel status.[3] But for the association to be a "close, *continuing*, personal" one, the retired partner had to remain active in the practice of law, with frequent, "if not daily," contact with the firm.[4]

Such a reading imposed unnecessary limitations on the traditional Of Counsel arrangement.[5] A "close, continuing, personal" relationship was not found where the retired partner was available for occasional consultation only, resided in another city or state for all or part of the year, or merely maintained an office with the firm.[6] Even if the retired partner remained in frequent contact with the office, there was no "close, continuing, personal" relationship if the Of Counsel was not active in the practice of law, or if the retiree was not required to perform any duties for the firm. Merely going

---

3. ABA Comm. on Ethics and Professional Responsibility, Formal Op. 330 (1972).

4. ABA Formal Op. 330 at 69.

5. *See* ABA Informal Op. 678.

6. This interpretation is based on an earlier opinion rendered by the committee. In Informal Opinion 1189, the committee reaffirmed Informal Opinion 1173 and stated:

> 4. It is our opinion that the continuing relationship necessary for the designation "Of Counsel" referred to in DR 2-102(A)(4) which we have defined as close daily in house association is susceptible to one exception which permits such classification to the designee if he had a previous continuing relationship with such other lawyer or law firm and during such relationship was physically present in the same office and/or suite with such other lawyer or law firm but which association of many years has been interrupted by the designee's inability to come to the office or his removal from the city or geographical area of his prior practice providing he is not associated with or holding himself out as being associated with any other lawyer or law firm.

Thus, even though the committee acknowledged specific instances in which a lawyer would not be required to practice in the same office of the lawyer or law firm, those instances are so limited that they would not cover most present-day Of Counsel relationships.

to the office because it was a place to stay away from home did not create an Of Counsel relationship.[7]

Thus, in *Mutual of Omaha Insurance Co. v. Chadwell,*[8] a federal district court, relying on the language of Formal Opinion 330, questioned whether an Of Counsel relationship existed where the retired partner merely maintained an office on the premises with no expectation that the retired partner would continue to render any legal services for the firm. The Of Counsel contract did not require the lawyer to fulfill a minimum number of work hours per week, nor was a physical presence in the office required for practicing law. But the contract did require the firm to provide the lawyer with office space, secretarial support, group insurance coverage, and a fixed annual compensation. The court, relying on 330, doubted whether the relationship in question was in fact a "close" or "continuing" one.[9]

Today, many Of Counsel are retired partners who continue to serve the firm full-time as consultants on various matters. A retired partner may continue with the firm as Of Counsel, practicing law on a diminished basis. Or the retired partner may relocate to another area and become Of Counsel with a firm there, as well as with the former firm. In other arrangements, the retiring partner might maintain an office with the same or a different firm, while pursuing independent interests. Most observers saw the "close, continuing, personal relationship" required by Formal Opinion 330 as much too restrictive for many situations in which a retired partner desired to branch out and do other things independently of the law office at which he or she was once partner.

Formal Opinion 90-357 has changed these rules, so that a retired partner now has many options. The new perspective in 90-357 is reflected in the following language of the committee:

> Formal Opinion 330 may be read as limiting the permissible use of the term "of counsel" by retired partners of a firm, because of possible implications from language in that opinion that an of counsel lawyer must be compensated for such legal

---

7. Corinne Maskaleris, *"Of Counsel"—Defined* at 14 (compilation from transcript of *Of Counsel: Revisited,* a program presented by the Senior Lawyers Division of the American Bar Association at the Annual Meeting, Aug. 6, 1980) (available from Senior Lawyers Division, ABA).

8. 426 F. Supp. 550 (N.D. Ill. 1977).

9. *Id.* at 552.

> work as the lawyer does, but only for that legal work—which, if strictly read, would exclude both a retired partner whose sole income from the firm is the partner's pension or other retirement benefit and counsel who share in some degree in the firm's profits. *See also* Informal Opinion 710. It is the Committee's view that, other conditions just described having been met, it is not relevant to the permissibility of use of "of counsel" what the compensation arrangements are. Similarly, some retired partners might be deemed to be excluded by the suggestion in Formal Opinion 330 that an of counsel's relationship to the firm must be "so close that he is in regular and frequent, if not daily, contact with the office of the lawyer or firm" (citing Informal Opinion 1134). Again, insofar as Formal Opinion 330 carries any implication that the contact must be so frequent as to verge on daily, the Committee now disavows it.[10] (Footnotes omitted.)

Most states have followed the rules established by Formal Opinion 90-357 as they pertain to retired partners. Since the publication of the first edition of this book, many states have modified their ethics rules to comply with the changes brought about by 90-357. For example, in Ohio, a retired lawyer may remain Of Counsel to a law firm so long as he or she remains an active member of the bar and provided the firm letterhead lists the lawyer as "retired."[11] In Arizona, a retired partner may be designated Of Counsel even if only an office is maintained on the premises of the former firm.[12] In Iowa, a retired partner need not be "active" in the practice of law to establish a proper Of Counsel relationship.[13]

Whatever the scope of the retired partner's activities, when that person becomes Of Counsel, rights and duties vis-à-vis the

---

10. ABA Formal Op. 90-357 at 4.

11. Opinion No. 91-18, The Supreme Court of Ohio, Bd. of Commissioners on Grievances and Discipline (August 16, 1991).

12. Arizona State Bar Ethics Opinion 81-2 (1981).

13. Iowa State Bar Ethics Opinion 80-27 (1980). But that state's ethics committee noted:

> Retired attorneys need not be active to be listed as "of counsel" on the firm stationery. Whether the retired lawyers "practice law" so as to require compliance with the rules governing the Client Security and Attorney Disciplinary Commission and/or the Commission on Continuing Legal Education, is a question each lawyer must determine for himself.

firm should be spelled out in detail in writing and should include matters such as compensation and the extent of income from participation in a particular matter and/or activities of the firm.[14]

The Part-Time Practitioner

Formal Opinion 90-357 describes a part-time practitioner this way:

> [One] who practices law in association with a firm, but on a basis different from that of the mainstream lawyers in the firm. Such part-time practitioners are sometimes lawyers who have decided to change from a full-time practice, either with that firm or another, to a part-time one, or sometimes lawyers who have changed careers entirely, as for example former judges or government officials.[15]

In many situations, the category of the lawyer who changes from full-time to part-time practitioner will overlap with that of the retired partner. The ethics committee makes it clear that any lawyer may change from full-time to part-time practice and use the Of Counsel designation to describe that new status. The committee defines the part-time practitioner as one "who practices law in association with a firm, but on a basis different from that of mainstream lawyers in the firm."[16] There is no requirement that the Of Counsel designation be reserved only for lawyers who change from full-time practice to part-time practice with the same firm. Such a part-time practitioner is subject to all the rules governing lawyers generally with the limitations that arise because of the limited amount of time involved in practice.

The second subcategory described in 90-357—the lawyer who changes careers—is quite a different species. Although Formal Opinion 90-357 mentioned only judges and government officials as lawyers who would fit into this category, corporate counsel and tenured professors are a couple of the other types of lawyers who

14. In *Trittipo v. O'Brien* (Ill. App., 1990) No. 1-88-2455, it was held that law firms need not purchase the shares of partners upon their retirement from a professional service corporation or partnership. Because of this holding, a lawyer moving from partner to Of Counsel status should be certain to place everyting in writing.

15. ABA Formal Op. 90-357 at 3.

16. *Id.*

may have to change careers because they are required to retire at a certain age. In this last category, the change may just as likely be to a full-time as to a part-time law practice.

The propriety of persons who have changed careers entirely to become Of Counsel centers around quite different issues from those dealing with lawyers who have decided to change from a full-time practice to a part-time one. Typically, the arrangement between the lawyer and the firm has only recently been formed, so there is not a "close, regular, personal" relationship. Yet Formal Opinion 330 appeared to relax the requirement of a "close, continuing, personal" relationship—at least when the lawyer was a retired public official. It required that, for there to be a "close and continuing" relationship, a retired public official need only be "regularly and locally available for consultation and advice." But this revision still implied that the retired public official's contact with the firm had to be frequent, "if not daily," as in the case of the retired partner.

The former official who becomes Of Counsel today will no doubt wonder whether the Formal Opinion 330 definition of a "close and continuing relationship" will apply under Formal Opinion 90-357 now that Formal Opinion 330 has been withdrawn. If we apply the 90-357 language dealing with the retired partner[17] to the situation of the public official, it would appear that the new rules have eliminated much of the earlier restrictions. Under 90-357, however, firms are unlikely to return to the old practice of decorating the letterhead by using names of former public officials who have only a minimal relationship with the firm. Such an arrangement would not satisfy the requirement of a "close, regular, personal" relationship under Formal Opinion 330 or 90-357.

The Probationary Partner

In Formal Opinion 90-357, the ethics committee selected a third category of lawyers for specific mention as qualifying for the Of Counsel designation: the probationary partner-to-be. The ethics committee has described a "probationary partner-to-be" as "a lawyer brought into the firm laterally with the expectation of becoming partner after a relatively short period of time."[18]

---

17. *See* the earlier discussion of the retired partner in this chapter.
18. ABA Formal Op. 90-357 at 3.

In drafting agreements, lawyers and law firms both will welcome the committee's permission to use the Of Counsel designation for the probationary partner. Such an arrangement enables Of Counsel and the law firm to try out one another. If the arrangement is a success, the probationary partner moves to full partner status. If it should fail, Of Counsel can move on to another arrangement without embarrassment either to himself or to the firm.

In one important respect, 90-357 has adopted a new rule affecting both probationary partners and senior attorneys. Formal Opinion 330 implied that Of Counsel could not be an employee of the firm. Formal Opinion 90-357 recognizes that both of these categories "involve, as a technical matter the status of an employee."[19] The committee has now stated:

> Insofar as Formal Opinion 330 may be read to conclude that either the probationary partner model or the permanent between-partner-and-associate model are not permissibly designated of counsel, that conclusion is disavowed.[20]

Obviously, the most important concern of probationary partners who are Of Counsel will be their relationship with their new professional association. As with an antenuptial agreement, the terms of such a relationship should be reduced to writing. Since a probationary partner normally comes into the firm because of some special expertise or long experience, each agreement should be custom-tailored to the particular Of Counsel and the firm to be joined. Matters of status, compensation, pension rights, and the like should be handled with great care.[21]

The Senior Attorney

Like the probationary partner, the senior attorney is technically an employee of the law firm. But unlike the probationary partner, the senior attorney is expressly denied the traditional goal of partner. As the ethics committee has noted, the senior attorney's status is a relatively new development:

> A fourth, relatively recent, use of the term [Of Counsel] is to designate a permanent status between those of partner and as-

19. *Id.* at 4.
20. *Id.*
21. *See* Chapter 11 and Appendixes A through G.

> sociate—akin to the category just described, but having the quality of tenure, or something close to it, and lacking that of an expectation of likely promotion to full partner status.[22]

An Of Counsel lawyer in this in-between status, the committee notes, is often referred to as a "senior attorney" or "principal attorney."

The growth of this particular category of Of Counsel is not surprising in view of the changing needs of the lawyers and the law firms on opposite sides of the arrangement. Many lawyers welcome the security that such a position would offer. Typically, the senior attorney receives a guaranteed income for life, without enjoying the possible profits or assuming any of the risks of loss that accompany the status of partner. The law firm will welcome the senior attorney's presence in that it will be guaranteed to have this person's expertise without having to involve the nonpartner in the management of the firm or give him or her a share of the general profits. The arrangement may well be very desirable for all concerned.

In discussing the use of the term "Of Counsel" generally, the ethics committee has emphasized that many terms are used within the profession to describe "Of Counsel":

> [A]lthough "of counsel" appears to be the most frequently used among the various titles employing the term "counsel," it is by no means the only use of that term to indicate a relationship between a lawyer and a law firm. Other such titles include the single word "counsel," and the terms "special counsel," "tax [or other specialty] counsel," and "senior counsel." It is the Committee's view that, whatever the connotative differences evoked by these variants of the title "counsel," they all share the central, and defining, characteristic of the relationship that is denoted by the term "of counsel," and so should all be understood to be covered by the present opinion.[23]

Thus, 90-357 governs all forms of Of Counsel, including such groups classified as "senior attorneys." Some firms seek to use different terminology for the various categories of Of Counsel. The word "counsel" might be used to describe the senior attorney, so that the term "Of Counsel" could be reserved for retired partners.

---

22. ABA Formal Op. 90-357 at 3.
23. *Id.*

Although the use of different terminology may be necessary for different contractual arrangements within the firm, we believe that the use of "Of Counsel" on the letterhead and other notices to the general public is the better practice. This is particularly true now that Formal Opinion 90-357 has officially recognized these many and varied relationships.

Specifically Prohibited Of Counsel Relationships

In Formal Opinion 90-357, the ethics committee first provided four "safe harbors" for those entering Of Counsel relationships.[24] But it also proscribed four situations that the drafters of Of Counsel agreements must avoid:

> [I]t is not ethically permissible to use the term "of counsel" to designate the following professional relationships: a relationship involving only an individual case, *see* Informal Opinion 678, Formal Opinion 330; a relationship of forwarder or receiver of legal business, *see* Formal Opinion 330; a relationship involving only occasional collaborative efforts among otherwise unrelated lawyers or firms, *see id.*; and the relationship of an outside consultant, *see id.*[25]

The common thread that runs through these four prohibited categories is their transitory nature.

The Lawyer Associated in a Single Case

In Informal Opinion 678, the ethics committee noted that the Of Counsel relationship cannot exist if it was based on consultation in only one particular case.[26] In proscribing the use of the Of Counsel designation in a single case, the committee was primarily concerned with Of Counsel's posture vis-à-vis the general public:

> The reference here is not to the appearance of a lawyer or firm on the court filings of a particular case, but rather to representation of an "of counsel" relationship on firm letterhead, professional cards, and the like on the basis of collaboration on a single case.[27]

24. *See* Chapter 3.

25. ABA Formal Op. 90-357, reprinted *infra*, Appendix I, at 242 (footnote omitted).

26. *See* the later discussion of the law firm as Of Counsel in this chapter.

27. ABA Formal Op. 90-357 at 4 n.7.

Avoidance of the representation that a lawyer was Of Counsel where the association was only for a single case would present a potential misrepresentation of the lawyer's status to the general public. Of Counsel are free to use the designation in court filings, appellate briefs, and the like, which the general public, as distinct from the litigants, would normally never see.

The Forwarder-Receiver of Legal Business

The Of Counsel designation does not apply where the relationship consists of nothing more than the referral of prospective clients to the other lawyer or firm.[28] The designation requires a close, regular, and personal relationship with the other lawyer or law firm, qualities that are not ordinarily found in a typical forwarder-receiver relationship.

A relationship that is limited to the referral of prospective clients between lawyers will not satisfy the requirements of an Of Counsel relationship, regardless of the past relationship between the lawyers or their future anticipated relationship. Where the relationship is only that of forwarder-receiver, the designation is not proper, even if the lawyer is a former partner of the firm[29] or the lawyers anticipate a merger in the near future.[30] This is true even if the referral of clients is used as a means of handling a recurring problem of overflow work. The Of Counsel designation has also been held improper where a national "law firm" advertises and refers cases to the lawyer in return for a percentage of fees generated.[31]

The Occasional Collaborator

When a lawyer occasionally collaborates with otherwise unrelated lawyers or firms, the absence of a regular or continuing relationship again prompts a prohibition against the use of the Of Counsel

28. ABA Formal Op. 330 (1972); Alabama State Ethics Opinion 86-28 (1986); Arizona State Ethics Opinion 81-1 (1981), *aff'd*, Opinion 87-24 (1987); Illinois State Ethics Opinion 87-12 (1988); Michigan Informal Ethics Opinion CI-536 (1981); New Jersey State Ethics Opinion 476 (1981); New York City Ethics Opinion 81-109 (undated); Philadelphia State Ethics Opinion 80-114 (undated).

29. Philadelphia State Ethics Opinion 80-114 (undated).

30. ABA Comm. on Ethics and Professional Responsibility, Informal Op. 1378 (1976).

31. New Jersey State Ethics Opinion 476 (1981); Illinois State Ethics Opinion 840 (1981).

designation. These collaborative efforts are isolated in-and-out situations in which the Of Counsel does not continue to provide day-to-day professional advice to a law firm or lawyer.

Of Counsel or Outside Consultant?

After retirement, partners frequently remain available to the firm as consultants, often to ensure continuity of cultivated business relationships. Likewise, a retired judge may become Of Counsel to be available to review briefs of the firm. A lawyer with expertise in a particular field of law may join a firm as Of Counsel to fill a need to compete against larger firms for clients.[32]

In the earlier Formal Opinion 330, the committee recognized that Of Counsel are often used as consultants:

> [The Of Counsel] relationship with the lawyer or law firm must be a close, regular, personal relationship like, for example, the relationship of a retired or semi-retired former partner who remains available to the firm for consultation and advice, or a retired public official who regularly and locally is available to the firm for consultation and advice.[33]

The committee stipulated that Of Counsel must be a "member or component part of the law office."[34] In the headnote, the committee concluded that the Of Counsel relationship must be "one that is not that of a partner, associate, or *outside consultant*."[35] But the committee failed to define what it meant by the phrase "outside consultant." Formal Opinion 90-357 fails to throw any additional light on the meaning of "outside consultant." Through custom, the word "consultant" has come to refer to one who has particular expertise and who is used by a lawyer or law firm, either generally or on a case-by-case basis.[36] But there is no definition of "outside consultant" in the Model Code or the Model Rules. And, since the committee failed to define when a consultant becomes an "outside consultant," its use of the phrase remains ambiguous.

---

32. M. ALTMAN & R. WEIL, HOW TO MANAGE YOUR LAW OFFICE, § 2.12 (Matthew Bender 1988) (quoting Flaherty, *The Many Roles for Of Counsel*, NAT'L L.J., Sept. 13, 1982).

33. ABA Formal Op. 330.

34. *Id.*

35. *Id.* (emphasis added).

36. *See* ABA Comm. on Professional Ethics, Informal Op. 1189 (Sept. 1971).

This is particularly troublesome for Of Counsel whose primary role may be limited to that of consultation. If the lawyer's activities with the firm are limited to consultation, is the term "outside consultant" appropriate? If the lawyer has a close association with the firm but resides in another city or state, is that lawyer considered an "outside consultant"? Is the lawyer an "outside consultant" who has a separate office from that of the law firm or other lawyer? Or is the lawyer considered an "outside consultant" only if he or she was not formerly associated with the lawyer or law firm as a partner or associate?

Some general guidelines can be gleaned from prior informal opinions. Informal Opinion 678[37] stated that an Of Counsel relationship cannot exist if the relationship is based on consultation in only one particular case. The facts that gave rise to the opinion were these: A firm proposed to designate an out-of-state lawyer Of Counsel for purposes of one case. The lawyer was in the office of the firm during the trial but was not admitted to practice in the state where the firm was located. He did not desire to become a member of the bar of that state, and intended to return to his home state at the end of the trial. The committee stated:

> [I]t seems to us it would be misleading if the relationship existed only as to one particular case even though it might be one of great importance which would require the very active participation of the outside counsel over an extended period of time, and even though a great deal of that time was actually spent in the office of the local firm.[38]

Informal Opinion 678 indicated that an Of Counsel relationship can exist between a lawyer and a law firm or another lawyer even though the first lawyer's activities are limited to consultation. But if the lawyer is not frequently available on an ongoing basis, the correct appellation would be "outside consultant," and the Of Counsel designation cannot be used. Given the 90-357 requirement of a "close, regular, personal" relationship, it appears that the same reasoning would apply today.

Several state bar panels addressing the question of when a consultant is an "outside consultant" appear to follow the reasoning of Informal Opinion 678. Indeed, in some states, the Of Counsel

---

37. ABA Comm. on Professional Ethics, Informal Op. 678 (1963).
38. *Id.*

relationship requires something more than mere consultation, regardless of the frequency of contact between the lawyer and firm. In New York, for example, mere consultation, regardless of the frequency, is insufficient to establish an Of Counsel relationship.[39] In Texas, an Of Counsel relationship does not exist if the lawyer is available only for consultation with firm members.[40]

Other state ethics committees are very lenient. In Arizona, for example, an Of Counsel relationship can exist where, at the minimum, the lawyer is available for general consultation, regardless of frequency.[41]

As far as we can discern, 90-357 continues the basic philosophy of prior ABA informal and formal opinions. The "outside consultant" is precluded from using the Of Counsel designation because that person does not have the sufficient continuing relationship with the law firm or lawyer to satisfy the committee's concept of Of Counsel.

Since the emphasis in Formal Opinion 90-357 is on the closeness and regularity of the relationship, consultation limited to a particular area of law will not preclude the existence of an Of Counsel relationship. Prior ABA informal opinions and several state bar opinions have expressed the view that a consultant specializing in tax law or in patent, trademark, and copyright law may be designated Of Counsel, provided the consultant maintains a close and continuing relationship with the other lawyer or firm.[42] Arizona has held that a lawyer available for consultation in a particular field of law can be designated Of Counsel, but that "more

---

39. New York State Bar Ethics Opinion 81-3 (undated).

40. Texas State Bar Ethics Opinion 402 (1982).

41. Arizona State Bar Ethics Opinion 87-24 (1987).

42. ABA Comm. on Professional Ethics, Informal Op. 1132 (1970) and 901 (1965); Arizona Ethics Opinion 87-24 (1987); Philadelphia Ethics Opinion 86-143 (1986) (holding that the lawyer may even be designated "tax counsel"); South Carolina Ethics Opinion 81-2 (1981) (patent, trademark, and copyright law). After Formal Opinion 330 was issued, questions remained concerning whether the firm could list the particular lawyer's specialty in legal lists or on the firm's letterhead. ABA Informal Opinion 901 prohibited the lawyer from being designated "Tax Counsel" on the firm's letterhead, even though the lawyer would handle all tax matters for the firm. A better designation, the committee wrote, would be that the lawyer is "Of Counsel or Counsel" for the firm. Formal Opinion 90-357 resolves this question by allowing Of Counsel to list their areas of specialty on the letterhead.

descriptive language should be included to explain the true nature of the relationship."[43] The Of Counsel designation is also permitted where the consultant does not practice law but, in his employment as a government official or university professor, has acquired expertise in a certain area of law.[44]

Other Of Counsel Relationships

Having specifically approved four categories of Of Counsel and prohibited four others, the ethics committee in Formal Opinion 90-357 provided some guidance for several situations that it did not directly address but that may, nonetheless, satisfy the requirements necessary for using the Of Counsel designation. In reaching our conclusions whether the designation is or is not appropriate, we shall also consider the informal opinions and the state bar ethics decisions.

The Public Official

In 90-357, the ethics committee's discussion of the use of the Of Counsel designation by former judges and public officials was in connection with second careers—that is, where the lawyer gave up a public position and title to practice law. As a practical matter, many lawyers want to maintain or develop a professional working arrangement with a law firm or individual lawyer while still in public office.

The more complicated case, and one not specifically addressed by 330 or 90-357, occurs where the lawyer wants to maintain an Of Counsel relationship with a firm or other lawyer while *currently* holding a public office. The questions raised by this scenario are twofold: First, does a public official's duties interfere with an ability to develop and maintain a continuing relationship with a firm or other lawyer to the extent required by 90-357? Second, would the person's current status as a public official create an unjustified expectation in third persons that an undue influence might be exerted to achieve a desired result?

The ABA informal opinions do not prohibit per se a public official from entering into an Of Counsel relationship; instead, per-

43. Arizona State Ethics Opinion 87-24 (1987).

44. Iowa State Ethics Opinion 87-12 (1987).

missive use of the term appears to turn on whether the lawyer has established a close, personal, and continuing relationship with the lawyer or law firm. ABA Informal Opinion 1134[45] addressed the question of whether the term could be used to describe a relationship between a firm and a United States Senator. The Senator wished to become affiliated with the firm as Of Counsel. Because of his senatorial duties, his practice of law was limited. He did, however, practice law whenever his duties permitted. Although he had an established continuing relationship with the firm, he had never been a member of the firm. The committee allowed the Senator to be designated Of Counsel, so long as he engaged in the practice of law, practiced in the offices of the firm, and rendered legal advice to the firm's clients.[46] By this view, in the case of the *current* officeholder, a continuing relationship exists and the Of Counsel designation is proper where his official duties allow sufficient time to engage in the practice of law with that firm.

Some states follow the requirements set out in the ABA Informal Opinion. Michigan prohibits current political officeholders from using the Of Counsel designation if the officeholder does not "actively and regularly engage in the practice of law with that firm."[47] Mississippi has a similar provision that prohibits public officeholders from using the Of Counsel designation to describe their relationship with law firms, unless they actively practice law in the firm or render legal advice to the clients of the firm.[48] The fact that an officeholder may have at one time been a former partner in the firm and thus had established a close relationship was irrelevant. If the former partner would not now be active in the practice of the firm, the designation was inappropriate, and the former partner could no longer be listed on the firm's letterhead.[49]

Other states have adopted a different standard: The designation is appropriate if the public official's past relationship as a partner with a firm satisfies the requirement of a continuing relationship. For example, Maryland allows current officeholders to be listed as Of Counsel to firms in which they were once partners, even though they are not currently and actively engaged in

45. ABA Comm. on Professional Ethics, Informal Op. 1134 (1969).

46. *Id.*

47. Michigan State Bar Ethics Opinion CI-886 (1983).

48. Mississippi State Bar Ethics Opinion 66 (1981).

49. *Id.*

the practice of law with the firm.[50] Some states' standards are even more relaxed. Illinois allows current officeholders to be designated Of Counsel to a firm even if they do not actively and regularly practice law as a member of the firm.[51]

The Law Professor

Closely related to the situation of the public official is that of the full-time law professor who practices with a law firm on a part-time basis. As long as there is a close, continuing, and personal relationship between the firm and the law professor, there is no objection to the professor's being considered Of Counsel to the firm. A law school may restrict the extent of activity of a member of its full-time faculty; but more often than not, the law firm and the law school both will find that the designation of one of their faculty as Of Counsel to the firm will be to the advantage of both.

The Out-of-State Of Counsel

Several ABA informal opinions have held that it is not per se improper for a lawyer in one state to be Of Counsel to a lawyer or law firm in another state.[52] The primary questions addressed by these informal opinions is whether Of Counsel must be licensed to practice in the state where he or she is listed as Of Counsel, and if not, whether the lawyer must list such jurisdictional limitations on the letterhead of the firm.[53]

The states have developed diverse and conflicting rules regarding out-of-state Of Counsel. Some states favor a requirement that Of Counsel be admitted to practice in the state where the affiliated lawyer or firm is located. Alaska, for instance, requires out-of-state Of Counsel to be licensed in the jurisdiction where the firm or other lawyer is located, unless the Of Counsel's activities are limited to advising the firm on legal matters in the out-of-stater's own jurisdiction.[54] In North Carolina, an out-of-state lawyer may maintain an Of Counsel relationship with a firm located in North Caro-

---

50. Maryland State Bar Ethics Opinion 83-50 (1983).

51. Illinois State Bar Ethics Opinion 817 (1982).

52. ABA Comm. on Professional Ethics, Informal Ops. 83-1499 (1983), 1315 (1975), and 1173 (1971).

53. *See* Chapter 9.

54. Alaska State Ethics Opinion 84-5 (1984).

lina only if the lawyer is licensed to practice in North Carolina.[55] The State of Washington requires Of Counsel to be an active member of the state bar association.[56] Other jurisdictions, such as Michigan[57] and Alabama,[58] without directly confronting the issue, have noted that a proper Of Counsel relationship can exist with out-of-state lawyers only when they are admitted to practice in the same state as the affiliated lawyer or law firm.

Still other states do not require Of Counsel to be licensed in the same state as the affiliated firm, but these states may require that jurisdictional limitations be noted on the firm's letterhead. In California, where law firms may be listed as Of Counsel to other lawyers or firms,[59] a lawyer or law firm may list an out-of-state firm as Of Counsel even if none of the out-of-state firm's lawyers are licensed to practice in California.[60] To avoid misleading the public, all listings must negate the impression that the firm or lawyer resides in California or is licensed to practice in California.[61] In New York and South Carolina, a lawyer may be designated Of Counsel to an in-state firm even though the lawyer is not admitted to practice in that state, provided that jurisdictional limitations are listed on the firm letterhead.[62]

Expense-Sharing Arrangements

Lawyers often enter into loose arrangements with other lawyers. Some of these arrangements may be for long-term sharing of overhead expenses. Or one lawyer may associate with another lawyer

---

55. North Carolina Ethics Opinion 34 (1987).

56. Washington State Bar Ethics Opinion 178 (1984).

57. Michigan State Ethics Opinion CI-1018 (1984).

58. Alabama State Ethics Opinion 426 (1981); *see also* Alabama State Ethics Opinion 86-86 (1986) (A lawyer may include on his or her letterhead the name of an out-of-state law firm with which the lawyer has an Of Counsel relationship. The law firm's letterhead must indicate any lawyers who are not licensed to practice law in this state).

59. *See* Chapter 3 for a discussion of using the term to describe a relationship between law firms.

60. California State Bar Formal Opinion 1986-88 (undated).

61. *Id.*

62. *See* New York City Ethics Opinion 80-66 (undated); New York City Ethics Opinions 80-22 (undated) and 81-3 (undated); *see also* South Carolina Ethics Opinion 81-2 (1981).

on a temporary basis,[63] particularly where the lawyer experiences a short-term increase in work. An older lawyer may, instead of fully retiring, enlarge his or her office to provide reduced rental space for a younger lawyer in return for that lawyer's promise to devote a fixed number of hours per week to the older lawyer's practice. Two or more solo practitioners, while otherwise maintaining complete autonomy, may agree to share office space and the expenses incurred in the practice of law. In all of these arrangements, the associated lawyers may share office space and expenses.

Can these office-sharing arrangements ever create an Of Counsel relationship? In general, the answer is no. The mere sharing of office space and expenses is insufficient to establish a true Of Counsel relationship.[64] To be closely related for purposes of satisfying the first aspect of the core characteristic of the Of Counsel relationship, most states require that lawyers currently "practice together."[65] In Kansas, lawyers who once practiced together, but who now only share office space, may not designate each other as Of Counsel unless they intend to continue to work closely together.[66]

Liberalized Rules Governing Of Counsel Relationships

Although much of Formal Opinion 90-357 is devoted to a discussion of varying fact situations that may, or may not, give rise to an Of Counsel relationship, the opinion articulated a number of rules affecting all Of Counsel relationships. For the most part, these rules are less restrictive than those reflected in Formal Opinion 330 or the informal opinions of the ABA's ethics committee.

---

63. A. Wolfson, *State High Court Approves Temporary Lawyers With Restrictions*, COURIER JOURNAL (Louisville, Ky.), Nov. 19, 1989, at B1.

64. ABA Comm. on Ethics and Professional Responsibility, Informal Op. 84-1506 (1984); *see also* Washington State Ethics Opinion 178 (1984).

65. Kansas State Ethics Opinion 83-34 (1983) and 83-34A (1984); Maine State Bar Ethics Opinion 86 (1988) (holding that a law firm composed of one full-time lawyer and one Of Counsel lawyer available for consultation on a regular basis may use a firm name that incorporates both lawyers' names provided the arrangement is more than an office-sharing arrangement; they must practice together, cooperate and consult, and share significant mutual responsibility for legal services); Washington State Ethics Opinion 178 (1984).

66. Kansas State Ethics Opinion 83-34 (1983) and 83-34A (1984).

The Law Firm As Of Counsel

A good example of such liberalization is the change that now allows a law *firm,* as distinct from an individual lawyer, to be Of Counsel to another lawyer or law firm. In Informal Opinion 1173,[67] the committee relied on the literal language of DR 2-102(A)(4) of the Model Code and, in part, on a rule pertaining to law lists and legal directories found in DR 2-102(A)(6) (which was later deleted from the Model Code) in finding that a law firm located in one city could not be designated Of Counsel to a lawyer in another city. DR 2-102(A)(4) provides:

> A lawyer may be designated "Of Counsel" on a letterhead if he has a continuing relationship with a lawyer or law firm other than as a partner or associate.

The committee held that "the very omission of the words 'law firm'" precludes a law firm from using the Of Counsel designation. The committee further held that, because "the practice of law is personal in nature and a law firm as such is never admitted to practice in any state," the phrase should not encompass law firms.[68]

The holding of Informal Opinion 1173 was later affirmed in Formal Opinion 330, but was subsequently overruled in part in Formal Opinion 84-351. Formal Opinion 84-351, which was written after several United States Supreme Court decisions expanded First Amendment protections for lawyer advertising,[69] acknowledged that there can be no per se bar against one firm being Of Counsel to another.[70] But the opinion stopped short of allowing the phrase "Of Counsel" to describe a continuing relationship between law firms. Instead, the committee authorized the terms "as-

---

67. ABA Comm. on Professional Ethics, Informal Op. 1173 (1971), *aff'd,* ABA Comm. on Ethics and Professional Responsibility, Formal Op. 330 (1972).

68. ABA Comm. on Professional Ethics, Informal Op. 1173 (1971).

69. *In re* R.M.J., 455 U.S. 191 (1982); Bates v. Arizona State Bar Ass'n, 433 U.S. 350 (1977). After these decisions, Model Code provisions DR 2-101 through DR 2-105 were substantially revised. DR 2-102(A)(4) was retained, but DR 2-102(A)(6) was deleted. The Model Rules, adopted after *R.M.J.,* prohibit any "false or misleading communication about the lawyer or the lawyer's services." *See* MODEL RULES OF PROFESSIONAL CONDUCT, Rules 7.1 and 7.5.

70. ABA Comm. on Professional Ethics, Formal Op. 84-351 (1984).

sociated" or "affiliated" to describe such a relationship.[71] An "affiliated" or "associated" law firm, the committee wrote, must be available to the other firm and its clients for consultation and advice, much as the individual Of Counsel is.[72] The committee, in fact, stated:

> The type of relationship that is implied by designating another firm as "affiliated" or "associated" is analogous to the ongoing relationship that is required by Model Code DR 2-102(A)(4) when using the designation "Of Counsel" as amplified by the guidelines in Formal Opinion 330 and Informal Opinion 1315.[73]

Many state ethics committees adhere to the traditional rule and disallow law firms from using the Of Counsel designation to describe their relationship with another law firm.[74] But other states do not impose a per se prohibition.[75] In Alabama, the designation can be used to describe a relationship between an Alabama law firm and an out-of-state law firm, provided the relationship between the two firms is close and involves frequent contact.[76] The Alabama committee noted that the phrase "Of Counsel" usually denotes an individual lawyer's relationship with a firm. But it could find no explicit Model Code provision prohibiting the relationship be-

---

71. *Id.*

72. *Id.*

73. *Id.*

74. Iowa State Ethics Opinion 83-12 (1983) (two law firms may not be of counsel to each other); New York City Ethics Opinion 81-3, 81-3 amended (undated) (a law firm may not be listed as Of Counsel on the letterhead of another firm, since only an individual may develop the personal nature of the relationship necessary for the designation Of Counsel); Wisconsin State Ethics Opinion E-86-10 (1986) (a law firm may not be designated Of Counsel to another law firm).

75. Alabama State Ethics Opinion 86-28 (1986); Arizona State Ethics Opinion 87-24 (1987) (a law firm may be listed as Of Counsel on the letterhead and other communications of another law firm as long as the designation is consistent with the actual relationship between the firms); California State Bar Formal Opinion 1986-88 (undated); Kentucky Ethics Opinion 311 (1986); Massachusetts State Bar Ethics Opinion 82-10 (1982); Michigan Informal Ethics Opinion CI-1029 (1984).

76. Alabama State Ethics Opinion 86-28 (1986).

tween law firms.[77] California allows law firms to use the phrase "Of Counsel" to describe their relationship.[78] Massachusetts has allowed a professional corporation of lawyers to be Of Counsel to another firm or lawyer.[79] Michigan allows law firms to be designated as Of Counsel to other lawyers or law firms whether located in Michigan or out-of-state.[80]

Other states recognize that a continuing relationship can exist between law firms, but nonetheless do not allow the phrase "Of Counsel" to describe that relationship. The District of Columbia and Wisconsin prohibit the use of the "Of Counsel" designation to describe a relationship between law firms.[81] These states permit firms to use only the terms "associated" or "affiliated" for this purpose.

Formal Opinion 90-357 overruled all prior ABA opinions that prevented a law firm from being Of Counsel to another law firm or lawyer. In the committee's words:

> The Committee has also previously held that a *firm* cannot be of counsel to another lawyer or law firm, *see* Informal Opinion 1173, Formal Opinion 330. The reasoning here was that the term connotes an individual rather than a firm. This may be still so as a matter of current usage, but semantics aside, the Committee's prior opinions do not suggest, and the Committee does not now perceive, any reason of [sic] policy why a firm should not be of counsel to another firm. Moreover, the Committee held in Formal Opinion 84-351 (1984) that two law firms could ethically present themselves as "affiliated" or "associated" with each other, and in Informal Opinion 1315 (1975), the Committee gave its approval to arrangements whereby two firms effectively became "of counsel" to each

77. *Id.*

78. California State Bar Formal Opinion 1986-88 (undated).

79. Massachusetts State Ethics Opinion 82-10 (1982).

80. Opinion No. RI-102, State Bar of Michigan, Standing Committee on Professional and Judicial Ethics (October 1, 1991).

81. District of Columbia Ethics Opinion 192 (1988); Wisconsin State Ethics Opinion E-86-10 (1986). *But see* New York City Ethics Opinion 81-78 (undated) (prohibiting a law firm from listing on its letterhead as an "associated" firm the name of another firm that handles numerous matters for the firm but is otherwise unrelated; the term "associated" is imprecise in its meaning and therefore is misleading).

other, by each designating a partner of the other firm as "of counsel" to itself. As with multiple of counsel relationships of a single lawyer, the relationships between firms addressed in Formal Opinion 84-351 and Informal Opinion 1315 would of course entail complete reciprocal attribution of the disqualifications of all lawyers in each firm.[82]

Allowing law firms to serve as Of Counsel to one another is a welcome change that has caused some state bar ethics committees to reconsider their positions. For states that have not yet taken a position on this point, 90-357 represents the sounder view from a policy standpoint, as long as law firms are aware of the attribution and disqualification rules inherent in these arrangements.[83]

Multiple Of Counsel Relationships

Another example of the liberalization of the Of Counsel rules in Formal Opinion 90-357 is the change with respect to a lawyer (or law firm) serving as Of Counsel to multiple firms or lawyers. Formal Opinion 330 held that it was improper for a lawyer to be Of Counsel to more than two law firms. This view was first expressed in ABA Informal Opinion 1173,[84] in which the committee stated:

> [I]t is not proper, in our opinion, for any lawyer or law firm to be designated "Of Counsel" to more than one lawyer or law firm . . . especially because the continuing relationship . . . connotes a close, daily, in-house association, free and clear of problems of conflict.

Informal Opinion 1189 affirmed the view that a lawyer cannot be Of Counsel to more than one lawyer or law firm.[85] These opinions were modified in the text of ABA Formal Opinion 330, which stated:

> While it would be highly unusual for a lawyer to be able to maintain simultaneously with two law firms the close, personal relationship indicated by the term "Of Counsel," it may not be impossible for such a situation to exist. It is obviously

82. ABA Formal Op. 90-357 at 5-6.
83. *See* Chapters 7 and 8.
84. ABA Informal Op. 1173 (1971).
85. ABA Informal Op. 1189 (1971).

impossible, however, for one to maintain such a relationship with more than two law firms.[86]

The headnote of Formal Opinion 330 concluded that a lawyer could not be Of Counsel to more than *two* law firms. Although the headnote did not precisely comport with the view that the committee expressed in the text, many states held that a lawyer may be Of Counsel to no more than two firms.[87] At least one state set a limit of one.[88]

Although at some point the number of Of Counsel relationships may be too great to maintain the close relationship necessary for use of the designation, the committee that issued 330 was not warranted using an arbitrary number to set a limit. In allowing a lawyer or law firm to be Of Counsel to multiple lawyers or law firms, the committee that wrote 90-357 recognized that it was quite possible to maintain a continuing relationship with multiple law firms. In adopting this more liberal approach, the committee stated:

> [T]he Committee's initial view, expressed in Informal Opinion 1173, was that a lawyer could not be of counsel to more than a single firm; and this was modified in Formal Opinion 330 to set a limit of two firms. On further consideration, the Committee finds the conclusion it reached on this subject in Formal Opinion 330 to be a doubtful one. The proposition that it is not possible for a lawyer to have a "close, regular, personal relationship" with more than two lawyers or law firms is not a self-evident one. A lawyer can surely have a close, regular, personal relationship with more than two clients; and the Committee sees no reason why the same cannot be true with more than two law firms. There is, to be sure, some point at which the number of relationships would be too great for any of them to have the necessary qualities of closeness and regularity, and that number may not be much beyond two, but the

---

86. ABA Formal Op. 330 (1972).

87. Connecticut State Ethics Opinion 88-13 (1988) (a lawyer who is designated Of Counsel at two different law firms may use his name and designation on the letterhead of each firm); Texas State Ethics Opinion 402 (1982).

88. Iowa State Ethics Opinion 87-9 (1987) (lawyers may not hold themselves out as Of Counsel to more than one firm located in different towns in the state).

controlling criterion is "close and regular" relationships, not a particular number.[89]

Formal Opinion 90-357 has caused some state ethics committees to reconsider their prior positions with respect to multiple Of Counsel relationships. In Ohio, for example, a retired lawyer may serve as Of Counsel to different law firms formed by the retired lawyer's former partners.[90] The Board of Commissioners on Grievances and Discipline of the Supreme Court of Ohio ruled:

> The ABA view is that an attorney may be "of counsel" to more than one firm. In Formal Opinion 90-357 (1990) the ABA committee stated that "[a] lawyer can surely have a close, regular, personal relationship with more than two clients; and the Committee sees no reason why the same cannot be true with more than two law firms." That advice is a departure from its earlier views in Formal Op. 330 (1972) that an attorney may be "of counsel" to only two firms and in Formal Op. 1173 (1971) that an attorney may not be "of counsel" to more than a single firm.

In Michigan, a lawyer may be designated Of Counsel to one or more lawyers or law firms whether in Michigan or out of state.[91]

Of Counsel's Name in the Firm's Name

Among the states, opinions diverge as to whether Of Counsel's name can be included in the firm's name. Much of the desire to use Of Counsel's name in the firm's name may be attributed, in part, to the goodwill value associated with Of Counsel's name. But when Of Counsel's name is included in the firm's name, there is a likelihood that third persons will misconstrue the true nature of Of Counsel's relationship and accompanying responsibilities among the lawyers. Against this backdrop, many states have developed specific guidelines concerning firm names and Of Counsel lawyers.

A few states allow the firm to include Of Counsel's name in the firm's name, at least where the Of Counsel is a former name

89. ABA Formal Op. 90-357 at 5.

90. Opinion No. 97-2, Supreme Court of Ohio, Bd. of Commissioners on Grievances and Discipline (April 11, 1997).

91. Opinion No. RI-102, State Bar of Michigan, Standing Committee on Professional and Judicial Ethics (October 1, 1991).

partner.[92] The Vermont Ethics Committee justified the use of the former partner's name in the firm's name, reasoning that as long as the departing lawyer maintains a close relationship with the firm, the public is not misled about the identity of the firm or the responsibilities of its principals.[93] But one state even allows the firm to include in the firm name the name of a newly associated Of Counsel, at least where the law firm is composed of one full-time lawyer and one Of Counsel who is available for consultation on a regular basis, and there is a mutual sharing of responsibility.[94]

Other states do not allow the firm name to include Of Counsel's name, even though Of Counsel may have at one time been a partner in the firm.[95] Relying on the false-and-misleading standard, the Los Angeles County Ethics Committee prohibits any nonpartner's name from being included in the firm name.[96] Including a nonpartner's name in the firm's name would be misleading about the nature of the relationship and the responsibilties of the lawyers practicing in the firm.[97] The Philadelphia Ethics Committee also was concerned that including Of Counsel's name in the firm's name would be misleading, since it would connote partnership, with all the accompanying rights and responsibilities.[98]

Formal Opinion 330 did not address whether the Of Counsel's name could ethically be included in the firm's name. Formal Opinion 90-357 allows the Of Counsel's name to be included in the firm's name in limited circumstances.[99] Under 90-357, two different results occur when the firm to which the lawyer is Of Counsel wants to include his or her name in the firm's name. The committee distinguished the familiar situation that occurs when a name partner of the firm retires from active practice and thereafter assumes an Of Counsel position with the same firm. The second situation occurs when the parties have only recently become affiliated, but the firm or individual lawyer wants to include Of Counsel's

---

92. Vermont State Ethics Opinion 83-7 (undated); Virginia State Ethics Opinion 660 (1985).

93. Vermont State Ethics Opinion 83-7 (undated).

94. Maine State Ethics Opinion 86 (1988).

95. Los Angeles County Ethics Opinion 421 (1983); Michigan Ethics Opinion CI-1001 (1984); Philadelphia Ethics Opinion 88-31 (1988).

96. Los Angeles County Ethics Opinion 421 (1983).

97. *Id.*

98. Philadelphia Ethics Opinion 88-31 (1988).

99. *See* Chapter 3, *supra,* at 40.

name in the firm's name. The committee noted that both of these situations raise the same issue: whether including Of Counsel's name in the firm's name entails implicit misrepresentations of the sort that would mislead the public. In the case of a new or recent affiliation, "there is no escaping an implication that a name in the new firm name implies that the lawyer is a partner in the firm, with fully shared responsibility for its work."[100] But there is no similar misrepresentation in the use of a retired partner's name in the firm name "while the same partner is Of Counsel, where the firm name is long-established and well-recognized."[101]

Aside from the ethical mandates imposed by the states and the ABA committee, Of Counsel should exercise careful consideration before allowing his or her name to be included in the firm's name. Inclusion in the firm's name may connote partnership status, with vicarious liability to Of Counsel for torts committed by other members of the firm.[102] Although 90-357 allows Of Counsel's name to be included in the firm's name in limited circumstances, in footnote 11 of the opinion, the committee refused to express a view concerning any possible exposure to general partnership liability for malpractice when the name of the Of Counsel is included in the firm's name.

Summary

Of Counsel arrangements take a variety of forms. Formal Opinion 90-357 discarded the approach of Formal Opinion 330, which distinguished two forms of Of Counsel arrangements: (1) where the lawyer practices in the same office as the other lawyer or firm and (2) where the lawyer does not practice in the same office but is in regular and frequent contact with the other lawyer or firm. Although a close, personal, and continuing relationship is still essential, 90-357 is far less restrictive than 330. Under 90-357, four categories of Of Counsel are specifically recognized: the part-time practitioner, the retired partner, the probationary partner, and the senior attorney. Four other categories are specifically prohibited: the lawyer on a single case, the forwarder or receiver of legal business, the occasional collaborator, and the outside consultant. Be-

100. ABA Formal Op. 90-357 at 6.

101. *Id.*

102. *See* generally Chapter 9.

tween these two groups lie countless other situations more or less comparable to one or the other of the two extremes.

Under 330, if Of Counsel was a retired partner, he or she was deemed to have a close association with the lawyer or firm. This lawyer did not need to practice *in the offices* of the lawyer or firm. But, to satisfy the notion of a "continuing" relationship, there was an implied requirement to remain active in the practice of law and to remain in *daily contact* with the lawyer or firm. While 90-357 removed any requirement of daily contact with the law firm or lawyer, it retained a requirement of a continuing relationship.

The ABA permits the Of Counsel designation to be used by current political officeholders and other public officials, provided they actively practice law in the same offices as the lawyer or firm, regardless of their prior affiliation with the firm. Some states follow the view of the ABA opinions; others do not. In the latter jurisdictions, Of Counsel need not actively engage in the practice of law with the firm, provided the parties' past relationship satisfies the requirement of a continuing relationship.

Some arrangements contemplate that Of Counsel will not practice law in the same office as the lawyer or firm. An out-of-state lawyer, a lawyer who acts as a consultant to one firm while maintaining a full-time position with a corporation or other law firm, or a lawyer who engages in multiple Of Counsel relationships cannot be physically present on a full-time basis in the office of the lawyer or firm with which he or she is affiliated as Of Counsel. Despite this, 90-357 would seem to allow these relationships, where they might have been prohibited under 330. Of Counsel must be available to the lawyer or firm on a frequent, ongoing, and continual basis. Consultation on a single case is insufficient to establish an Of Counsel relationship, even where the consultant is a former partner of the firm. Some state bars follow the mandates established by the ABA; others are more liberal.

Some arrangements can never be designated Of Counsel relationships. The sharing of office space and expenses is insufficient to satisfy the requirement of a continuing relationship. The lawyer who refers or forwards clients to another lawyer or firm cannot be considered Of Counsel to that lawyer or firm.

The ABA now permits law firms to use the Of Counsel designation. It also permits a lawyer to be Of Counsel to more than two law firms. Probationary partners and senior attorneys who normally have an employee relationship with the firm are now recognized as appropriate candidates for the Of Counsel designation.

Checklist

Retired Partners

1. To what extent does the retired partner maintain a continuing relationship with the other lawyer or law firm?
   (a) Is the retired partner active in the practice of law, or is the retiree merely maintaining an office with the firm to have a place to go? Does the retired partner maintain an independent client base? Does the Of Counsel agreement require the retired partner to perform certain duties for the firm or its clients? Is the retired partner available to the firm or its clients for consultation and advice on an ongoing basis?
2. Does the retired partner's name appear in the firm's name? Is the firm's name "long-established and well-recognized"?

Former Public Officials

1. Is the former public official available for consultation and advice?
2. Does the firm specify the Of Counsel's former status on its letterhead? If so, does the state in which the firm is located allow the former status to be listed on business communications? If the state does allow it, does it require that the public official's retired status be included on the communication?

Public Officials

1. Is the public official currently engaged in the "practice of law"? Does the official render legal advice to clients of the other lawyer or firm? If not, is he or she a former partner of the firm?
2. Does the public official practice in the offices of the firm or other lawyer?

The Of Counsel As Consultant

1. Is Of Counsel available only for consultation? If so, is Of Counsel a member or component part of the law office?
2. Is Of Counsel frequently available for consultation on an ongoing basis? Is the relationship between Of Counsel and the firm limited to one particular case?

Out-of-State Of Counsel

1. Is Of Counsel admitted to practice in the state in which the other lawyer or law firm is located? Does that state require that out-of-state Of Counsel be admitted to practice there before being listed on the firm's or other lawyer's business communications?
2. If the state allows out-of-state Of Counsel to be listed on business communications, does the state require that Of Counsel's jurisdictional limitations be listed?

Expense-Sharing Arrangements

Is the relationship between the lawyers limited to the sharing of an office and expenses? Do the lawyers "practice law" together?

Law Firms As Of Counsel

Does the state, or states, in which the law firm is located allow firms to be listed as Of Counsel to each other? If not, does it allow firms to be listed as "associated" or "affiliated" with each other?

Forwarder-Receiver of Legal Business

1. Is the relationship between the lawyer and the law firm or other lawyer limited to the referral of prospective clients?
2. Alternatively, is the relationship between the parties such that the lawyer involved is performing professional service for the law firm or other lawyer, rather than for the client?

Multiple Of Counsel Relationships

1. Does the state in which the Of Counsel practices law allow multiple Of Counsel relationships? If so, are there any geographical limitations?
2. If the state permits multiple Of Counsel relationships, is it wise for Of Counsel or the law firm or other lawyer to enter into a particular relationship in light of potential conflicts and vicarious liability?

Of Counsel's Name in the Firm's Name

1. Is Of Counsel's name included in the firm's name?
2. If so, does the state in which the firm is located allow the name of the Of Counsel to be included in the firm's name? Does the state only allow the firm's name to include Of Counsel's name if Of Counsel was formerly a partner of the firm?

CHAPTER V

Distinguishing Of Counsel from Other Legal Relationships after Formal Opinion 90-357

Many firms now identify some lawyers by terms such as "special counsel," "senior counsel," or "resident counsel." These terms counter the prevailing notion that Of Counsel is a retired partner.[1] This change in language also indicates that many Of Counsel serve in functions other than the traditional ones of consultation and advice. They may resemble an employee of the firm, performing specialized tasks, such as coordinating the firm's in-house training program, or they may be used on a regular basis, carrying a work load similar to that of an associate in the firm.[2] Or, if such an employee is treated as a probationary partner-to-be, he may resemble a partner and be on the firm's "partnership track."

Under the prior Formal Opinion 330, "Of Counsel" could not be used to describe an employee of the firm. While Formal Opinion 90-357 made it clear that "Of Counsel" can never be used to describe a partner or associate, the committee recognized that some Of Counsel relationships, such as probationary partners-to-be and senior attorneys, always involve an employer-employee relationship. In these limited situations, Of Counsel may have employee status without interfering with their ability to use the designation.

1. Wagner, *Variations on the "Of-Counsel" Theme*, 6 CAL. LAW. 59, 60 (July 1988).

2. *Id.*

Formal Opinion 90-357 also recognizes that the Of Counsel designation is appropriately used for various kinds of specialty counsel:

> [A]lthough "of counsel" appears to be most frequently used among the various titles employing the term "counsel," it is by no means the only use of that term to indicate a relationship between a lawyer and a law firm. Other such titles include the single word "counsel," and the terms "special counsel," "tax [or other specialty] counsel," and "senior counsel." It is the Committee's view that, whatever the connotative differences evoked by these variants of the title "counsel," they all share the central, and defining, characteristic of the relationship that is denoted by the term "of counsel," and so should all be understood to be covered by the present opinion.[3] (Footnotes omitted.)

Although the committee withdrew Formal Opinion 330 when it issued Formal Opinion 90-357, it continued to rely on it for purposes of defining the "core characteristic" of the Of Counsel relationship:

> That core characteristic properly denoted by the title "counsel" is, as stated in Formal Opinion 330, a "close, regular, personal relationship"; but a relationship which is neither that of a partner (or its equivalent, a principal of a professional corporation), with the shared liability and/or managerial responsibility implied by that term; nor, on the other hand, the status ordinarily conveyed by the term "associate," which is to say a junior non-partner lawyer, regularly employed by the firm.[4] (Footnotes omitted.)

The fact that the Of Counsel relationship may be analogous to an employee, partner, or outside-consultant relationship raises significant issues. Especially important is the area of vicarious liability for malpractice in which third parties try to hold Of Counsel liable for the unlawful acts of the firm, or the firm for the unlawful acts of Of Counsel. Also, classification of their relationship may determine

---

3. ABA Comm. on Professional Ethics, Formal Op. 90-357 at 3.
4. *Id.* at 4-5.

whether Of Counsel can be included as an employee of the firm in the firm's health insurance coverage.

To determine whether a lawyer can be designated as Of Counsel, the relationship must be contrasted with these other legal relationships. This task may prove difficult, since all of these varying relationships may, and often do, contain common and overlapping characteristics, and one might reach different conclusions with respect to the appropriate classification for different purposes. Yet each relationship contains essential elements or core criteria that distinguish it from other legal relationships.

In establishing an Of Counsel relationship, the firm must identify and contrast the essential elements of these various relationships. This chapter examines the basic core criteria necessary to the relationships of partner, associate, and outside consultant, and contrasts these with the requirements needed to establish a permissible Of Counsel relationship.

Of Counsel Contrasted with Partner

Under Formal Opinion 90-357, the Of Counsel relationship is not that of a partnership.[5] This requirement stems from one clause found in the Model Code of Professional Responsibility, which states:

> A lawyer may be designated "of counsel" on a letterhead if he has a continuing relationship with a lawyer or law firm, other than as partner or associate.[6]

This Model Code provision addressed the concern that some professional arrangements might be misleading to the public. Lawyers should not explicitly or implicitly hold themselves out as being partners if they are not in fact partners.[7] Explicit misrepresentation occurs when a lawyer expressly states that he or she is a partner in the firm. Implicit misrepresentation arises when Of Counsel's status is not properly indicated in professional listings, letterheads, or professional cards, or where Of Counsel's name is included in the firm name. Misrepresentation also arises where the

5. *Id.*

6. Model Code of Professional Responsibility DR 2-102(A)(4) (1969, amended 1980). There is no counterpart to DR 2-102(A) in the Model Rules.

7. Model Code of Professional Responsibility EC 2-13 (1969, amended 1980).

relationship itself contains traits common to a partnership, such as Of Counsel's assumption of management responsibilities or sharing in firm profits. As to the latter concern, the earlier Formal Opinion 330 stated:

> It would be misleading to refer to a lawyer who shares in the profits and losses and general responsibility of a firm as being "Of Counsel."[8]

The Of Counsel designation is improper where the parties' outward acts manifest or imply that a partnership relation exists,[9] or where the relationship itself contains characteristics essential to a partnership.[10] For example, one of the essential elements of a partnership is the partner's right to share in the profits of the business. When there is a sharing of profits coupled with other elements essential to a partnership, most courts would conclude that a true partnership relation exists, regardless of the words chosen by the parties to describe it. Thus, Of Counsel who shares in the profits of the firm clearly risks vicarious liability as a partner.

Even if the relationship does not contain any of the common elements of a partnership, caution must be taken so that an implied partnership does not arise. There are many ways in which a nonpartner may be held out as a partner. The nonpartner, or other persons in the business with the consent of the nonpartner, may be referred to as a partner. The nonpartner's name may be included in the firm's name, letterheads, signs, and other advertisements, or in pleadings, motions, and appearances.

---

8. ABA Comm. on Professional Ethics, Formal Op. 330 (1972); *see also* Arizona State Bar Ethics Opinion 81-1 (1981); California State Bar Ethics Opinion 1986-88 (1987); Michigan State Bar Ethics Opinion CI-617 (1981); New York City Ethics Opinion 80-66 (undated); Pennsylvania State Bar Ethics Opinion 87-171 (1988); Washington State Bar Ethics Opinion 178 (1984).

9. The elements of an implied partnership are: (1) representations, either public or private, that tend to imply the existence of a partnership; and (2) reasonable reliance on the representation by the person seeking enforcement.

10. These elements include: (1) the intention to form a partnership; (2) an agreement to carry out a business for profit; (3) a sharing of profits and losses; (4) co-ownership of the business; and (5) general responsibility through joint management and control of the business. Unif. Partnership Act § 6.

Avoiding the Appearance of a Partnership

The Of Counsel relationship need not be created through a written agreement, but good planning requires that the arrangement be in writing. A written agreement defines the rights and duties of the parties and raises a rebuttable presumption of their intention to create an Of Counsel, rather than a partnership, relation. It is possible for the drafters to create an agreement that will satisfy both Of Counsel and the law firm without causing Of Counsel to be treated as a partner.

The drafters should eliminate any of the identifying traits of partnership. For example, Of Counsel should not share in the profits of the firm. Nor should the agreement give Of Counsel any of the duties and responsibilities of a partner, such as the authority to manage or control the business. Such responsibilities could cause Of Counsel to be personally liable for the torts of the firm. In one such agreement, Of Counsel appeared to assume the duties of a partner:

> [Of Counsel] shall perform legal services on behalf of the Firm and, except as otherwise provided herein, shall, with respect to the rendering of legal services, have all of the duties and *responsibilities as if he were a partner of the Firm* as provided in [the Firm Partnership Agreement].[11] (Emphasis supplied.)

That same agreement contained other indicia of a partnership, instead of an Of Counsel, relation between the parties:

> In consideration of the services performed by (Of Counsel], the Firm shall pay to [Of Counsel] an amount equal to the amount to which [Of Counsel] would be entitled, pursuant to provisions of [the Firm Partnership Agreement], if he were a partner of the Firm. . . .[12]

Even though the agreement clearly set forth the lawyer's status as Of Counsel,[13] the specific terms of the agreement could have been used as evidence that a partnership relation actually existed between the parties. Instead, the agreement should clearly negate

---

11. *See* Appendix A at § 4.1.
12. *Id.* at § 5.
13. *Id.* at § 2.

any elements of a partnership relation. The following provision is commonly used to achieve this result:

> As [Of Counsel], Lawyer is not required to contribute capital to the Firm, nor will he have any formal voting rights at any Partnership meetings. Otherwise, he will be welcome to participate in discussions and meetings of the Firm and of the Partnership, except as to Partnership meetings or portions of meetings where only Equity Partners may participate.... Lawyer will not share in or be liable for any profits or losses of the Firm, including any malpractice liability not arising from his acts.[14]

To avoid liability as an implied partner, Of Counsel should not present to the public as a partner of that firm. The name of an Of Counsel who is not a former partner should not be included in the firm's name,[15] and the Of Counsel status should be clearly communicated in the firm letterhead,[16] professional announcement cards, shingles, and directories or law lists such as the Martindale-Hubbell directory.[17] The agreement should contain provisions stating the parties' intention to list the lawyer as Of Counsel. A common provision would state:

---

14. Appendix B at § 6.

15. *See* Tennessee State Bar Ethics Opinion 84-F-64 (1984). *But see* Virginia State Bar Ethics Opinion 660 (1985) (a law firm may continue to use the name of a former partner in the name of the firm or professional corporation, provided the former partner is engaged in part-time law practice with the firm on an Of Counsel basis).

16. American Casualty Co. v. Costello, 174 Mich. App. 1, 435 N.W.2d 760 (1989). For ethical rules and opinions relating to the "Of Counsel" designation in letterheads and other advertising, see CODE OF PROFESSIONAL RESPONSIBILITY DR 2-102(A)(4); and ABA Comm. on Professional Ethics, Formal Op. 330 (1972), which states:

> The term "Of Counsel" may be used, if it correctly describes the existing relationship, on letterheads and professional announcement cards and in law lists and directories.

See also ABA Comm. on Professional Ethics, Formal Op. 84-351 (overruling in part Formal Opinion 330 and Informal Opinion 1265, and holding that letterhead designation of "affiliated" or "associated" law firms is not prohibited).

17. Missan v. Schoenfeld, 95 A.D.2d 198, 465 N.Y.S.2d 706 (Sept. 1, 1983); *Costello*, 435 N.W.2d 760.

> During the term of this agreement, the Corporation shall, at its sole expense, cause [Of Counsel's] name to be listed as "Of Counsel" on the Corporation's stationery, in the Martindale-Hubbell Directory, [state and county] Bar directories, telephone directories and in other listings or directories, in which the Corporation may from time to time list its name and the names of its members and associates of the Corporation.[18]

In addition, the Of Counsel status should be clearly set out in pleadings, memoranda, opinion letters, and court appearances.[19]

Of Counsel Contrasted with Associate

Formal Opinion 90-357 makes it clear that Of Counsel has a continuing relationship with a lawyer or law firm that is neither that of a partner nor that of an associate. An associate is usually described as a regular full-time nonpartner lawyer employee of the firm.[20] The term "associate" has acquired a special significance within law firms, as distinct from the firm's other lawyer-employees. Indeed, 90-357 states, "[T]he status ordinarily conveyed by the term 'associate,'. . . is to say a junior non-partner lawyer, regularly employed by the firm."[21]

A generation ago, law firms classified lawyers within the firm as partners or associates. Associates were lawyers who aspired to become partners of the firm. But with the many changes that have affected the law practice in the last three decades, law firms today often have different classes of partners. Two tiers of partners are sometimes established for management and control. Different arrangements for lawyer-employees have also been created, depending upon the objectives of the lawyer and the firm. Some lawyers are hired or promoted into a permanent nonpartner position and given such titles as "resident counsel," "senior attorney," "special counsel," or just "counsel." The relatively simple structure of a law

---

18. Appendix D at § 12.

19. *Costello*, 435 N.W.2d at 760; 59A AM. JUR. 2d Partnerships § 673

20. *In re* Sussman, 241 Or. 246, 405 P.2d 355 (1965). *Webster's New Collegiate Dictionary* (1981) defines "associate" as "a fellow worker, partner, colleague." As an adjective, it is defined as: "1: closely connected with another, 2: closely related esp. in the mind, 3: having secondary or subordinate status." ABA Comm. on Ethics and Professional Responsibility, Formal Op. 84-351 at 4, n.6 (1984).

21. ABA Formal Op. 90-357 at 5.

firm with just two classes of lawyers—partners and associates—is now confined to the smaller firms. Thus, although associates are employees, not all employees of a law firm are "associates."

Formal Opinion 90-357 permits an employer-employee relationship in two specific types of Of Counsel arrangements: (1) where the lawyer is a probationary partner-to-be; and (2) where the term designates a permanent status between those of partner and associate. Whether the committee permits elements of the employer-employee relationship to exist in other Of Counsel relationships is not clear from the wording of the opinion.

Of Counsel As Employee or Independent Contractor

Many persons find that their legal relationships with others are enhanced if they are considered to be "independent contractors" rather than "employees." The law of agency developed primarily in the nineteenth century in response to the demands of the industrial revolution. Before that time, the laborer (artisan) supplied the necessary tools, worked independently, trained apprentices, and so forth. Then the law affecting the status of independent contractors was overshadowed by the development of the concept of the corporate entity, the doctrine of *respondeat superior,* the doctrine of apparent authority, and many other legal concepts that responded to the problems created by the growth of a capitalist society.

Today there are many advantages in being treated as an employee. Many firms provide their lawyer-employees with such fringe benefits as individual liability coverage, hospital and major medical insurance, and pension benefits. The firm shares the responsibility of paying the employee's social security taxes.[22] But there are also distinct disadvantages. As an employer, the firm can exercise considerable control and supervision over Of Counsel's services. The firm may require Of Counsel to perform a minimum number of hours per week or month. Or it may prohibit Of Counsel from performing legal services outside the firm.

Likewise, there are advantages and disadvantages in being treated as an independent contractor rather than an employee. For example, an independent contractor retains a greater amount of freedom. A lawyer in such an arrangement can devote any number of hours to the firm and use the balance to work independently. Although the independent contractor pays the full amount of social

22. See the discussion of income taxation later in this chapter.

security taxes, there are tax advantages in this arrangement.[23] By reporting income on Schedule C of Form 1040, an independent contractor has the advantage of deducting all business expenses before calculating adjusted gross income and therefore avoids the two-percent floor for deductions that might otherwise have to be itemized as miscellaneous deductions. The disadvantages of being treated as an independent contractor include the exclusion from the firm's employee benefits, such as medical and disability insurance and pension and profit-sharing plans.[24]

The factors that determine whether a particular relationship constitutes an employer-employee (that is, master-servant) or independent-contractor relationship have been listed in Section 220(2) of the Restatement of Agency, Second, as follows:

(a) the extent of control which, by the agreement, the master may exercise over the details of the work;
(b) whether or not the one employed is engaged in a distinct occupation or business;
(c) the kind of occupation, with reference to whether, in the locality, the work is usually done under the direction of the employer or by a specialist without supervision;
(d) the skill required in the particular occupation;
(e) whether the employer or the workman supplies the instrumentalities, tools, and the place of work for the person doing the work;
(f) the length of time for which the person is employed;
(g) the method of payment, whether by the time or by the job;
(h) whether or not the work is part of the regular business of the employer;
(i) whether or not the parties believe they are creating the relation of master and servant; and
(j) whether the principal is or is not in business.

When drafting a particular agreement with respect to the employer-employee or the independent-contractor relationship, the drafter should characterize the relationship by using as many of these factors as possible that point in the desired direction. If enough factors indicate an employer-employee or independent-contractor relationship, it is immaterial how the parties designate

23. See the discussion of income taxation later in this chapter.

24. For more complete discussion of the problem of the independent contractor, see *infra* Chapter 10.

it. In *Mutual of Omaha Insurance Co. v. Chadwell,*[25] the estate of a deceased Of Counsel lawyer claimed benefits under the firm's accident insurance policy by attempting to characterize the Of Counsel as an employee of the firm.[26] Upon his retirement from the partnership, the lawyer had agreed to continue with the firm on an Of Counsel basis. In return, the firm agreed to compensate him for past services. In addition, it provided him with office space and group insurance.[27] But the Of Counsel agreement specified no duties expected of the lawyer in return. This indicated a lack of control over the lawyer. The court found that the lawyer was not an employee, and the lawyer's estate could not claim any benefits under the accident policy.[28]

The Of Counsel relationship does not fit perfectly into the conventional categories of principal and agent or master and servant. Nor would it be desirable that it do so. On the contrary, one of the blessings of the Of Counsel relationship is that it can be whatever the contracting parties want it to be. In drafting such an agreement, however, the parties must be constantly aware of the pros and cons of the independent-contractor versus the employee status.

In three areas—contracts, torts, and taxation—the parties may find that they would prefer the relationship between the Of Counsel and the contracting firm to be more closely related to the law of independent contractor than to the law of agency.

Of Counsel and Contractual Liability

In the area of contracts, much of the traditional doctrine of agency law centers around such doctrines as apparent authority, authority

25. 426 F. Supp. 550 (N.D. Ill. 1977).

26. The insurance policy limited eligibility to "[a]ll lawyers associated with the Policyholder [law firm] as a partner or employee." *Chadwell*, 426 F. Supp. at 551.

27. *Id.* at 552.

28. *Id.* at 552; *see also* Rev. Rul. 68-324, 1968-1 C.B. 433 (law firm exerted sufficient control over lawyer to establish employer-employee relationship when it furnished lawyer with a place to work and required him to work certain hours) *and* Technical Advice Memorandum 8013016 (Dec. 27, 1969) (lawyers were employees of law partnership, not independent contractors, even though they were not required to work a specified number of hours; because firm retained right to control lawyers' work, lawyers were not permitted to engage in practice of law in their spare time, and lawyers worked under direct supervision of law partner).

by estoppel, implied authority, and the like. The independent contractor will want to negate these relationships. A law firm might wish to be held responsible for the acts of Of Counsel only to the extent that Of Counsel's actions were specifically authorized by the firm. So long as third parties have adequate notice of the precise terms of the relationship between the firm and Of Counsel, there is no reason why the parties could not operate in this fashion. Similarly, by providing third parties with adequate notice of the extent of Of Counsel's authority—whether acting as an independent contractor or employee—Of Counsel may avoid potential liability for the firm's acts and omissions. The contractual relationship of the parties must be carefully spelled out in an agreement designed to protect both Of Counsel and the firm.

Of Counsel and Tort Liability

A law firm would have a more difficult time limiting the scope of its liability for the tortious acts (for example, malpractice) of Of Counsel. Normally, the firm would be vicariously liable for the acts and omissions performed by Of Counsel within the scope of employment. It is doubtful that the firm would be liable when Of Counsel is an independent contractor. Whether Of Counsel is an employee or an independent contractor (instead of being a partner), he or she would normally not be responsible for the torts of partners or associates of the firm. In footnote 6 of Formal Opinion 90-357, the ethics committee avoided making any comment on Of Counsel's potential malpractice liability:

> The Committee expresses no view, however, on whether an arrangement under which the of counsel lawyer shares in the profits of the firm may expose the lawyer to malpractice liability as a partner.[29]

Of Counsel must seek protection against the potential of malpractice liability through proper malpractice insurance. Of Counsel will expect the law firm to pay for this insurance. In many Of Counsel agreements, the parties provide that the firm will be responsible for this cost. Such an arrangement is appropriate whether Of Counsel is an independent contractor or an employee.

29. ABA Formal Op. 90-357, n.6.

Of Counsel and Income Taxation

Many lawyers have found that retaining independent-contractor status is especially important in the tax area. The tax status of such a person is different from that of an employee. The independent contractor normally reports business income on Schedule C to Form 1040, Profit or Loss from Business (Sole Proprietorship). The use of this form, in contrast with treating the Of Counsel as an employee, presents some major tax advantages.

BUSINESS DEDUCTIONS

All of the independent contractor's business expenses may be taken "above the line"—that is, deducted in determining the taxpayer's adjusted gross income. By contrast, an employee determines adjusted gross income by deducting only those business deductions that are specifically listed in Section 62 of the Internal Revenue Code.

A lawyer filing Schedule C reports only the net profit (or loss) from the business, and all business deductions are taken on Schedule C. The lawyer can still choose to itemize deductions or take the standard deduction *after* the net profit from business has been included in adjusted gross income.

Since all business deductions are taken on Schedule C, the lawyer who reports income taxes in this fashion need not be concerned with the floor of two percent of adjusted gross income that applies to the miscellaneous business deductions of an employee.

SOCIAL SECURITY TAXES

Independent contractors pay social security tax on their net annual income from self-employment, if that income exceeds $400.[30] A special tax form, Form SE, is used to compute the amount of social security tax. Beginning in 1990, the tax rate for independent contractors is 15.30 percent. The maximum taxable amount (in 1998) for self-employed persons is the same as for employees, $68,400. Half of the social security tax can be deducted as a business expense for federal income tax purposes.

In contrast, the amount of social security taxes that an employee pays each year is 7.65 percent of the maximum taxable

30. GUIDE TO SOCIAL SECURITY AND MEDICARE at 9 (William M. Mercer-Meidinger-Hansen, Inc., 1998).

amount[31] of $68,400.[32] In 1998, an employee and employer each pay social security taxes of 7.65 percent on the first $68,400 of the worker's wages.[33] For employees, social security taxes are not deductible for federal income tax purposes.

What constitutes wages of the employee is important in determining the amount of social security taxes owed. "Wages" means the gross amount of pay an employee received for employment covered by the Social Security Act unless the pay is specifically excluded by law. Pay that is not for covered employment is not wages for social security purposes, even though the amounts are included for purposes of determining the annual earnings. Wages include payments by the employer, whether the payment is made in cash, or by check, promissory note, or in noncash forms such as goods or clothing. Food and lodging are included unless they are furnished by or on behalf of the employer. The first six months of sick pay or accident disability pay are considered wages.[34] Items of little value, such as the use of the company parking lot or medical clinic, are excluded from wages.[35] Amounts received under certain deferred-compensation plans are, however, treated as wages for purposes of the social security tax,[36] as is the cost of employer-provided group term life insurance if such insurance is includable in gross income for federal income tax purposes.[37]

---

31. The tax rate quoted here is actually the sum of two taxes deducted from payroll. The first tax, Old-Age, Survivors, and Disability Insurance, or OASDI, is the tax that funds cash amounts payable to beneficiaries. The current tax rate on OASDI is 6.20 percent. The second tax funds the Hospital Insurance (HI) part of Medicare. The current tax rate on HI is 1.45 percent. Although the taxes on these two programs may be withheld separately from the employee's wages, for most purposes the amounts are added together and deducted as one tax. *See* GUIDE TO SOCIAL SECURITY AND MEDICARE at 6 (William M. Mercer-Meidinger-Hansen, Inc., 1998).

32. *See* 20 C.F.R. § 404.1047.

33. *See* 42 U.S.C.A. § 409 and 20 C.F.R. §§ 404.1041–60. *See also* 20 C.F.R. § 404.429 for definition of "earnings."

34. *See* 42 U.S.C.A. § 409(b) and 20 C.F.R. § 404.1051.

35. GUIDE TO SOCIAL SECURITY AND MEDICARE at 8 (William M. Mercer-Meidinger-Hansen, Inc., 1998).

36. 26 U.S.C.A. §§ 403, 457, 3121, 3201, 3316; 29 U.S.C.A. § 1002; § 209 of the Social Security Act, as amended, 42 U.S.C.A. § 409.

37. See § 9003 of the Omnibus Budget Reconciliation Act of 1987, Pub. L. No. 100-203, amending clause 3 of § 209(b) of the Social Security Act, as amended, and subparagraph (C) of § 3121(a)(2) of the Internal Revenue Code. *See also* Technical and Miscellaneous Revenue Act § 8013 (1988).

Right to Discharge, Right to Terminate

The associates in a law firm know that under the employment-at-will doctrine of the common law, the employer has the right to discharge them and terminate the relationship at any time. This traditional doctrine is now disappearing with the growth of the tort of wrongful discharge, which requires that employees be discharged only for just cause. Formal Opinion 90-357 recognized the permanent status of the senior attorney "in between those of partner and associate—akin to the last category just described [in other words, associate], but having the quality of tenure, or something close to it, and lacking that of an expectation of likely promotion to full partner status."[38]

By contrast, an independent contractor is not subject to discharge as long as the work performed complies substantially with contract specifications. The law firm or lawyer with which the independent contractor has contracted may terminate the contract, but the independent contractor has a remedy for any damages suffered for breach of contract.

Of Counsel Contrasted with Outside Consultant

Unlike the terms "partner" and "associate," the phrase "outside consultant" has not acquired a precise meaning, and the committee did not attempt to define it. The requirement that Of Counsel *not* be like an outside consultant restates in negative terms the requirement that lawyers who are Of Counsel *must* be members or component parts of the law office.

Although the committee in 90-357 did not further elucidate the meaning of "outside consultant," the determination of whether Of Counsel is a member or component part of a law office should depend on whether there is a "close, continuing, personal" relationship with the lawyer or law firm.[39] Whether a relationship limited to consultation and advice satisfies the requirements of a "close, continuing, personal" relationship has important legal consequences, particularly in the areas of imputed disqualification and fee splitting. Being treated as a member of the firm may expose Of

38. ABA Formal Op. 90-357 at 3 (1990).
39. *See* Chapter 4.

Counsel to conflicts of interest. Furthermore, treating Of Counsel as a member of the firm influences the forms of compensation allowable.

Conflicts of Interest

Of Counsel must withdraw from the law firm or the law firm must withdraw from its current representation of a client if that representation conflicts with the interests of other current or former clients of Of Counsel.[40]

Compensation

In Formal Opinion 90-357, the committee specifically stated that "it is not relevant to the permissibility of use of 'of counsel' what the compensation arrangements are."[41] Although this gives both the law firm and Of Counsel the freedom to contract for whatever arrangement they deem appropriate, the lessons of Formal Opinion 330 should not be overlooked. In the earlier opinion, the committee said:

> [T]he lawyer who is "Of Counsel" may be compensated either on a basis of division of fees in particular cases or on a basis of consultation fees. He is compensated as a *sui generis* member of that law office, however, and not as an outside consultant.[42]

In other words, Formal Opinion 330 implied that Of Counsel could split fees with the firm, but only for cases in which he or she rendered services. Lawyers in an Of Counsel relationship were treated as *members* of the law office. Outside consultants, on the other hand, were not members of the law office, and their compensation had to be directly related to the work performed for each client.

40. Georgia State Bar Ethics Opinion 33 (1983); Michigan State Bar Ethics Opinion CI-1071 (undated); New Jersey State Bar Ethics Opinion 541 (1984); Pennsylvania State Bar Ethics Opinion 88-6 (undated); Texas State Bar Ethics Opinion 445 (1987); *see generally*, Chapters 7 and 8, *infra.*

41. ABA Formal Op. 90-357 at 7.

42. ABA Formal Op. 330.

Under 90-357, the liberalization of the rules regarding compensation arrangements for Of Counsel have similarly liberalized the rules governing outside consultants. The relationship of the firm with outside consultants and Of Counsel is entirely contractual, with the result that drafters can negate either one of these objectives depending upon their goals.

Currently, many states allow Of Counsel to split fees with the firm without regard to the amount of services performed.[43] Other states prohibit Of Counsel from splitting fees with the firm or other lawyer. In these states, Of Counsel must be compensated as an outside consultant.[44]

Normally, outside consultants are not allowed to split fees unless the firm and the outside consultant comply with the Model Code or Model Rules.[45] The Model Code and the Model Rules both prohibit a lawyer from splitting fees with another lawyer who is *not* a member of the law firm, unless the fee-sharing arrangement is

---

43. Alabama State Bar Ethics Opinion 81-536 (undated) (A law firm may share legal fees with a lawyer who is Of Counsel to the firm pursuant to a contract or agreement providing for such division. The Model Code provision prohibiting fee division with another lawyer who is not a partner or associate without the client's consent after full disclosure is inapplicable); Texas State Bar Ethics Opinion 450 (1987) (The Model Code provision governing division of legal fees is not applicable to a law firm that intends to share a fee with a lawyer who is publicly represented to be Of Counsel to the firm. The Of Counsel lawyer is considered to be a member of the firm for purposes of this Model Code provision); Virginia State Bar Ethics Opinion 442 (1983) (A lawyer who does part-time legal work for a law firm may be designated Of Counsel on the firm's stationery and may divide legal fees with the firm).

44. Arizona State Bar Ethics Opinion 86-3 (1986) (a law firm and a lawyer who is Of Counsel to the law firm may share fees only on the basis of the amount of work done by each on behalf of the other's clients); *see* California State Bar Ethics Opinion 1986-88 (undated); District of Columbia Ethics Opinion 151 (1985) (the Model Code provisions prohibiting fee splitting apply to the Of Counsel relationship, unless the lawyer's relationship with the firm or other lawyer is "akin to that of a partner or associate").

45. MODEL CODE OF PROFESSIONAL RESPONSIBILITY DR 2-107(A); *see also* Illinois State Bar Ethics Opinion 776 (1982) (law firm may pay outside legal consultants and keep portion of fee billed to the client for the consultant's time, provided the client has consented in writing to the employment of the outside lawyer after written disclosure of facts relating to the referral and the firm discloses that it will receive a referral fee).

fully explained to the client, the client consents, and the fee is divided in proportion to the services rendered.[46]

Summary

Formal Opinion 90-357 is an improvement over Formal Opinion 330. The later opinion (90-357) focuses on what the relationship *can,* rather than cannot, be. It articulates several relationships (the part-time practitioner, the former judge or governmental official, the retired partner, the probationary partner, and the senior attorney) as falling within the Of Counsel concept. It specifically excludes others: the lawyer in the individual case, the forwarder or receiver of legal business, the lawyer who occasionally collaborates, and the outside consultant.

Yet, apart from its positive, flexible approach to defining an Of Counsel relationship, Formal Opinion 90-357 relied on one negative aspect contained in Formal Opinion 330. It mandated that the relationship must *not* be like that of partner or associate. If the relationship has facets commonly found in one of these other relationships, use of the Of Counsel designation is improper. When the relationship more nearly resembles that of partner or associate, Of Counsel is exposed to other problems, particularly in the area of

---

46. DR 2-107(A) states:

> A lawyer shall not divide a fee for legal services with another lawyer who is not a partner in or associate of his law firm or law office, unless:
> (1) The client consents to employment of the other lawyer after full disclosure that a division of fees will be made.
> (2) The division is made in proportion to the services performed and responsibility assumed by each.
> (3) The total fee of the lawyers does not clearly exceed reasonable compensation for all legal services they rendered the client.

Rule 1.5(e) of the Model Rules of Professional Responsibility states:

> [A] division of fee between lawyers who are not in the same firm may be made only if:
> (1) the division is in proportion to the services performed by each lawyer or, by written agreement with the client, each lawyer assumes joint responsibility for the representation;
> (2) the client is advised of and does not object to the participation of all lawyers involved; and
> (3) the total fee is reasonable.

vicarious liability. Thus, Of Counsel should never share in the firm's general profits, or assume management and control of the business. Likewise, Of Counsel should be careful to avoid the *appearance* of a partnership. An implied partnership could exist when the parties represented to the public that a partnership existed, and there was reasonable reliance upon that representation by the person seeking to establish the partnership. If an implied partnership is found, Of Counsel will be liable to an injured third party for torts committed by the firm.

Formal Opinion 90-357 has made it clear that Of Counsel is a special contractual relationship. The drafter of an Of Counsel agreement must be sensitive to Of Counsel's need for freedom of action, and draft an agreement that will satisfy the needs of all parties.

Checklist

Does the Relationship Resemble a Partnership?

1. Does the Of Counsel relationship contain characteristics essential to a true partnership? Does Of Counsel share in the profits and losses of the partnership? Does Of Counsel have general responsibility in the management of the firm? Is the lawyer a member of the firm's executive committee? Does Of Counsel possess joint management and control in other areas of the firm?
2. Is there an implied partnership between Of Counsel and the firm? Do the parties publicly or privately hold themselves out as partners? Is Of Counsel's name included in the firm's name? Is the Of Counsel status clearly represented on the firm's letterheads, advertisements, law listings, professional announcement cards, firm directory, court appearances, legal briefs, and other documents filed with the court?

Is Of Counsel More Like an Associate?

1. Does the Of Counsel relationship contain indicia common to the employer-employee relationship? Does the firm or other lawyer have the right to exercise control over Of Counsel?
   (a) Does the firm or other lawyer require Of Counsel to work in the firm's or other lawyer's offices?

(b) Does the firm or other lawyer supply Of Counsel with materials and supplies (including telephone, desk, computer services, law library) or support staff (secretaries, paralegals, and so forth)?
(c) Does the firm or other lawyer bill clients for services performed by Of Counsel?
(d) Is Of Counsel required to work full-time or a specified number of hours exclusively for the firm?
(e) Is Of Counsel compensated with a fixed salary?
(f) Does the firm or other lawyer pay for Of Counsel's business or travel expenses?
(g) Does the firm or other lawyer have the right to discharge Of Counsel at any time?
(h) Does Of Counsel work under the direction or supervision of another lawyer in the firm?
(i) Does Of Counsel automatically have certain desirable benefits, such as life, health, or malpractice insurance?

2. Is there any expectation that Of Counsel will attain partnership status within the near future? Is the Of Counsel designation being used to describe a probationary position?

Is Of Counsel More Like an "Outside Consultant"?

Is the relationship with the firm or other lawyer limited to one particular case? Is Of Counsel compensated in the same way as an outside consultant? Does the state in which his practice is located permit Of Counsel to split fees with the firm without regard to work performed? If so, do the parties desire a fee-sharing arrangement?

CHAPTER VI

Of Counsel and Legal Malpractice

Introduction

Since the publication of the first edition of this book, the law with respect to both Of Counsel and legal malpractice has seen substantial development. In the first edition, we stated that there was little or no case authority with reference to the liability of Of Counsel for legal malpractice. Nor was there any authority regarding the extent of liability of a law firm or lawyer by reason of Of Counsel's wrongdoing. It is still difficult to find judicial authority dealing directly with malpractice liability of Of Counsel or the law firm to which he or she is attached. But a number of cases dealing with Of Counsel or associated counsel point in the general direction of the law, particularly with respect to vicarious liability. In this chapter, we consider some of these illustrations of the application of familiar principles of common law to similar fact patterns. In passing, we note some of the more obvious trends in the law:

- In tort, the law firm or lawyer will be responsible for the tortious conduct of Of Counsel either because of *respondeat superior,* or because it was negligent in the selection or control of Of Counsel. Liability in contract will depend upon the specific contractual arrangements between the firm and Of Counsel. While Of Counsel will normally seek to be an independent contractor, the law firm may still be vicariously liable where it has clothed Of Counsel with actual or apparent authority.

- Of Counsel will normally not be liable for the errors or omissions of partners, associates, or employees of the firm. But factual patterns may negate the usual independent contractor status. Characterization of the relationship between Of Counsel and the firm as partnership by estoppel, joint venture, or employer-employee can enter into a particular situation to vary the result.
- Legal malpractice may be based on breach of fiduciary duty, negligence, and/or breach of contract. The application of any one or all of these doctrines in typical fact situations appears to be on the increase.
- Privity of contract is required for a law firm or lawyer to be held liable for negligence or breach of fiduciary obligation, but this doctrine is being eroded where lawyers have reason to believe that third parties will be relying on their work.
- The rules with respect to conflicts and imputed disqualification continue to play an important role in all litigation involving legal malpractice.[1]

Vicarious Liability in Tort

Law firms and lawyers are responsible for the torts committed by their employed lawyers and office staff. If Of Counsel is characterized as an employee, rather than an independent contractor, the liability of the law firm is premised on the doctrine of respondeat superior. The tort must have been committed by the employee while acting within the scope of employment.[2] Apart from liability under respondeat superior, the firm may also be liable for its failure to control or supervise the employee adequately. In various cases, the firm or employer has been held liable for the acts and omissions of another lawyer employed by them.[3]

---

1. We defer the discussion of these matters until later. *See infra* Chapters 7 and 8.

2. McGarity v. Craighill, Rendleman, Ingle & Blythe, 63 N.C. App. 106, 349 S.E.2d 311 (1986).

3. Walker v. Stevens, 79 Ill. 193 (1875); Young v. Bridwell, 20 Utah 2d 332, 437 P.2d 686 (1968); Mahoney v. Middlesex County Comm'rs, 144 Mass. 459, 11 N.E. 689 (1887).

Liability Based on Contractual Arrangements

Where liability is based on breach of contract or breach of fiduciary relationship, the act of the agent done within the scope of the actual or apparent authority is binding upon the principal. Apparent authority exists when the agent's acts or omissions are ordinarily perceived to be within the agent's scope of authority. For example, a lawyer can be held liable for the negligence of his or her secretary in filing a client's papers.[4]

But apparent authority does not exist if the acts or omissions are not ordinarily within the scope of the agent's duties. A former member of a law firm was not acting within the scope of his apparent authority when he misappropriated funds borrowed from the law firm's clients. There was no evidence that the law firm was in the business of investing, or that it had benefited from the former member's acts.[5]

Independent Contractors

The individual lawyer or law firm is generally not vicariously liable for the torts committed by an "independent contractor" hired by the lawyer or firm. In *Bockian, Esanu, Katsky, Korins & Siger*,[6] the court ruled that a law firm and its partners were not vicariously liable for the acts of a process server in his attempt to effect personal process, since he was an "independent contractor" of the firm.

Despite this general rule, vicarious liability may still be imputed to a lawyer or law firm for the acts of its independent contractor where the lawyer or firm expressly directs the independent contractor to commit the wrongs or where the lawyer or firm knew that the independent contractor was untrustworthy.

---

4. DeVaux v. American Home Assurance Co., 387 Mass. 814, 444 N.E.2d 355 (1983).

5. *McGarity*, 83 N.C. App. 106, 349 S.E.2d at 313.

6. 124 Misc. 2d 607, 476 N.Y.S.2d 1009 (1984). *See also* Kirschenbaum v. Rehfield, 539 So. 2d 12 (Fla. Dist. Ct. App. 1989) (law firm not vicariously liable for criminal attack by former investigator employee; attack was outside any apparent agency relationship and in no way furthered the interests of the firm); Noble v. Sears Roebuck & Co., 33 Cal. App. 3d 654, 109 Cal. Rptr. 269 (1973).

The Of Counsel Relationship

A 1993 case from Maryland illustrates the liability of both Of Counsel and the law firm for misrepresentation and breach of fiduciary relation. In *Homa v. Friendly Mobile Manor, Inc.*,[7] Leonard S. Homa, a member of the Maryland Bar, contracted with the law firm of Levan, Schimel, Richman and Belman, P.A. (LSRB) to perform services "as counsel/manufactured housing consultant . . . on behalf of Friendly . . . in connection with the sale of [mobile parks]. . . . "[8]

Friendly Mobile Manor, Inc. (Friendly) owned two mobile home parks. John S. Weiner, a real estate lawyer, and Kenneth Rossignol, a real estate broker, owned all of its stock. Weiner and Rossignol sold one of the two parks without the aid of Homa. Homa then offered to buy the second mobile home park.

In October 1986, Homa and Friendly entered into a contract whereby Homa was to purchase[9] the second mobile park, with a provision that, at closing, the buyer would assume responsibility for the payment of installment loans on specified financed mobile homes. Homa prepared the written contract on the law firm stationery of LSRB, on which his name appeared as "Of Counsel."

William T. Poole, a stockholder of Pascal Turner, Ltd. II (P/T), a corporation to be formed, agreed to take an assignment of Homa's contract to buy the second mobile home park, provided the assignment excluded any "contracts or agreements affecting the park for any matter for which the Purchaser will be required to assume or will become obligated."[10]

On December 3, 1986, the parties (Poole, Homa, Rossignol, and Weiner) met to settle the transaction. When a dispute arose concerning the assumption of the loans, Poole left the room, and Homa told Rossignol and Weiner that "he didn't think it really made any difference whether Mr. Poole signed the bill of sale with that assumption language in it, . . . that Mr. Poole had taken the assignment of the contract, and that . . . P/T was responsible under the contract of

7. 93 Md. App. 337, 612 A.2d 322 (1992).

8. *Homa*, 93 Md. App. 337, 612 A.2d at 325 (ellipsis in the original).

9. Homa presumably intended to resell the property, since the parties had a handwritten agreement that provided "Homa was entitled to a commission whether he bought the park or whether an assignee purchased it, in which case the commission was to be paid by the assignee." 93 Md. App. 337, 612 A.2d at 325.

10. *Id.*

sale to assume the loans."[11] The parties then deleted the language about assuming the installment loans from the bill of sale.

Prior to the settlement, Poole and Homa discussed the possibility of Homa becoming an investor in P/T. At the time of the settlement, Homa's son was employed by Poole. On December 2, 1986, the day before the settlement, Homa attended a meeting of the investors. P/T was incorporated in January 1987, and Homa began to do consulting work for it. In February, he became a shareholder.

In a declaratory judgment action by P/T against Friendly, the court ruled that P/T was not obligated to assume the installment loans.[12] Friendly then sued Homa and LSRB for breach of the October 1986 purchase contract, and for fraud.

Sitting without a jury, the trial court first bifurcated the two actions, and found Homa liable for fraud and breach of his legal services contract. The court awarded Friendly a judgment of $159,948.16 in compensatory damages, plus $31,440.00 in punitive damages.

In sustaining the lower court, the Maryland Court of Special Appeals concluded that Homa was guilty of fraud by virtue of the common law of misrepresentation:

- Friendly had proven a case of fraud as against Homa by showing:
  1. that Homa had made a false representation of a material fact;
  2. that Homa either knew of the falsity, or acted with reckless disregard of the truth;
  3. that Homa intended that Friendly would rely on the false representation;
  4. that Friendly did in fact rely upon it;
  5. that Friendly's reliance was justified; and
  6. that Friendly had suffered damages in reliance on the representation.[13]

The court then dealt with the fiduciary responsibility of a lawyer:

- The fiduciary relationship between lawyer and client placed upon Homa an affirmative duty to disclose all known facts

---

11. *Id.*

12. P/T Ltd. II v. Friendly Mobile Manor, 79 Md. App. 227, 556 A.2d 694 (1989).

13. *Homa,* 612 A.2d at 326 (paraphrase).

> material to their relationship. Failure to disclose constitutes fraud.[14]

Homa sought a reversal of the trial court's holding with respect to legal malpractice, because of Friendly's failure to produce any expert testimony with respect to Homa's alleged breach of fiduciary duty. The appellate court recognized that expert testimony may be required in some legal malpractice cases to establish the standard of care for negligence, but not where legal malpractice is based upon breach of fiduciary duty:

> Homa's failure to inform Friendly of his impending financial interest in P/T was a clear violation of his fiduciary duty as Friendly's attorney, was easily recognizable as such by a lay person, and most certainly was recognizable by a judge acting in the capacity of factfinder.[15]

Homa also contended that he was not liable on his contract with Friendly because a novation had occurred wherein P/T had been substituted for Homa on his contract with Friendly. The court responded:

> Even though the assumption language in the bill of sale was deleted, Weiner, based on Homa's counsel, believed P/T was responsible nonetheless to assume the loans. Because Friendly believed P/T was obligated to assume the loans, it is clear that Friendly did not agree to excuse the performance of this duty and did not agree to substitute the new agreement with P/T for its agreement with Homa. There was not a novation because the evidence does not establish a clear and definite intent to substitute one contract for another.[16]

As noted earlier, the appellate court bifurcated the case, treating Homa's appeal as to his liability to Friendly separate from Friendly's appeal regarding the liability of LSRB. On the latter aspect of the case, the trial court ruled that Friendly had failed to prove that Homa acted with the authority of LSRB.

In affirming this result, the Maryland court first discussed the common law of agency. Agency is a fiduciary relationship wherein

---

14. *Id.* at 327 (paraphrase).

15. *Id.* at 329.

16. *Id.* at 330. The appellate court also ruled that an award for punitive damages was appropriate, and that Homa's egregious conduct constituted gross fraud. *Id.* at 332.

the agent acts under the control and with the actual or apparent authority of the principal. The three elements integral to the relationship are:

1. the agent is subject to the principal's right of control;
2. the agent acts primarily for the benefit of the principal; and
3. the agent has the power to alter the legal relations of a principal.

Homa had no actual authority to act on behalf of LSRB:

> Although the agreement was on LSRB letterhead, the express contents of the [engagement] letter, and the testimony of Weiner and Rossignol, leave no doubt that the agreement was made with and for the services of Homa personally and exclusively and not with or for the services of LSRB or any employee thereof. . . . [The letter] also lists the services that "Consultant" will perform personally and provides that Friendly will pay to "Consultant" directly the fee for services rendered. . . . There is no indication in the agreement that LSRB would in any manner manage, supervise, or otherwise control Homa's performance under the agreement. The agreement was signed by Homa individually, and without reference to the title of his position with LSRB.[17]

Homa was not engaged in this transaction for LSRB's benefit; nor was LSRB to receive any benefit for Homa's services. Until he received the engagement letter, Rossignol was unaware of Homa's relationship with LSRB; the relationship, however, helped him "sell the idea" of using Homa's services to Weiner. But Weiner would have hired Homa regardless of his association with LSRB. From all this evidence, the appellate court concluded that the trial court properly held that Homa was acting for himself, and not for LSRB.

The trial court was equally correct in determining that Homa had no apparent authority, since there was no evidence that LSRB knew or should have known about this particular transaction.

Homa was the first decision to discuss the liability of a law firm for legal malpractice based on an agreement between the firm and Of Counsel. The case is useful in delineating the area where a law firm would *not* be subject to liability because of contractual arrangements that Of Counsel might make with clients. It is of less

17. *Id.* at 334.

help as a precedent for the typical Of Counsel situations outlined in Formal Opinion 90-357.[18]

The first part of *Homa* provides an analysis of the liability of the lawyer to the client for malpractice:

- Homa was guilty of intentional misrepresentation by virtue of his representation to Friendly that P/T had agreed to assume the installment loans.
- Homa breached his fiduciary relationship with his client by his failure to disclose a conflict of interest because of his relationship with Poole and P/T. This nondisclosure of a material fact constituted fraud.
- Expert testimony was not required to prove the standard of care "where the common knowledge of laymen is extensive enough to recognize or infer negligence [or an intentional violation] from the facts."[19]
- Punitive damages were recoverable by the client against the lawyer "where the wrong involved some violation of duty springing from a relationship of trust or confidence, or where the fraud is gross, or the case presents extraordinary or exceptional circumstances clearly indicating malice and wilfulness."[20]

The second part of the *Homa* decision, by negative inference, is helpful in establishing the extent of liability of a law firm for Of Counsel's wrongdoing. There is little in the opinion of the court to indicate the extent of the relationship between Homa and LSRB. The contract between them indicated that the reason for the Of Counsel arrangement was to effect the sale of the mobile home parks to the best advantage for Friendly. This was not the "close, continuing, and personal relationship" required of Of Counsel by Formal Opinion 90-357. In finding an absence of apparent authority, the court commented:

> Friendly presented no evidence of any contact with or reliance upon any conduct by LSRB that would establish that LSRB authorized Homa to act on its behalf in this transaction or that LSRB stood to benefit in any way from the agreement between Friendly and Homa. Even though there is one piece of corre-

---

18. *See supra*, Chapter IV, pp. 43 *et seq.*

19. *Homa*, 93 Md. App. 337, 612 A.2d at 328.

20. *Id.* at 331, quoting Loyola Federal S. & L. Ass'n v. Trenchcraft, 17 Md. App. 646, 663, 303 A.2d 432 (1973).

> spondence on LSRB letterhead, and as Friendly notes Homa shared office space with LSRB, there is no evidence LSRB knew or should have known about this particular transaction. No fees were to be paid to LSRB; moreover, fees were to be paid to Homa only if he personally procured a bona fide qualified purchaser for Friendly Manor (the agreement did not provide a separate fee for his legal services). In addition, . . . the evidence is sufficient to support the finding that Homa was not hired by Rossignol and Weiner because of his association with LSRB and would have been hired even if not associated with LSRB.[21]

From all appearances, the relationship between Friendly and Homa was for a single transaction, and not the "close, continuing, and personal relationship" required by Formal Opinion 90-357; but the case delineates the scope of liability for legal malpractice of both Of Counsel and the law firm.

Although *Homa* was concerned with a single transaction, rather than the "close, continuing, and personal relationship" required by 90-357, the same principles apply where a lawyer is serving as Of Counsel. In *Staron v. Weinstein*,[22] a New Jersey appellate court reversed a summary judgment for defendant, holding that the related firm (or lawyer) was liable, if the plaintiff could show that Of Counsel acted negligently with the firm's apparent authority.

Plaintiff Mariuz Staron was injured in an automobile accident. A friend referred him to Sheldon G. Weinstein, a lawyer practicing in Summit, New Jersey. Weinstein missed a two-year statute of limitations, thereby causing plaintiff to lose a substantial amount of potential damages covered by liability insurance.

On November 7, 1985, plaintiffs Mariusz and Elzbieta Staron, husband and wife,[23] entered into a retainer agreement with Weinstein, on the second page of which a law firm was listed as "Robert C. Thelander, Esq." above Weinstein's signature. On the day after the execution of the agreement, Weinstein wrote the insurer, on Thelander stationery, that "we represent" Mariuz Staron, and requested personal injury protection benefits. On the same day, also on Thelander stationery, he made a claim based on the driver's

---

21. *Homa,* 93 Md. App. 337, 312 A.2d at 335.

22. 305 N.J. Super. 236, 701 A.2d 1325 (1997).

23. Elzbieta was not involved in the automobile accident, but apparently joined with her husband for any potential damages, such as loss of services, to which she might be entitled by virtue of her marital status.

negligence. On the top right hand corner of the Thelander stationery, Weinstein was listed as "Of Counsel." Weinstein sent copies of both letters to the plaintiffs.

On August 15, 1986, Thelander advised Weinstein that he was terminating their Of Counsel relationship. He also advised those of Weinstein's clients of whom he had knowledge, of the termination, giving them Weinstein's home address. Thelander never knew of the relationship between the Starons and Weinstein until a summons and complaint was filed against him.

The lower court granted Thelander's motion for summary judgment, finding that there was no apparent authority by which Weinstein could bind Thelander or his firm. In reversing, the appellate court said:

> Proper resolution of the issues in this case requires a detailed evaluation of the facts including whether plaintiffs intended to retain only Weinstein to represent them as their attorney; whether his relationship with Thelander became relevant to their decision to sign the retainer agreement; whether Thelander was to be involved in the handling of Weinstein's trials and in whose name the pleadings were to be filed; what fees, if any, Thelander was to receive upon recovery; whether plaintiffs knew of the dissolution of the Thelander relationship before the malpractice occurred and continued to have Weinstein represent them, and why Thelander failed to notify plaintiffs of the dissolution.[24]

That the use "Of Counsel" on Thelander's letterhead was significant is indicated by the following comment of the court:

> In the context of a motion for summary judgment, plaintiffs made a sufficient showing that Thelander's firm became counsel for plaintiffs by virtue of both the retainer agreement and the fact that defendant [Weinstein] had at least apparent authority to enter into such agreements on behalf of the firm.[25]

Similarly, *Hirsch v. Weisman*[26] was a single transaction situation, wherein personal injury plaintiffs sought recovery against lawyer Weisman for his failure to bring their personal injury suit in a timely manner. Weisman had contracted with the law firm of

---

24. 701 A.2d 1325, 1327, 305 N.J. Super. 236, 240 (A.D. 1997).
25. 701 A.2d 1325, 1327, 305 N.J. Super. 236, 241 (A.D. 1997).
26. 189 A.D.2d 643, 592 N.Y.S.2d 337 (1st Dept. 1993).

Zuller & Bondy, and one of its partners, Thomas Bondy, to serve as trial counsel. In January 1988, Bondy negotiated a favorable settlement in the amount of $80,000, on behalf of Weisman, under the mistaken belief that the policy limits of the defendants' liability insurance policy was $100,000.

When the plaintiffs learned that the limit was actually $500,000, they sought leave of court to amend their pleadings and to serve the amended pleadings on the Bondy defendants. The trial court granted leave to amend, and held that the action was governed by the six-year statute of limitations for contracts, rather than the three-year malpractice statute, which would have barred the action.

The appellate court reversed, stating that the only damages recoverable in an action beyond the three-year period, but within the six-year period, would be those attributable to a breach of contract. It added:

> [A] plaintiff had better be able to point with specificity to some contractual agreement, express or implied, that has been breached in order to avail himself of the additional time in which to bring an action for damages.
>
> Here, there was no contractual relationship between plaintiffs and the Bondy defendants. Plaintiffs were in privity only with Weisman, their retained counsel. At best, the Bondy defendants had an "of counsel" relationship with plaintiffs. Historically, such a relationship has been held not to provide a basis for recovery by the retained trial counsel directly from the client, . . . even where the client may ultimately have benefited from the services performed. . . . The lack of privity runs both ways, and without showing knowledge of the contractual agreement between Weisman and the Bondy firm, plaintiffs cannot be considered third-party beneficiaries of that arrangement.[27]

---

27. *Hirsch,* 592 N.Y.S.2d at 338. In New York, Of Counsel must be in privity with the client to recover directly from him. Kiser v. Bailey, 92 Misc. 2d 435, 400 N.Y.S.2d 312 (1977) (Of Counsel retained to assist in litigation could not recover from client's estate). *See also In re* Muscillo's Estate, 159 N.Y.S.2d 253 (Sur. 1957); Levy v. Jacobs, 5 Misc. 2d 994, 148 N.Y.S.2d 607 (1955); *In re* Loomis, 273 N.Y. 76, 6 N.E.2d 103 (1937); Grennan v. Well Built Sales of Richmond County, Inc., 35 Misc. 2d 905, 231 N.Y.S.2d 625 (1962) (lawyers retained as trial counsel are entitled to withdraw because they never had a contractual relationship with the client).

Unlike *Homa* and *Hirsch, Bankers Trust Company v. Cerrato, Sweeney, Cohn, Stahl & Vaccaro*[28] involved a continuing relationship between a law firm and Of Counsel. During the period in question, defendant LoCasio was listed as a member of the firm, and then as "Of Counsel." He negotiated a settlement of a law suit on behalf of his client, Bernard. The proceeds of the settlement were assigned to the plaintiff, Bankers Trust Company, but defendants paid the proceeds directly to Bernard.

The Appellate Division ruled that material issues of fact were presented by LoCasio's knowledge of the settlement, and his misrepresentation thereof, thereby facilitating the misappropriation. This knowledge was chargeable to Cerrato, Sweeney, "if it clothed him with the apparent authority to act on its behalf."[29]

Associated Counsel

When a law firm or lawyer associates outside counsel for a particular matter, with the client's knowledge and consent, the first lawyer is ordinarily not vicariously liable for the second lawyer, provided the latter's negligence was an independent act. In the agreement between the firm and outside counsel, the parties should specify their respective duties to avoid any misunderstanding and protect each other from possible joint liability.[30]

The courts are reluctant to impose liability on the delegating lawyer for the errors and omissions of outside counsel. But if the associated lawyers are practicing together, sharing equal responsibility and authority, or sharing in the profits of the matter, there is a strong rationale for imposing vicarious liability on the lawyers for the torts of each other.[31] Liability may be premised on a theory that the parties were engaged in a joint venture.[32] At the other end of the scale, if the outside lawyer acts in a limited and passive role,

---

28. 187 A.D.2d 384, 590 N.Y.S.2d 201 (1st Dept. 1992).

29. 590 N.Y.S.2d at 202.

30. ABA DIVISION OF EDUCATION, PROFESSIONAL RESPONSIBILITY: A GUIDE FOR ATTORNEYS 311, 315 (1978). *See* Chapter 11, *Planning and Drafting the Of Counsel Agreement*, p. 187.

31. Ortiz v. Barrett, 222 Va. 118, 278 S.E.2d 833 (1981); *see also* C. WOLFRAM, MODERN LEGAL ETHICS, § 5.6, at 237-38 (West 1986).

32. Fitzgibbon v. Carey, 70 Or. App. 127, 688 P.2d 1367 (1984). *See also* discussion of *Duggins infra.*

such as cocounsel for one aspect of a case[33] or a pro hac vice lawyer hired to advise on matters of local law,[34] courts are reluctant to impose vicarious liability on outside counsel for the errors and omissions of the delegating firm or lawyer.[35]

In *Duggins v. Guardianship of Washington*,[36] for example, the mother and guardian of a five-year-old boy sought to recover damages in a medical malpractice action for the inadequate treatment of a traumatic injury to her son's eye. She executed a contingent fee contract with a lawyer, Duggins, providing that he could employ additional counsel at no additional expense to the guardianship. Duggins employed Barfield, a specialist in medical malpractice litigation.

While pretending to file suit, Barfield settled the case with the insurer without informing it of his cocounsel relationship with Duggins. He then misappropriated $53,089 of the insurance proceeds from the guardianship, and ultimately went to prison for the commission of a felony. The guardian sought to recover from Duggins this amount, plus prejudgment interest, to reconstruct the guardianship.

The Supreme Court of Mississippi treated the relationship between Duggins and Barfield as one of joint venture, and held Duggins liable for the restoration of the guardianship. But the court noted that even in the absence of partnership liability, Duggins would be accountable because he had procured Barfield's involvement in the litigation.

Tormo v. Yormark[37] presented a fact pattern similar to that of *Duggins*. A New York lawyer associated a New Jersey negligence specialist in a personal injury case. Unbeknownst to the first lawyer, the specialist obtained a settlement from the insurer, who delivered two checks to him. He forged the client's endorsement on one of the checks and applied the proceeds to his own use. Whether the New York lawyer was guilty of negligence by virtue

---

33. Some courts have held that co-counsel are liable for each other's acts. *See* Floro v. Lawton, 187 Cal. App. 2d 657, 10 Cal. Rptr. 98 (2d Dist. 1960); Livingston v. Cox, 6 Pa. 2d 360 (1847).

34. *See* Misner, *Local Associated Counsel in the Federal Courts: A Call for Change*, 67 CORNELL L. REV. 345 (1982).

35. *See* WOLFRAM, MODERN LEGAL ETHICS, *supra* note 27 at 238.

36. 632 So. 2d 420, 35 ALR5th 909 (Miss. 1993).

37. 398 F. Supp. 1158 (D.N.J. 1975).

of the specialist's misappropriation of the client's funds was a fact question for the jury. The New York lawyer's only inquiry was to look into a lawyers' directory to make sure that the New Jersey lawyer was licensed in New Jersey.

Similarly, in *Cohen v. Lipsig*,[38] where a lawyer retained outside trial counsel to pursue the client's cause, the Appellate Division reversed the granting of defendant's motion for summary judgment, holding that there were several fact questions for the jury:

- Was the outside counsel negligent?
- Did the lawyer obtain the informed consent of the plaintiff about the choice of trial counsel?
- Did the lawyer use reasonable care in the selection of trial counsel?
- Should the lawyer be estopped from denying the derivative liability for the alleged negligence of his chosen trial counsel?

Express or Implied Partnership

All members of a law partnership are jointly and severally liable for the torts committed by other members of the partnership or its agents within the scope of their authority.[39] Partnership assets may be reached to satisfy the judgment, as may the personal assets of each individual partner, if the partnership assets are insufficient. But individual partners must be named as parties, or they will not

38. 92 A.D. 536, 459 N.Y.S.2d 98 (2nd Dept. 1983).

39. *See, e.g.,* Williams v. Burns, 463 F. Supp. 1278 (D. Colo. 1979); Peterson v. Harville, 445 F. Supp. 16 (D. Or. 1977); *aff'd,* 623 F.2d 611 (9th Cir. 1980); Blackmon v. Hale, 1 Cal. 3d 548, 463 P.2d 418, 83 Cal. Rptr. 194 (1970) (former member of partnership held liable for law partner's misappropriation of funds, since law partner was acting within scope of apparent authority); Moore v. State Bar, 62 Cal. 2d 74, 396 P.2d 577, 41 Cal. Rptr. 161 (1964); Husted v. Gwin, 446 N.E. 2d 1361 (Ind. App. 1983) (law partnership liable and estate of deceased partner liable for other partner's misrepresentation of settlement and misappropriation of funds); Model Bldg. & Loan Ass'n v. Reeves, 114 Misc. 137, 186 N.Y.S. 759 (N.Y. Sup. Ct. 1921), *rev'd on other grounds,* 201 A.D. 329, 194 N.Y.S. 383 (1st Dept. 1922), *rev'd,* 236 N.Y. 331, 140 N.E. 715 (1923). *But see* Jackson v. Jackson, 20 N.C. App. 406, 201 S.E.2d 722 (1974) (malicious prosecution outside scope of partnership business); Tennent Shoe Co. v. Birdseye, 78 S.W. 1036 (Mo. App. 1904) (fraudulent or unfair dealings by law partner are individual acts not imputable to entire partnership).

personally be liable for a judgment.[40] If Of Counsel is guilty of legal malpractice, there is a likelihood that the law firm or lawyer to whom he or she is attached will also be held liable. The reverse of this situation, that is, whether Of Counsel will be liable for the wrongdoing of the partners or associates of the firm, is much less likely. But the contractual arrangements among the parties must make it clear that Of Counsel acts completely independently of the firm or lawyer.

A legal malpractice action raises the issue of whether a partner or agent acted within the scope of his authority. Because lawyers practice law in a variety of business arrangements, there is always the recurrent issue of whether an actual partnership existed. Although a partnership in fact may not have existed among the lawyers, an ostensible or apparent partnership may exist for purposes of liability to third persons.[41] If a partnership is established, Of Counsel may be just as liable for the wrongdoing of the partners

---

40. *See* R. MALLEN & J. SMITH, LEGAL MALPRACTICE, § 5.3, at 265 & n.4 (3d ed. 1989).

41. Section 16 of the Uniform Partnership Act states:

(1) When a person, by words spoken or written or by conduct, represents himself, or consents to another representing him to anyone, as a partner in an existing relationship or with one or more persons not actual partners, he is liable to any such person to whom such representation has been made, who has, on the faith of such representation, given credit to the actual or apparent partnership, and if he has made such representation or consented to its being made in a public manner he is liable to such person, whether the representation has or has not been made or communicated to such person so giving the credit by or with the knowledge of the apparent partner making the representation or consenting to its being made.

(a) When a partnership liability results, he is liable as though he were an actual member of the partnership.

(b) When no partnership liability results, he is liable jointly with the other persons, if any, so consenting to the contract or representation as to incur liability, otherwise separately.

(2) When a person has been thus represented to be a partner in an existing partnership, or with one or more persons not actual partners, he is an agent of the persons consenting to such representation to bind them to the same extent and in the same manner as though he were a partner in fact, with respect to persons who rely upon the representation. Where all the members of the existing partnership consent to the representation, a partnership act or obligation results; but in all other cases it is the joint act or obligation of the person acting and the persons consenting to the representation.

and associates of the firm, as the firm would be liable for Of Counsel's torts.

Under more limited circumstances, the partnership by estoppel doctrine operates to prevent lawyers from denying that a partnership existed, with the result that liability will attach. To prevail under this doctrine, a plaintiff must prove: (1) that the lawyer has been held out as a partner; (2) that such holding out was done directly by the lawyer, or with the lawyer's knowledge and consent; and (3) that the plaintiff relied on the apparent partnership to his detriment.

Ordinarily, the sharing of office space and profits, or the use of a joint name on a letterhead alone, will not create a "holding out," or partnership by estoppel. In *Brown v. Gerstein,*[42] for example, the court found the evidence insufficient to apply the doctrine. There, the plaintiff sued a lawyer for malpractice and deceit in a foreclosure action, and attempted to hold a second lawyer derivatively liable because he had practiced law with the first lawyer. The two lawyers had practiced in the same offices and had used each other's name on office stationery. But there was no evidence that the uninvolved lawyer had consented to, or had knowledge of, the transactions that gave rise to the dispute. The court said:

> [T]he use of a person's name in business, even with that person's knowledge, is too slender a thread to warrant a favorable finding on the consent element.[43]

Despite this holding, there is a risk in the use of a joint name on office doors and letterheads, particularly where other acts foster the impression of a partnership.[44] In *Bonavire v. Wampler,*[45] the court found that a lawyer's acts in defrauding prospective investors were attributable to a law firm from which the pieces of evidence, taken together, supported the conclusion that a "holding out" had occurred. Throughout the course of a fraudulent investment scheme, the plaintiffs had met with the lawyer at the law

---

42. 17 Mass. App. 558, 460 N.E.2d 1043 (1984). The common law doctrine of partnership by estoppel, reflected in this case, has been codified in most jurisdictions. See Uniform Partnership Act § 16, *supra*.

43. 17 Mass. App. 558, 460 N.E.2d 1043, 1053.

44. Hart v. Commercial Bank, 957 F. Supp. 958 (E.D. Mich. 1997); MALLEN & SMITH, LEGAL MALPRACTICE, *supra* n.40, § 5.3, at 271.

45. 770 F.2d 1010 (11th Cir. 1985).

firm's offices, the names of the lawyer and the law firm appeared, the lawyer's name was included on the law firm's letterhead, and an agreement with the client was prepared on the law firm's stationery.[46] In addition, the lawyers had advertised in the yellow pages together as a "full service law firm," and the defrauding lawyer had introduced the other lawyer to the client as his partner.[47]

On these facts, the court concluded that the law firm had not dispelled the notion of a partnership and had, in fact, ratified the lawyer's acts, thereby making itself liable for compensatory and punitive damages.[48]

Partnership by Estoppel

In *Myers v. Aragona*,[49] the court relied on the doctrine of partnership by estoppel to hold a lawyer liable under the Uniform Partnership Act to the plaintiff for funds misappropriated by another lawyer working for him. The nonparticipating lawyer was estopped to deny the existence of a partnership in which the two lawyers had listed themselves on their letterhead and had openly referred to themselves as "partners." Since the lawyers had displayed themselves as though they were partners in fact, and the third person had relied on such representations, the nonparticipating lawyer was jointly and severally liable for the torts of the misappropriating lawyer.[50]

Even though the mere use of a joint name and the sharing of office space will not in itself create liability under the estoppel theory, a prudent lawyer should specify on all communications the precise nature of his or her relationship with the firm or associated lawyers. The same rules apply whether Of Counsel is practicing primarily as a solo practitioner, with a firm, or with another lawyer. Of Counsel should detail the nature of his or her relationship

---

46. *Id.* at 1016.

47. *Id.*

48. *Id.* at 1011.

49. 21 Md. App. 45, 318 A.2d 263 (1974).

50. *See* Cottman v. Cottman, 56 Md. App. 413, 468 A.2d 161 (1983) (concept of partnership by estoppel not basis for liability where outward representations of partnership were not made until after occurrence of acts that gave rise to litigation); *see also* Duggins v. Guardianship of Washington, 632 So. 2d 420, 35 ALR5th 909 (Miss. 1993) (partnership by estoppel applied where two lawyers held to have entered into a joint venture).

with the firm or other lawyer in all communications, including letterheads, pleadings, shingles, law lists, legal directories, firm brochures, and professional announcement cards.[51] It is also advisable for Of Counsel to follow his or her signature on all business communications with the words "Of Counsel."[52] Use of terms such as "in association with" or "special tax counsel" may be misleading in that the lawyer's relationship with the firm is not clearly stated.[53]

Prudence dictates that Of Counsel's name be dropped from the firm's name upon withdrawing from the partnership. Although ethically permissible in some jurisdictions,[54] the retention or inclusion of Of Counsel's name in the firm name may signify to the public that Of Counsel shares mutual responsibility for legal services rendered.[55]

The retainer agreement with the client should describe the nature of Of Counsel's relationship with the firm or other lawyer. It should also delineate the extent of the lawyer's services and the services of other lawyers, if such services are needed.

---

51. It is good practice to apply these same principles to modern electronic communications, such as e-mail. In the office of one of the authors, the secretary-receptionist identifies his relationship to the firm when answering the telephone.

52. *But see* New York County Lawyers' Association Opinion 663 (1985) (holding it is unnecessary for Of Counsel to follow name with the words "Of Counsel").

53. *See* California Ethics Opinion 1986-90 (undated) (criticizing the description "a legal association" as being vague and misleading); Michigan State Ethics Opinion CI-657 (1981) (criticizing the designation "special tax counsel" as misleading, since Michigan does not recognize specialties in the area of tax law, and the designation does not clearly state the lawyer's relationship with the firm). By contrast, the use of the term "Of Counsel" has a word-of-art meaning, spelled out in Formal Opinion 90-357, and also conveys the nature of the relationship between the lawyer and the firm.

54. Maine Ethics Opinion 86 (1988); Vermont State Ethics Opinion 83-7 (undated).

55. *See* Los Angeles Ethics Opinion 421 (1983); Michigan Ethics Opinion CI-1001 (1984); Philadelphia Ethics Opinion 88-31 (1988). If Of Counsel is a former member of the firm who has retired, it is proper to leave that name in the firm name. See discussion, *supra* Chapter IV, at pp. 66 *et seq*. But if Of Counsel becomes an active practitioner in another firm upon retirement, his or her name should be removed from the former firm's name.

Since there is a risk that the partnership by estoppel doctrine can exist after the lawyer's withdrawal or dissolution of the partnership,[56] Of Counsel should promptly announce a separation from the former firm or any new status within the same firm. Of Counsel's name should be removed from the former firm's letterhead, office doors, and windows, as well as from the firm's checking and other accounts.

For purposes of vicarious liability, a 1997 case illustrates the distinction between partnership and partnership by estoppel. Monon Corporation retained Henry J. Price to pursue a claim of patent infringement against Wabash. Despite Monon's specific instructions not to release Wabash from any agreement which the parties might reach, Price did so. As a result, Monon brought suit against Price for legal malpractice.

At the time Price was retained, he was a partner of Barnes & Thornburg. He then joined Townsend, Yosha, Cline & Price, where he completed the work for Monon, and drafted the release. Monon also joined the individual lawyers in the firm (the Attorneys) as defendants. One of the lawyers was the sole shareholder of a professional corporation, Louis Buddy Yosha Professional Corporation. The Attorneys contended that they were employees of the corporation. The trial court granted their motion for summary judgment, but the appellate court reversed:

> Although the Attorneys indicate that the evidence shows that they worked within the framework of the professional corporation, the evidence supports the view that they carried on as co-owners of a business for profit. We conclude a genuine issue of fact exists about whether the firm really was a partnership for the purposes of vicarious liability.[57]

---

56. Royal Bank & Trust Co. v. Weintraub, Gold & Alper, 68 N.Y.2d 124, 506 N.Y.S.2d 151, 497 N.E.2d 289 (1986) (partnership remained liable for money misappropriated by former partner where partners continued to maintain all outward appearances of the partnership entity for purposes of winding up). *But see* Ventro v. Darlson, 468 So. 2d 463 (Fla. App. 4 Dist. 1985) (failure of lawyer to remove old firm's name from window of office he continued to occupy with his new firm was insufficient to create liability under estoppel doctrine where transactions were initiated well after the lawyer left the firm, and plaintiff knew that he had done so).

57. Monon Corporation v. Townsend, Yosha, Cline & Price, et al. (Ind. App. 1997), discussed *supra*, Chapter 1, at 9.

The court rejected the concept that the firm was a partnership by estoppel:

> . . . Monon hired Price before he joined the firm of Townsend, Yosha, Cline & Price. Although it certainly kept Price as its lawyer despite his move to the new firm with new attorneys, Monon has not demonstrated that it acted upon any representations that the firm was a partnership such that it was "influenced thereby to do some act" in reliance on the representations. . . . Monon has identified sufficient evidence to support the conclusion that the firm in question was, in fact, a partnership but has not established that it is entitled to insist upon an estoppel.[58]

Summary

Tort liability often reaches beyond the lawyer who actually committed the wrong to make other nonparticipating lawyers vicariously liable. Since Of Counsel relationships commonly contain characteristics of partner and other legal relationships, there is the risk that third parties might attempt to hold Of Counsel vicariously liable for the torts of other members of the firm. This liability can be avoided by careful drafting of the agreement between Of Counsel and the firm and advising a prospective client of the nature of this arrangement.

Because of the doctrines of respondeat superior, apparent authority, and partnership by estoppel, the law firm may find it more difficult to avoid vicarious liability for the wrongdoing of Of Counsel.

Of Counsel should make provisions for protection (for both self and assets) by negating any inference to third parties that a partnership relation exists between the parties. This necessarily means that Of Counsel's name should not be included in the firm's name. Of Counsel status should be clearly designated on all firm communications. Finally, Of Counsel should never practice law without adequate coverage under a legal malpractice policy. Coverage under such a policy, and who should be responsible for the payment of the premium, should be one of the terms negotiated and included in the Of Counsel agreement.

58. *Id.* at 10.

Checklist

Of Counsel's Acts as Employee

1. Is the firm vicariously liable for Of Counsel's acts as an employee?
2. Was the tort committed within the scope of Of Counsel's actual authority? Was the tort committed while Of Counsel was acting within the scope of employment? Can liability attach because of the firm's failure to supervise Of Counsel adequately?
3. Were the acts committed within Of Counsel's apparent authority? Was the third party reasonable in believing that Of Counsel performed the tortious acts within the scope of employment?
4. Was the transaction one that the firm routinely provided for its clients?

Of Counsel's Acts as Independent Contractor

1. Is the firm liable for acts of Of Counsel as an independent contractor? Did the firm cloak Of Counsel with such actual or apparent authority that he or she could bind the firm?
2. Did the firm expressly direct Of Counsel to commit certain acts? Did the firm know or should it have known that Of Counsel was untrustworthy?

Partnership

1. May the agreement be construed as making Of Counsel a partner? Is the conduct of the parties such as to give the appearance of the existence of a partnership?
2. Was Of Counsel held out as a partner? Did Of Counsel have knowledge of the holding out? Did Of Counsel consent to it?
3. Did the plaintiff reasonably rely on the implied partnership to his or her detriment?
4. Did the parties use a joint name on office doors, letterheads, and other business communications?
5. Where Of Counsel is a retired partner, has the separation from the firm as a partner been clearly announced?

CHAPTER VII

Of Counsel and Conflicts of Interest

A lawyer who becomes Of Counsel may find that the interests of a new client are adverse to the interests of a client he or she presently represents or may have previously represented. Conversely, the firm may have a conflict with one or more of Of Counsel's present or former clients. If a lawyer maintains multiple Of Counsel relationships, the potential for such conflicts increases exponentially.

This chapter explores what Of Counsel or a law firm should do when it discovers such a conflict. The Model Rules of Professional Conduct[1] provide the necessary guidelines to determine the existence of a conflict. If Of Counsel finds a conflict, he or she must decline or withdraw from representing the client. Similarly, the firm may not represent a client where the representation would adversely affect its relationship with another client.

It is often difficult to determine whether Of Counsel's conflict should be imputed to the firm or the firm's conflict to Of Counsel. A proper analysis of this "imputed disqualification" requires two steps: (1) Does Of Counsel or the law firm have a conflict when ei-

1. Hereinafter, THE MODEL RULES. The Model Rules, promulgated by the American Bar Association (ABA) in 1983, replaced the earlier Model Code of Professional Responsibility (the Model Code), adopted in 1969, and amended in 1980. The basic principles underlying the Model Rules and the Model Code are the same. Most jurisdictions have adopted one or the other. State and local bar associations have also published their own bar rules, which may or may not be consistent with the Model Rules or the Model Code. A lawyer or law firm must refer to all these sources to determine a potential conflict.

ther is asked to represent a client because of a present or past representation? (2) If the answer is yes, is the conflict of Of Counsel or the firm imputed to the other party that could cause a disqualification? We examine the first of these issues in this chapter, and defer the issue of imputed disqualification to the next chapter.

The Duties of the Lawyer

Loyalty and confidentiality are essential elements in a lawyer's representation of a client. But fulfillment of these duties may be threatened when Of Counsel represents two or more clients with adverse interests, or when representing a client with interests adverse to a former client. These duties are also threatened when a lawyer's obligations to the client conflicts with the lawyer's own personal or financial interests, or when the lawyer is asked to appear as a witness at trial where Of Counsel or the firm represents one of the parties.

If a lawyer has reason to believe that his or her representation will be directly adverse to another client, the lawyer should decline the representation, or withdraw if the agreement has already been made to represent the client.[2] But withdrawal may work undue hardship on the client.[3] As a result, the Model Rules permit the lawyer to represent the client if (1) he or she "reasonably believes that the representation will not adversely affect the relationship with the other client," and (2) "each client consents after consultation."[4] Consultation requires the lawyer to make a full disclosure of the ramifications of the representation that might make it adverse.

In addition to possible adverse client situations, the lawyer must not represent a client if the representation might be "materi-

---

2. Note, *Developments in the Law: Conflicts of Interest in the Legal Profession*, 94 HARV. L. REV. 1243, 1284 (1981).

3. *See, e.g.*, Nemet v. Nemet, 112 A.D.2d 359, 491 N.Y.S.2d 810 (2d Dept. 1985), appeal dismissed, 66 N.Y.2d 602 (1986) (attorney disqualified from representing wife in a divorce action, despite her alleged hardship).

4. MODEL RULES OF PROFESSIONAL CONDUCT (1983), Rule 1.7(a), provides:

> A lawyer shall not represent a client if the representation of that client will be directly adverse to another client, unless:
>
> (1) The lawyer reasonably believes the representation will not adversely affect the relationship with the other client; and
>
> (2) Each client accepts after consultation.

ally limited" by his or her own interests or by "responsibilities to another client or third person."[5] Again, the lawyer may still represent the client in the belief that the representation will not be adversely affected, and the client consents after consultation. As part of the consultation, the lawyer must explain "the implications of the common representation and the advantages and risks involved."[6]

Common Conflict Problems under the Model Rules

Conflict problems may arise at any time once a client seeks a lawyer for help. Even if the client elects not to retain the lawyer, the duty of confidentiality remains.[7] For conflicts purposes, the prospective client would become a "former client."[8] The lawyer may not act as an advocate against a person represented in another matter, even though it is unrelated. But the lawyer is free to represent persons or entities whose interests are only generally adverse, such as competing businesses.[9]

The lawyer may not represent a client where the interests of another client or third person, or the lawyer's own interests, might "materially limit" the lawyer's representation.[10] For example, a

---

5. MODEL RULES OF PROFESSIONAL CONDUCT (1983), Rule 1.7(b), provides:

> A lawyer shall not represent a client if the representation of that client may be materially limited by the lawyer's responsibilities to another client or to a third person, or by the lawyer's own interests, unless:
> (1) The lawyer reasonably believes the representation will not be adversely affected; and
> (2) The client consents after consultation. When representation of multiple clients in a single matter is undertaken, the consultation shall include explanation of the implications of the common representation and the advantages and risks involved.

6. *See supra*, note 2.

7. *See* ABA Legal Ethics Opinion 90-358 (1990), holding that if a prospective client consults a lawyer to obtain legal representation or advice, the duty of confidentiality continues even though no lawyer-client relationship is ultimately agreed upon. A lawyer or firm may not reveal information learned from a prospective client to an existing client.

8. *See infra*, Chapter 8, pp. 130 *et seq.*, for discussion of the difference between current and former clients in the conflicts setting.

9. MODEL RULES OF PROFESSIONAL CONDUCT (1983), Rule 1.7, comment [2].

10. MODEL RULES OF PROFESSIONAL CONDUCT (1983), Rule 1.7(b).

lawyer may not undertake work for a client that he or she cannot handle competently and at a reasonable fee simply to gain needed income. Or the lawyer may not refer a client to a business in which he or she has an undisclosed interest.[11]

Rule 1.7(a) prohibits representation of opposing partisan litigation. Such conflicts are readily discernible. Difficulties may arise where the parties are on the same side, as coplaintiffs or codefendants. There may be substantial differences in the parties' testimony, incompatibility in their positions with reference to an opposing party, or different possibilities with regard to settlement of the overall dispute.[12]

Such conflicts are not uncommon in estate planning and estate administration. A lawyer may be called upon to represent several family members whose interests may prove to be adverse. Some jurisdictions take the position that a lawyer represents the fiduciary; others hold that the client is the estate or trust, including the beneficiaries. In either event, the lawyer should make clear his or her relationship to each of the parties.[13] If there is a conflict between the beneficiaries and the fiduciary, or among the beneficiaries, the lawyer should advise them to retain appropriate counsel.

May a lawyer represent another lawyer in a legal malpractice action, where the two lawyers are adversaries in another litigation? The representation of the colleague might materially limit the representation of the client in the other litigation. In determining whether to withdraw from representing the adversary, the lawyer should consider:

- The relative importance of the matter to the represented lawyer.
- The relative size of the fee expected by the representing lawyer.
- The relative importance to each lawyer and to his or her client of the matter involving the third-party clients.

---

11. MODEL RULES OF PROFESSIONAL CONDUCT (1983), Rule 1.7, Comment [5].

12. MODEL RULES OF PROFESSIONAL CONDUCT (1983), Rule 1.7(b), Comment [6]. In criminal cases, the potential for conflict among criminal defendants is "so grave that ordinarily a lawyer should decline to represent more than one codefendant." *Id.*

13. MODEL RULES OF PROFESSIONAL CONDUCT (1983), Rule 1.7, comment [12].

- The sensitivity of the matter.
- The substantial similarity between the subject matter or issues of the two representations.
- The nature of the relationship of one lawyer to the other and of each lawyer to his or her third-party client.[14]

The potential for conflict in this situation is apparent: One or both of the lawyers may fail to provide their respective clients zealous representation; or the demands of their regular clients may jeopardize their own lawyer-client relationship. A case-by-case analysis "taking into account the knowledge of the colleagues, and the nature of the matter in which the represented lawyer is represented," is essential.[15]

Where a lawyer represents multiple clients on the same side, conflicts often arise because of discrepancies in the parties' testimony, incompatible positions as to the opposing party, or different possibilities for settlement. For the lawyer to continue to represent these parties, he or she must explain the ramifications and intricacies of all persons and entities involved in the litigation, and obtain their consents. Sometimes the lawyer may act as an intermediary to resolve the differences among such parties; but, if that fails, he or she may have to withdraw from representing any of the parties.[16]

Effect of Formal Opinion 90-357 on Conflict Problems

A conflict-of-interest problem may arise in several ways, but most conflict problems are caused by the lawyer's simultaneous or successive representation of clients with adverse interests. After Formal Opinion 90-357, conflict problems are also likely to arise from a lawyer's ability to maintain Of Counsel relationships with more than two law firms at the same time.

---

14. ABA Ethics Committee, Formal Op. 97-406 (1997); Rhode Island Supreme Court Ethics Advisory Panel Opinion 96-23 (1996) (semble); Committee on Professional Ethics of the Association of the Bar of the City of New York, No. 1996-3 (1996); Alabama State Bar Opinion RO-96-06 (1996).

15. Formal Op. 97-406 (1997); Restatement of the Law Governing Lawyers, Proposed Final Draft No. 1, § 206, Comment [g] (1996).

16. MODEL RULES OF PROFESSIONAL CONDUCT (1983), Rule 2.2. Where a lawyer is acting as an intermediary, any party to the intermediation can seek his or her withdrawal. Upon withdrawal, he or she may not represent any of the clients in the matter subject to the intermediation. Rule 2.2(c).

Although Formal Opinion 90-357 eliminated the prohibitions against lawyers entering into multiple Of Counsel relationships, it emphasized that one must guard against too many Of Counsel relationships because of the rules governing disqualification:

> As a practical matter, nonetheless, there is a consideration that is likely to put a relatively low limit on the number of "of counsel" relationships that can be undertaken by a particular lawyer: this is the fact that . . . the relationship clearly means that the lawyer is "associated" with each firm with which the lawyer is of counsel. In consequence there is attribution to the lawyer who is of counsel of all the disqualifications of each firm, and, correspondingly, attribution from the of counsel lawyer to each firm, of each of those disqualifications. *See* Model Rule 1.10(a). In consequence, the effect of two or more firms sharing an of counsel lawyer is to make them all effectively a single firm, for purposes of attribution of disqualifications.[17]

Additional conflict problems will likely result from law firms being able to enter into Of Counsel relationships with other law firms. Under these circumstances, lawyers and law firms should be very careful about entering into multiple Of Counsel relationships. The additional potential for imputed disqualification will deter lawyers from entering into too many Of Counsel relationships.

Conflicts in Simultaneous Representation

Both the Model Code and the Model Rules prohibit the lawyer from simultaneously representing multiple clients with interests that are directly adverse to one another. Model Code DR 5-101(A) provided that a lawyer must decline to represent a client if, in the lawyer's independent professional judgment, the client could be adversely affected by the lawyer's acceptance of the proffered employment, or if such representation might involve the lawyer in representing differing interests. Model Rule 1.7(a)[18] bars representation of a client if that representation will be "directly adverse" to another client, even if that representation is wholly unrelated. Model Rule 1.7(b) prohibits multiple representation if the lawyer's ability to represent one client will be "materially limited by the

17. *See supra* note 2.

18. Model Rules of Professional Conduct (1983), Rule 1.7(a).

lawyer's responsibilities to another client or to a third person, or by the lawyer's own interests."[19]

Both Rule 1.7(a) and Rule 1.7(b) provide for a waiver of these rules where the lawyer reasonably believes that the representation will not be adversely affected, provided there is a full disclosure and the client consents.

Lawyers often undertake representation of differing interests—for example, when giving advice to both the buyer and seller in drafting a contract, or to the husband and wife in a divorce proceeding. Sometimes the clients so trust the lawyer that they are willing to overlook their minor differences, and thereby reduce lawyer fees.[20] But a lawyer should proceed cautiously in representing both sides of a transaction; if hostility between the parties should arise, there will also arise an inability to represent either party.[21]

A law firm may ask, for example, whether its Of Counsel relationship with a lawyer who represents the majority ownership interests of a seller in a particular transaction precludes it from undertaking representation to document the sale. In one such situation raised before the State Bar of Michigan, a law firm had for several years represented two different clients, each engaged in the construction business. One client was a corporation involved in commercial construction. The other was a partnership involved in multifamily residential construction composed of two corporations. The majority shareowner of each partnership corporation was deceased, and the estate's personal representative and fiduciary was a retired partner of the law firm, who remained with the firm in an Of Counsel capacity. The law firm had appeared in probate court on behalf of the estate fiduciary.

Beneficiaries of the estate and the personal representative sought to sell certain partnership assets to the corporation client. The economic terms of the transaction had been negotiated between the partnership and the corporation with the Of Counsel

---

19. MODEL RULES OF PROFESSIONAL CONDUCT (1983), Rule 1.7(b).

20. *See* MODEL RULES OF PROFESSIONAL CONDUCT (1983), Rules 1.7(a) and (b), 1.9(a), 1.13(e), and 2.2; and Model Code, DR 5-105(C).

21. *Cf.* Nemet v. Nemet, 112 A.D.2d 359, 491 N.Y.S.2d 810, 811 (2d Dep't) (Of Counsel and law firm disqualified from representing wife where Of Counsel had been formerly employed by husband's law firm; "appearance of impropriety" evident in the Of Counsel arrangement).

lawyer's participation. The parties then sought counsel to document the terms of the transaction.

The law firm asked whether it may represent the purchaser corporation in documenting the transaction under the following circumstances:

1. Separate counsel would be retained to represent the interests of the partnership, the two partnership corporations, and the estate beneficiaries;
2. The purchasing corporation would retain separate counsel to advise it on the issue of conflict waiver;
3. All parties to the transaction would consent to the law firm's representation of the purchasing corporation in the matter after consultation with separate counsel; and
4. The terms of the transaction would be presented to the probate court for approval, and the consent of all estate beneficiaries.

Relying on Model Rule 1.7(b), the Michigan Standing Committee on Professional and Judicial Ethics[22] concluded that the fiduciary duties of the Of Counsel lawyer materially limited his ability to undertake representation to document the sale for the seller and purchaser.

> Having already represented the interests of the seller in determining the terms of the transaction, even though this "representation" was in a fiduciary capacity and not as counsel for the estate, the "of counsel" lawyer could not now switch sides and purport to impartially document the transaction for both parties. The conflict is not vitiated by the involvement of the probate court, since the estate fiduciary is responsible for recommending the matter to the court and is not impartial.[23]

Because Of Counsel's fiduciary duties would adversely affect his ability to document the sale, client consent would not vitiate the conflict.

The committee went further, holding that the law firm was precluded from representing the selling partnership and the estate fiduciary in the sale transaction.

---

22. State Bar of Michigan, Standing Committee on Professional and Judicial Ethics, Opinion No. RI-237 (June 6, 1995).

23. *Id.*

> Even if the proposed representation is seen as merely documenting the arrangements already agreed upon, a direct conflict is presented under the terms of MRPC 1.7(a).... Although the selling partnership and the estate fiduciary may be in agreement concerning the sale of assets to the purchasing corporation, the fact that both the selling partnership and the estate fiduciary are current clients of the law firm exacerbates the law firm's conflict in documenting the transaction impartially and independently for all parties.[24]

However, the committee found that, unlike the Of Counsel lawyer, the law firm might be able to undertake the documentation representation if no member of the law firm had been involved in the transaction on behalf of the seller if it obtained informed consent of the partnership and the purchasing corporation.

Conflict problems are often obvious from the moment the lawyer undertakes the representation.[25] Differing interests between clients can arise in many, often subtle, ways. For this reason, identifying a conflict problem often requires a careful and ongoing analysis of the facts, as well as the interests and expectations of the parties.

Conflicts in Successive Representation

Successive representation raises questions regarding the lawyer's dual duties of loyalty and confidentiality. A breach of these duties is generally confined to matters that are "substantially related."[26]

---

24. *Id.*

25. For example, a law firm was disqualified from representing a debtor-in-possession where Of Counsel to the law firm was the son of a partner of the debtor. *In re ZB Surfside Co.*, 1994 Bankr. LEXIS 1852 (Bankr. S.D.N.Y. 1994).

26. Model Rules of Professional Conduct (1983), Rule 1.9. The full text of the Rule is as follows:

> A lawyer who has formerly represented a client in a matter shall not thereafter:
>
> (a) represent another person in the same or a substantially related matter in which that person's interests are materially adverse to the interests of the former client unless the former client consents after consultation; or
>
> (b) use information relating to the representation to the disadvantage of the former client except as Rule 1.6 would permit with respect to a client or when the information has become generally known.

Although the Model Code did not specifically address this problem, case law developed the doctrine of the "substantial relationship" test, a two-part inquiry: First, are the former and present representations adverse in a material way? Second, are the matters substantially related? If the answer to both these questions is in the affirmative, the lawyer is prohibited from continuing in the matter.[27]

When there is a substantial relationship between the former and current representations, two basic presumptions arise: First, if there is a lawyer-client relationship, it is presumed the lawyer has access to and receives information from the client.[28] Second, when the matters are related, it is presumed that the lawyer will divulge former client confidences. The need for these presumptions stems from the view that the former client should not be forced to prove that confidential information was in fact given.[29]

Sometimes it is a close question as to whether a particular client is a current or former client. A current client can bar the lawyer from representing another client whose interests are "directly adverse." If the client is a former one, the substantial relationship test must be satisfied to disqualify a present representation.

In *Heathcoat v. Santa Fe International Corp.*,[30] for example, a law firm prepared a client's will. Later, it represented someone else who was adverse to its former client. During this adverse representation, it sent a form letter to the former client, inviting her to call the firm for advice in view of recent changes in the tax law. Despite this letter, the court characterized the client as a former client, and refused to disqualify the law firm.[31]

In a similar case, a New Jersey law firm performed tax and estate work for the president of a steel company. With the president's consent, it represented another business client in a transaction with the steel company. The firm continued to send form letters, similar to the letter in *Heathcote,* advising the president of tax law changes and suggesting that he update his will. When the transaction between the two companies failed, the other company sued the president of the steel company. The president sought to disqualify the

27. MODEL RULES OF PROFESSIONAL CONDUCT (1983), Rule 1.9(a).
28. *Supra* note 2, at 1328–29.
29. *Id.*
30. 532 F. Supp. 961 (E.D. Ark. 1982).
31. *Id.* at 963–64.

New Jersey firm. The court ruled that there was a current lawyer-client relationship, and that the president could bar the firm from representing the other business client.[32]

In still another case, a law firm represented a company and its president individually over a period of years. It eventually billed the company $785 for its last work, but never sought to collect the bill. Meanwhile, it sent out firm newsletters addressed to "clients and friends." It also retained the company's corporate minute books and the president's will. One of the firm's lawyers casually referred to the company and its president as his "clients." The court ruled that the mailings of the newsletters were "routine ministerial actions" and that the lawyer's comments about the company and its president still being clients were "ice-breaking" comments that could not be given "significant weight." It concluded:

> It is unreasonable to continue to demand an attorney's undivided loyalty for an indefinite period of time when the attorney's last bill is both disputed and unpaid, and when each of several opportunities to use the attorney's services is directed to another firm.[33]

Advancing Inconsistent Positions

May a lawyer take inconsistent positions on a legal question when representing two or more parties in different cases? Rule 1.7 allows this, unless "representation of either party would be adversely affected."[34] This may be proper in cases pending in different trial courts, but not in an appellate court.[35] Taking inconsistent positions in unrelated matters is improper if there is a substantial risk that a lawyer will undercut the position taken for one of his clients.[36] The lawyer should first obtain the consent of both clients after making a full disclosure of the potential ramifications.

---

32. Manoir-Electroalloys Corp. v. Amalloy Corp., 711 F. Supp. 188 (D.N.J. 1989).

33. Artromick International, Inc. v. Drustar, Inc., 134 F.R.D. 226, 231 (S.D. Ohio 1991).

34. Model Rules of Professional Conduct (1983), Rule 1.7, Comment [8].

35. *Id.*

36. Legal Ethics Opinion 377 (ABA 1993).

Determining Disqualification of Of Counsel

When a conflict arises from an Of Counsel's involvement in a former and current representation, the approach is the same as it would be for any other lawyer. The inquiry focuses upon whether or not there is a substantial relationship between the subject matter of the two representations.[37] A substantial relationship exists, for example, if the former representation is the same action at law as the current representation,[38] if there is a significant overlap between the services rendered in the two representations,[39] or if the factual contexts of the two representations are similar.[40] A finding of a substantial relationship will give rise to the initial presumption that Of Counsel received confidences during the prior representation, causing disqualification.

To prevent disqualification, Of Counsel must look at the subject matter of the two representations to determine whether the first presumption can be avoided altogether. This will turn on whether a substantial relationship exists. If a substantial relationship exists, Of Counsel must withdraw, unless Of Counsel can qualify under the "peripheral representation" exception.

The Peripheral-Representation Exception

Even if a substantial relationship is found between the former and current representations, Of Counsel may avoid disqualification if able to demonstrate that he or she was only "peripherally involved" in the former representation.[41] If the lawyer is disqualified because of matters that the firm handled, and not because of his or her own personal involvement, the court, in essence, allows the irrebuttable presumption to be rebutted.[42] Thus, an actively and heavily involved lawyer must be distinguished from one who "enter[ed] briefly on the periphery for a limited and specific purpose

---

37. Jenson v. Touche Ross & Co., 335 N.W.2d 720, 731 (Minn. 1983).

38. Atasi Corp. v. Seagate Technology, 847 F.2d 826, 829 (Fed. Cir. 1988).

39. *Jenson*, 335 N.W.2d at 732.

40. United States *ex rel.* Lord Elec. v. Titan Pacific Constr. Corp., 637 F. Supp. 1556, 1560 (W.D. Wash. 1986).

41. *Atasi*, 847 F.2d at 829.

42. *See* Trone v. Smith, 621 F.2d 994 (9th Cir. 1980); Silver Chrysler Plymouth, Inc. v. Chrysler Motors Corp., 518 F.2d 751 (2d Cir. 1975).

relating solely to legal questions."[43] In the latter case, the assumptions underlying the traditional notion of the lawyer-client relationship no longer apply.[44]

A "peripheral" lawyer may be one called in as a consultant on one aspect of a case, or an associate whose involvement in the matter was limited or sporadic. Such a lawyer's role would not be representation that would require disqualification.

Although some courts apply a rebuttable presumption if the lawyer was only "peripherally" involved,[45] a very strict standard of proof is normally needed to rebut the presumption.[46] The exception for peripheral involvement has been used in a case involving the disqualification of an Of Counsel lawyer. In *Atasi Corp. v. Seagate Technology,*[47] the conflict involved a classic case of a lawyer switching sides in the middle of the litigation. The court easily found that a substantial relationship existed between the lawyer's former and current representations. The lawyer involved had been Of Counsel to a firm representing the defendant, but, before the litigation concluded, became Of Counsel to a new firm representing the plaintiff. Of Counsel argued that he did not receive any confidential information while Of Counsel at the first firm.[48] But the court noted that the lawyer's disqualification did not rest upon proof of actual disclosure; the test "only depends on whether the former and current representations are substantially related."[49] Since the former representation was the very same action at law as the current representation, the substantial relationship test was satisfied.

Having found a substantial relationship, the court next considered whether the Of Counsel's personal involvement in the former representation warranted mitigating the irrebuttable presumption of shared confidences. The court noted that Of Counsel had per-

---

43. *Silver Chrysler*, 518 F.2d 751.

44. *See* MODEL RULES OF PROFESSIONAL CONDUCT (1983), Rule 1.9, comments, ¶ 2 ("The underlying question is whether the lawyer was so involved in the matter that the subsequent representation can be justly regarded as a changing of sides in the matter in question").

45. *Silver Chrysler*, 518 F.2d at 756–57.

46. LaSalle Nat'l Bank v. Lake County, 703 F.2d 252 (7th Cir. 1983).

47. 847 F.2d 826 (Fed. Cir. 1986).

48. *Id.* at 829.

49. *Id.*

sonally signed a pleading, helped prepare a brief, and twice visited the defendant's facility. As a result, the defense of peripheral representation failed, and Of Counsel and his new firm were disqualified from current representation.

Atasi illustrates that, by itself, the Of Counsel designation will not prevent disqualification under the exception for peripheral representation. The label attached to the relationship will not determine the success or failure of the defense. Rather, the lawyer's actual involvement, without regard to his or her status within the firm, is controlling. Where Of Counsel's signature appears on pleadings or briefs, or where personal appearances are made, it is unlikely that the involvement will be considered "peripheral."

The peripheral-representation exception is not limited to rebutting the presumption that the involved lawyer actually received confidential information. It has also been used to prevent firm-wide disqualification—that is, where the firm seeks to rebut the presumption that confidential information was divulged to the firm's current affiliates.

Summary

While conflict-of-interest problems are common in all professional relationships of lawyers, there is probably a greater chance of encountering such problems in the Of Counsel relationship. Most conflict problems arise from the lawyer's simultaneous or successive representation of multiple clients with adverse interests. If the conflict arises from simultaneously representing multiple clients with adverse interests, the lawyer is prohibited from undertaking the representation of such clients.

If the conflict arises from the lawyer's representation of a current client with interests adverse to those of a former client, the lawyer is prohibited from the current representation if the former and current matters are substantially related. If the matters are "substantially related," a presumption arises: Confidential information is deemed to have been obtained by the lawyer from the former client during the former representation. It is further presumed that the lawyer will use this information to the former client's disadvantage.

Most courts hold the substantial-relationship presumption to be irrebuttable. But some of these courts allow an exception where the lawyer was only "peripherally" involved in the former representation. A peripheral lawyer might be one called in as a consultant, or an associate whose involvement was limited to research in the library.

Lawyers who move between firms as Of Counsel or who maintain multiple Of Counsel relationships must guard against possible conflict-of-interest problems. Under these circumstances, the peripheral exception becomes important. Of Counsel are often used in a limited capacity within a law firm. To force Of Counsel to withdraw would work a hardship on their desire to practice as Of Counsel, and preclude their moving between firms, without serving any useful social purpose. Similarly, requiring the law firm to withdraw might be of little social utility. Where Of Counsel's name appears on pleadings and other court documents, or where Of Counsel makes personal appearances on behalf of a former client, the peripheral-lawyer exception cannot be used. But, in other situations, the courts should look closely at the extent of this actual involvement before requiring a withdrawal.

Thanks to the liberality of 90-357, lawyers and law firms may now enter into multiple Of Counsel relationships. But in view of the rules with regard to imputed disqualification, all parties to an Of Counsel agreement should carefully consider the effects of any new Of Counsel relationship on those already in existence. In the next chapter, we shall consider the effects of the Of Counsel relationship on imputed disqualification.

Checklist

Simultaneous Representation

1. Is Of Counsel simultaneously representing clients with adverse interests?
2. Are the clients coplaintiffs? Are they codefendants? Is it likely that the clients' interests will become adverse during litigation?

Successive Representation

1. Are there any facts that might cause the former client to be considered to be a current client?
2. Is Of Counsel or the lawyer's firm representing a client who has a direct conflict with a former client of Of Counsel or a former law firm?
3. Are the former and current representations substantially related? Are the representations related to the same contro-

versy? Does it appear that Of Counsel had access to confidential information of the former client? Are the legal or factual issues of the two matters related?

The Peripheral-Representation Exception

1. If the matters are substantially related, can the Of Counsel take advantage of the peripheral-representation exception?
2. Was Of Counsel actively involved in the former representation? Did he or she personally sign pleadings, briefs, or opinion letters? Did Of Counsel make personal appearances on behalf of the client? Was there participation in private conferences with the former client?
3. Was Of Counsel's involvement in the former representation peripheral? Was this involvement brief and for a limited purpose? Was Of Counsel called in as a consultant on one aspect of the case? Was this involvement limited to legal research or technical advice?

CHAPTER VIII

Imputed Disqualification and the Of Counsel Relationship

In general, when a lawyer is disqualified by a conflict, all lawyers "associated" with this lawyer are vicariously disqualified. As the Ethics Committee in Formal Opinion 90-357 pointed out, "There can be no doubt that an of counsel lawyer (or firm) is 'associated in' and has an 'association with' the firm (or firms) to which the lawyer is of counsel,"[1] for purposes of the rules of imputation of disqualification. But a broad and inflexible rule of vicarious disqualification may work hardship on lawyers in general, and on lawyers who are Of Counsel in particular. As the following sections illustrate, the general rule of imputed disqualification is subject to exceptions and modifications.

Rules Governing Imputed Disqualification

The Model Code applied a sweeping rule to disqualify all members of an affected lawyer's firm from continuing in the representation once a conflict had been found. If one lawyer was disqualified from representing a client because of a conflict of interest, every partner and associate in the law firm was also disqualified.[2]

---

1. ABA Comm. on Ethics and Professional Responsibility, Formal Op. 90-357 at 13.

2. MODEL CODE OF PROFESSIONAL RESPONSIBILITY DR 5-105(D) (1969, amended 1980) provides:

> If a lawyer is required to decline employment or to withdraw from employment under a Disciplinary Rule, no partner or associate, or any other lawyer affiliated with him or his firm may accept or continue such employment.

The Model Rules modified this approach somewhat by imposing firm-wide disqualification only where there is a special danger of conflicting representation by present or past associates of the same firm.[3] Model Rule 1.10(a) provides that, while lawyers are currently "associated" in a firm, none of them can represent a client if any one of them practicing alone would be disqualified from representing a client.[4] The application of this rule is limited to a lawyer disqualified in one of three situations: where the lawyer's representation would (1) offend the conflict-of-interest rule with regard to a former client (Model Rule 1.9); (2) offend the conflict-of-interest rule with regard to a present client (Model Rule 1.7); or (3) involve a lawyer in preparing an instrument in which the lawyer or a person related to the lawyer would receive a gift.

Imputed-disqualification issues frequently arise when there is a substantial relationship between representations that are adverse to a current or former client. We shall focus on the rules that have developed in this area, with emphasis on conflicts that arise due to a firm's multiple representation or conflicts that arise after a lawyer has left one firm and joined another that represents a client with interests adverse to a client of the former firm.

The Presumption of Shared Confidences

The substantial-relationship test (described in Chapter 7) triggers two presumptions. The first, related to the receipt of confidential information, causes disqualification of the individual lawyer. Under the second presumption, the disqualified lawyer is presumed to have conveyed the confidential information to all of the lawyers in the current firm, causing the disqualification of the entire firm. But whether this latter presumption is irrebuttable depends upon whether the lawyers are currently or formerly affiliated.

Present Affiliates: Irrebuttable Presumption

When lawyers work together, they are presumed to share confidences. The threat that confidential information may be disclosed warrants the application of an irrebuttable presumption.

---

3. MODEL RULES OF PROFESSIONAL CONDUCT Rule 1.10 (1983).

4. MODEL RULES OF PROFESSIONAL CONDUCT Rule 1.10(a) (1983) provides, "While lawyers are associated in a firm, none of them shall knowingly represent a client when any one of them practicing alone would be prohibited from doing so by rules 1.7, 1.8(c), 1.9 or 2.2."

Model Rule 1.10(a) imposes an irrebuttable presumption for conflicts that arise among currently associated attorneys. If a lawyer in a firm is disqualified from the representation, every other lawyer in the firm is also disqualified. Unlike Model Rule 1.10(b), discussed below, which provides for disqualification only if the representation presents a material risk to the client, Model Rule 1.10(a) creates a "per se rule for same-firm conflicts."[5] This reflects the general notion that the risk of even casual sharing is too great.[6]

These irrebuttable presumptions have been accepted by the courts,[7] the majority of which will not inquire into whether confidential information was in fact shared between the lawyers. As long as the matters are substantially related, the lawyer and the entire firm are disqualified. To prevent disqualification, the lawyer and firm must show that there is no substantial relationship between the multiple representations.

Former Affiliates: Rebuttable Presumption

Model Rule 1.10(b) provides that when a lawyer leaves a firm, no lawyer or firm with which the departing lawyer becomes associated shall represent a client whose interests are materially adverse to that of another client formerly represented by the departing lawyer or the firm.[8] When a lawyer leaves one firm and joins another, the problem of disqualification becomes more complicated. Then

5. C.W. WOLFRAM, MODERN LEGAL ETHICS: PRACTITIONER'S ED. § 7.6 (West Publ'g Co. 1986).

6. Note, *Developments in the Law: Conflicts of Interest in the Legal Profession*, 94 HARV. L. REV. 1243, 1372 (1981).

7. *See* Westinghouse Elec. Corp. v. Kerr-McGee Corp., 580 F.2d 1311 (7th Cir.), *cert. denied*, 439 U.S. 955 (1978); International Business Mach. Corp. v. Levin, 579 F.2d 271 (3d Cir. 1978); Fund of Funds, Ltd. v. Arthur Andersen & Co., 567 F.2d 225 (2d Cir. 1977).

8. MODEL RULES OF PROFESSIONAL CONDUCT, Rule 1.10(b) (1983) provides:

> When a lawyer becomes associated with a firm, the firm may not knowingly represent a person in the same or a substantially related matter in which that lawyer, or a firm with which that lawyer was associated, had previously represented a client whose interests are materially adverse to that person and about whom the lawyer had acquired information protected by Rules 1.6 and 1.9(b).

all of the disqualifications that afflicted every lawyer in the first firm are spread to all of the lawyers in the second firm.[9]

As the prohibition against representation is extended, the wisdom of an absolute rule of imputed disqualification becomes questionable. Competing interests must be considered: First, the client must be assured that the departing lawyer will maintain the duties of loyalty and confidentiality. Second, the lawyer should not be precluded from taking on new clients, particularly when the lawyer's involvement in the matter was limited or peripheral. A broad disqualification rule would hamper a lawyer's career opportunities with no substantial benefit to the client. Third, a broad rule of disqualification would preclude prospective clients from their first choice of counsel.

The courts are divided on the extension of the rule of imputed disqualification and whether a rebuttable or an irrebuttable presumption should be applied when the conflict involves a departing lawyer. The traditional rule was to apply an irrebuttable presumption that client confidences were shared between the departing lawyer and his or her current affiliates, and impose a firm-wide disqualification of the second firm.[10] The trend now is to use a flexible approach and allow the firm an opportunity to rebut the presumption of shared confidences.[11]

---

9. WOLFRAM, *supra* note 5, at § 7.6. It is sometimes helpful to separate out the possible situations that tend to give rise to problems involving imputed disqualification:

(1) a disqualification spread from an individual lawyer to another;
(2) a disqualification spread from an individual lawyer to the entire firm;
(3) a disqualification spread from the firm to its individual members, associates, or other affiliates; and
(4) a disqualification spread from one firm to another. *Id.*

10. Emle Indus. v. Patentex, Inc., 478 F.2d 562 (2d Cir. 1973); Marketti v. Fitzsimmons, 373 F. Supp. 637 (W.D. Wis. 1974); T.C. Theatre Corp. v. Warner Bros. Pictures, 113 F. Supp. 265 (S.D.N.Y. 1953).

11. *See* Panduit Corp. v. All States Plastic Mfg. Co., 744 F.2d 1564, 1580 (Fed. Cir. 1984); Schiessle v. Stephens, 717 F.2d 417 (7th Cir. 1983); Novo Terapeutisk Laboratorium A/S v. Baxter Travenol Laboratories, Inc., 607 F.2d 186 (7th Cir. 1979); Akerly v. Red Barn Sys., Inc., 551 F.2d 539 (3d Cir. 1977); City of Cleveland v. Cleveland Elec. Illuminating Co., 440 F. Supp. 193, 209 (N.D. Ohio 1976), *aff'd*, 537 F.2d 1310 (6th Cir. 1977), *cert. denied*, 435 U.S. 996 (1978); Silver Chrysler Plymouth, Inc. v. Chrysler Motors Corp., 518 F.2d 751 (2d Cir. 1975); United States *ex rel.* Lord Elec. Co. v. Titan Pacific Constr. Corp., 637 F. Supp. 1556 (W.D. Wash. 1986).

When the tainted lawyer is Of Counsel to the firm, a successful rebuttal may depend upon several factors:[12]

- The nature and extent of Of Counsel's former representation of the client;
- The time lapse between that representation and the present controversy;
- The nature of the Of Counsel arrangement, including work assignments and salary arrangements;
- The likelihood that Of Counsel has had contact with the firm's lawyers responsible for handling the present controversy; and
- The presence of any "specific institutional mechanisms" designed to prevent the passage of information between the tainted lawyer and the lawyers responsible for handling the instant controversy.

Several recent cases illustrate how these factors are applied. In *United States ex rel. Lord Electric v. Titan Pacific Construction Corp.*,[13] the court refused to disqualify the entire firm because of a conflict involving an Of Counsel. Several factors were important in the court's decision. Not only had the court found that the movants were using the motion to disqualify as a tool for harassment and delay, but the nature of Of Counsel's relationship with his current firm indicated that the other lawyers in the firm were not exposed to confidential information. Of Counsel worked less than full-time at the firm—he averaged approximately 70 hours per month[14]—and he did not participate in the general earnings of the firm. In describing the nature of Of Counsel's relationship, the court stated:

> [Of Counsel's] involvement in the firm as a non-participating attorney makes it less likely that he has disclosed confidences to other lawyers working on this and related suits against [the defendant].[15]

Another relevant factor was the prolonged time lapse between the current and former representations. Of Counsel had ceased working on matters related to the former client over a year before he left the firm. He then left the practice for a period of four years,

---

12. *Lord Elec. Co.*, 637 F. Supp. at 1565-66 (W.D. Wash. 1986).
13. *Id.*
14. *Id.* at 1559, 1566.
15. *Id.* at 1566.

after which he returned and joined his current firm as Of Counsel. This time lapse made it less likely that Of Counsel had retained any significant recollection of his former client's affairs, particularly since he had not taken any files or notes with him when he left his former firm.

In *Atasi Corp. v. Seagate Technology,*[16] the Ninth Circuit also focused on the nature of Of Counsel's relationship with his current firm. According to the court, the Of Counsel contract revealed an "active and very close relationship with the firm."[17] The contract provided that:

1. the firm would provide Of Counsel with a full-time secretary and an office;
2. the firm would handle all billing for Of Counsel;
3. the firm would cover his health insurance policies;
4. Of Counsel would receive his mail through the firm's office;
5. Of Counsel would do all his work in the name of the firm;
6. the firm would bill Of Counsel's clients for any postage, phone, and copying costs;
7. the firm would send Of Counsel legal work of its clients; and
8. the firm would provide backup help to Of Counsel, if needed.

Based on the terms of this contract, the court concluded:

> [W]e must observe that [Of Counsel] was more than a *de minimus* [sic] of counsel, an independent contractor working part-time for the firm.[18] (Emphasis in original.)

Since there was a significant relationship between the former and current controversies, a rebuttable presumption arose that Of Counsel had shared those secrets with his current affiliates. The entire firm was disqualified because it could not show that each lawyer in the firm had been notified of screening procedures before Of Counsel joined the firm.

Another relevant factor relied on by the courts is the nature and extent of Of Counsel's involvement in the prior controversy. The firm may be able to escape disqualification if it can show that Of Counsel was only "peripherally" involved in the former repre-

---

16. 847 F.2d 826 (Fed. Cir. 1988).
17. *Id.* at 831.
18. *Id.* at 830.

sentation.[19] Even if Of Counsel is found to have been only peripherally involved in the prior representation, the firm might still be required to demonstrate that appropriate screening mechanisms are established. For instance, in *Jenson v. Touche Ross & Co.*,[20] the plaintiffs sought to disqualify the defendant's firm because the firm's Of Counsel had previously acted as plaintiff's cocounsel in the same matter. Of Counsel argued that his prior involvement with the plaintiffs was limited to one aspect of the case and that his prior role did not bear a substantial relationship to the subject matter of his current representation.[21] The trial court agreed and denied the motion to disqualify Of Counsel's firm but prohibited Of Counsel from discussing the litigation with any of his current firm members.

On appeal, the Supreme Court of Minnesota agreed that Of Counsel's firm should not be disqualified, but attempted to clarify the trial court's application of the substantial-relationship test. In applying the test, the court explained, the trial court should consider the facts and issues involved to determine whether there is a substantial overlap between the two representations.[22] If a substantial relationship is found, an irrebuttable presumption arises that the lawyer received confidences, and a rebuttable presumption arises that the lawyer shared those confidences with his current affiliates. Finally, the trial court should weigh the competing equities.

Applying this approach, the court found that a substantial relationship existed between the two representations, but that the firm had rebutted the presumption that confidences had been conveyed to the current firm affiliates. The relevant factor was the lawyer's lack of involvement in the prior representation. The court accepted the trial court's findings that, in effect, Of Counsel's previous involvement was limited and that his subsequent representation would not disadvantage the plaintiffs. Of primary importance was the fact that (1) Of Counsel's prior connection to the plaintiffs was solely through their lead counsel and (2) his prior representation was limited to collection of the settlement made with the defendant. The degree of the lawyer's involvement in the prior matter is important when considering whether the presumption of

19. In this rebuttal, the inquiry focuses upon whether the first presumption—whether shared confidences were received by the lawyer in question—was rebutted.

20. 335 N.W.2d 720 (Minn. 1983).

21. *Id.* at 730.

22. *Id.* at 731.

shared confidences has been rebutted. Although the court made a passing reference to the Of Counsel arrangement, as well as the size of Of Counsel's firm, the lawyer's prior involvement was of paramount importance.

The Chinese Wall

Where a lawyer cannot show limited prior involvement in representation, other methods of rebuttal may still prevent firm-wide disqualification. One approach is to build a "Chinese wall" around the tainted lawyer to prevent the "spread" of confidential information to the rest of the firm.[23] The lawyer is, in effect, screened from discussing confidential information with the other members of the firm.

Use of the Chinese wall in the private sector in general and the Of Counsel context in particular has not met with widespread approval. Although it has been recognized in the limited area of conflicts involving former government lawyers, it has generally been characterized as a self-serving defense to escape the lawyer's ethical obligations. Even when the most stringent barriers are in place,[24] a Chinese wall cannot assure the client that confidential information will not be leaked. Although there is a split of authority on the Chinese wall as a viable defense, the trend has been to allow it in principle[25] but to require such stringent proof of "specific institutional mechanisms" that the defense rarely succeeds.[26]

---

23. WOLFRAM, *supra* note 5, at § 7.6.4.

24. Effective screening methods include both internal procedures and structural barriers. These include separating the affected lawyers to different offices or even cities, placing limitations on all interoffice correspondence and memoranda, and files. *See* Note, *Developments in the Law: Conflicts of Interest in the Legal Profession*, 94 HARV. L. REV. 1243, 1368-69 (1981).

25. Courts that have accepted the "Chinese wall" defense include: Smith v. Whatcott, 757 F.2d 1098 (10th Cir. 1985); EZ Paintr Corp. v. Padco, Inc., 746 F.2d 1459 (Fed. Cir. 1984); LaSalle Nat'l Bank v. Lake County, 703 F.2d 252 (7th Cir. 1983); Nemours Found. v. Gilbane, Aetna, Fed. Ins., 632 F. Supp. 418, 429 (D. Del. 1986); Kovacevic v. Fair Automotive Repair, Inc., 641 F. Supp. 237, 244 (N.D. Ill. 1986); *Lord Elec. Co.*, 637 F. Supp. 1556.

26. Smith v. Whatcott, 757 F.2d at 1101-02 (wall must be constructed in a timely and firm-wide manner); *EZ Paintr Corp.*, 746 F.2d at 1462 (wall must be timely implemented); *Schiessle*, 717 F.2d 417 (there must be a formal, institutionalized wall). The Ninth Circuit has not yet decided whether it would accept the "Chinese wall" defense, although it was accepted as one method for rebutting the presumption of shared confidences in *Lord Elec. Co.*, 637 F. Supp. 1556, and in *Haagen-Dazs Co.*, 639 F. Supp. at 287.

Only one court has allowed it as a viable defense in the Of Counsel context. In *United States ex rel. Lord Electric v. Titan Pacific Construction Corp.*,[27] the court was satisfied that no disclosures had taken place between the tainted lawyer and his current firm. The court found that appropriate screening measures had been in place when Of Counsel first joined the firm: Once Of Counsel's current firm learned of the conflict, the lead counsel instructed all lawyers at the firm to have no conversations with Of Counsel regarding the current matter. In addition, the lead counsel revealed the conflict to opposing counsel and requested their consent to allow Of Counsel to work on the matter. Screening mechanisms that are established at the time a tainted lawyer joins a firm are the most reliable objective evidence available to rebut the presumption of shared confidences. Satisfied that Of Counsel and his firm had acted in an ethical manner, the court refused the motion to disqualify. As a precaution that no confidences would be disclosed in the future, it decided that additional measures would be necessary. Each lawyer at the firm would be required to certify he or she had no conversation on the matter in the past with Of Counsel, and would not speak of the matter in the future with him.

Although the *Titan* court allowed the Chinese wall to rebut the presumption of shared confidences, other courts have not only disagreed with its reasoning, but have ruled that *Titan* does not adequately reflect the trend in the Ninth Circuit.[28] In applying the law of the Ninth Circuit, the Federal Circuit found that the Ninth Circuit had not yet ruled on the availability of the Chinese wall as a defense.[29] But even if the defense were available, the Federal Circuit found that the presumption could not be overcome because timely screening procedures were not established:

> [T]here is a complete lack of evidence before the court indicating that the *entire* . . . firm was also notified of this oral screening *before* [Of Counsel] assumed his "of counsel" position.[30] (Emphasis in original.)

27. 637 F. Supp. 1556 (W.D. Wash. 1986).

28. *See Atasi*, 847 F.2d at 832, n.7.

29. *Id.* at 831. The decision noted that two district courts in the Ninth Circuit had previously allowed the defense in *Lord Elec. Co.*, 637 F. Supp. 1556 and *Haagen-Dazs Co.*, 639 F. Supp. at 287.

30. *Id.* at 831.

Affiliated Law Firms

A difficult series of questions is presented in the conflict area raised by relationships between law firms. For the reasons described above, no hard and fast rule applies to all situations in which law firms become Of Counsel to one another. As a general proposition, however, where two law firms have a close, regular, and continuing relationship, it is highly unlikely that one could represent a client whose interests are adverse to clients of the other firm without following the procedure prescribed in Model Rule 1.7(b). In such a case, the law firm must make a good faith determination that the representation will not be adversely affected and, if that determination can be made, secure the informed consent of the client if the representation is to go forward.

Several examples from recent cases are instructive to evaluate the conflict situations raised by Of Counsel relationships between law firms.

In *Mustang Enterprises v. Plug-In Storage, Inc.*,[31] Hill, Steadman & Simpson (the Hill Firm), a Chicago-based intellectual property law firm of some 30 lawyers and Of Counsel to Bachmand & Lapointe, P.C., (the Bachman Firm), defendant's patent counsel, was disqualified from representing the plaintiff in the same patent action. Since 1991, the Bachman Firm, which consisted of four lawyers, had been retained by Plug-In as its patent counsel. When all the legal files were transferred to the Bachman Firm from the firm that had previously represented Plug-In, the files included a substantial number of documents dealing with patents currently in suit.

There was no question that the Bachman Firm could not take on the current lawsuit on behalf of Mustang against its current client, Plug-In. What remained for the court's resolution was whether that disqualification was also imputed to its "affiliated" law firm, the Hill Firm. For that purpose, the existence or nonexistence of a Chinese wall would make no difference whatsoever if the Hill Firm and Bachman Firm were regarded as the equivalent of two offices of the same law firm, because in that event the firm itself would be regarded as having switched sides.[32]

In legal terms, the question before the court was whether "affiliated firms" are to be treated as the equivalent of two offices of

31. 874 F. Supp. 881 (N.D. Ill. 1995).
32. *Id*. at 887.

the same firm as a matter of law. Relying on ABA Formal Opinion 84-351, the court noted that the question would be answered in the affirmative unless the "affiliated" designation was available on a limited basis.[33]

For example, availability may be limited if the "affiliated" or "associated" firm performs all of the tax, labor, patent, or other specialized work for the other firm. Availability may also be limited to performing legal services that have a relationship to or must be performed in another state. *Id.* (quoting ABA Formal Opinion 84-351).

In this case, the court noted that the Hill Firm and the Bachman Firm used the "affiliated firm" designation without limiting it in any respect. Having chosen to obtain those benefits that flowed from the public listings, the Hill Firm could not now complain that both firms should be treated as a two-office law firm for conflict-of-interest purposes:

> Whatever benefits Hill Firm and Bachman Firm may view themselves as deriving from holding each other out as an "affiliated firm," the price that must be paid for deriving those benefits is the inability of either firm to litigate against clients of the other firm under circumstances such as those presented here.[34]

Difficult questions are also raised when the professional relationship between the firms becomes more substantial. In *Complaint of Maritima Aragua, S.A.,*[35] an action involving parties with an interest in a vessel involved in a collision, the court refused to disqualify the law firms representing plaintiffs due to their prior representation of defendants' related entity. The plaintiffs' law firm, Watson Farley & Williams (WFW) of New York, was part of a Jersey Island partnership (WFW Jersey). The partners of the affiliated firm of WFW, with offices in London, England (WFW UK) were also members of WFW Jersey, but the New York partners of WFW Jersey were not members of WFW UK.

The underlying matter involved the collision in Venezuela between two vessels, the *Mar Coral* and the *Trade Resolve,* and a claim for damages filed by Maraven, a pipeline owner whose pipeline

33. *Id.* at 888.

34. Mustang Enterprises v. Plug-In Storage, Inc., 874 F. Supp. 881, 890 (N.D. Ill. 1995).

35. 847 F. Supp. 1177 (S.D.N.Y. 1994).

was damaged in the collision. The defendant, the *Trade Resolve*, was owned by a Panamanian corporation related in ownership to Gregory Callimanopulos, a well-known Greek shipowner. The complaint in the *Trade Resolve* litigation was answered by WFW Jersey. The *Trade Resolve* defendants filed a motion to disqualify WFW Jersey due to prior representation its affiliated firm, WFW UK, had given to Mr. Callimanopulos. WFW UK's prior representation included advice to in-house counsel of Brokerage & Management Corp., one of the *Trade Resolve* defendants, on the manner in which Mr. Callimanopulos's international holdings and activities should be structured in light of questions concerning legal responsibilities and liabilities. Confidences and secrets were imparted to WFW UK concerning Callimanopulos's business interests. In addition, the companies' in-house counsel met with partners of the New York office of WFW Jersey to discuss implications of the Oil Pollution Act of 1990 and certain taxation matters for companies associated with Callimanopulos, including the various entities that compose the *Trade Resolve* defendants.

The court acknowledged that there was a trend for lawyers and firms to practice in multiple states, and that this is often not done as s single firm with multiple offices, but through the structure of "associated" or "affiliated" law firms. With regard to the confidentiality that must be maintained between "affiliated" or "associated" firms, the court relied on ABA Formal Opinion 84-351 (October 20, 1984), which noted that potential clients are led to believe that lawyers of the "affiliated" or "associated" firms will not simultaneously represent persons whose interests conflict with the client's interests.

> When a firm elects to affiliate or associate another with it and to communicate that fact to the public and clients, there is no practical distinction between the relationship of affiliates under that arrangement and the relationship of separate offices in a law firm.[36]

The partners of WFW UK were partners of WFW Jersey, although the partners of the New York office of WFW Jersey were not partners of WFW UK. Although the law firms were not in an Of Counsel relationship, partners at each firm admitted the firms were, at a minimum, an affiliated partnership. As such, the court

36. *Id.* at 1181.

determined that WFW UK's prior representation of Trade & Transport and Brokerage & Management must be considered representation by WFW Jersey for which confidences were presumed to have been transmitted.

Disqualification would not follow unless the *Trade Resolve* defendants could demonstrate that the relationship between the two actions was "patently clear" or that the actions were "identical" or "essentially the same." Applying the substantial relationship test in this case, the court determined that the *Trade Resolve* defendants had not satisfied their burden of demonstrating that WFW's prior representation of Callimanopulos's interests was "substantially related" to the present matters. WFW UK's prior advice to Brokerage & Management was completely unrelated to the present action. Moreover, the meetings between Baldwin and various WFW lawyers discussed only general matters related to the Oil Pollution Act of 1990, citizenship, and taxes, and included no discussion of confidential information.

Whether conflicts have to be cleared between law firms and whether relationships have to be disclosed to clients of either turns on the substance of the relationship, not the name the law firms choose to call it. But if a particular representation may be materially limited by an existing relationship, the lawyer must decline the representation unless the lawyer believes the representation will not be adversely affected and the client consults after consultation.[37]

Former Government Employees

Another type of conflict-of-interest problem, a result of the classic "revolving door" situation,[38] arises frequently in the case of a retiring judge or other government employee who wishes to leave government employment and become affiliated with a law firm as Of Counsel. While in the role of prosecutor, a lawyer may have prosecuted an individual who is a client of the lawyer's current firm. Or a former judge may have participated in a court matter involving a client regularly represented by the current firm.

Although conflicts problems are inherent in these situations, competing interests, such as the need to encourage government service by lawyers and the public's desire to avoid professionalization of government service, have resulted in the development of

---

37. ABA Formal Op. 94-388 (December 5, 1994).

38. *See* Note, *Developments in the Law, supra* note 6, at 1425 n.43.

special rules.[39] The effect of the rules is to require that the former government employee be disqualified only in matters with which the lawyer was associated, or in which the lawyer had "substantial" responsibility,[40] while employed by the government.

---

39. As to government employees in general, DR 9-101(B) of the MODEL CODE OF PROFESSIONAL RESPONSIBILITY (1969, amended 1980) provides, "A lawyer shall not accept private employment in a matter in which he had substantial responsibility while he was a public employee." Rule 1.11 of the MODEL RULES OF PROFESSIONAL CONDUCT (1983) provides in pertinent part:

> (a) Except as law may otherwise expressly permit, a lawyer shall not represent a private client in connection with a matter in which the lawyer participated personally and substantially as a public officer or employee, unless the appropriate government agency consents after consultation. No lawyer in a firm with which that lawyer is associated may knowingly undertake or continue representation in such a matter unless:
>
> (1) the disqualified lawyer is screened from any participation in the matter and is apportioned no part of the fee therefrom; and
>
> (2) written notice is promptly given to the appropriate government agency to enable it to ascertain compliance with the provisions of this rule.

As to former judges and arbitrators, DR 9-101(A) of the MODEL CODE OF PROFESSIONAL RESPONSIBILITY provides, "A lawyer shall not accept private employment in a matter upon the merits of which he has acted in a judicial capacity."

Rule 1.12 of the MODEL RULES OF PROFESSIONAL CONDUCT (1983) provides in pertinent part:

> (a) Except as stated in paragraph (D), a lawyer shall not represent anyone in connection with a matter in which the lawyer participated personally and substantially as a judge or other adjudicative officer, arbitrator or law clerk to such a person, unless all parties to the proceeding consent after consultation. . . .
>
> (c) If a lawyer is disqualified by paragraph (a), no lawyer in a firm with which that lawyer is associated may knowingly undertake or continue representation in the matter, unless:
>
> (1) the disqualified lawyer is screened from any participation in the matter and is apportioned no part of the fee therefrom; and
>
> (2) written notice is promptly given to the appropriate tribunal to enable it to ascertain compliance with the provisions of this rule.

40. For a discussion of the substantial-relationship test in the context of former government officials, see Note, *Developments in the Law*, *supra* note 6, at 1433-39 (1981).

But the rules pertaining to imputed disqualification and the government employee are more uncertain. The Model Code extends vicarious disqualification to any situation in which the lawyer would be required to decline employment; the Model Rules extend vicarious disqualification to any government employee who "participated personally and substantially" in any matter involving a private client. These rules have not been interpreted literally, and resolution of the matter has been left for the courts.[41] One answer to this problem is through "screening" the former government employee from the matter.[42] This procedure has been endorsed by the ABA and, unlike the case of private sector employment, accepted by most courts.[43] The screening technique has been incorporated into the Model Rules as an alternative to complete withdrawal by the firm.[44]

Imputed Disqualification and the Lawyer As Witness

Another conflict-of-interests problem arises when the lawyer is asked to testify as a witness at a trial in which one of the parties is represented by the lawyer or a member of the firm. The lawyer, in the role of witness called by the opposing party, may present testimony directly adverse or prejudicial to the interests of the client. Or the lawyer may be called to act as witness on behalf of the client. In this situation, the lawyer's credibility may be called into question, thereby compromising and prejudicing the interests of the client. In 90-357, the committee stated:

> [An Of Counsel lawyer] is a lawyer in the firm for purposes of Rule 3.7(b), regarding circumstances in which, when a lawyer is to be a witness in a proceeding, the lawyer's colleague may nonetheless represent the client in that proceeding.[45]

---

41. *Id.* at 1439-40.

42. *Id.* at 1363 n.390.

43. ABA Comm. on Ethics and Professional Responsibility, Formal Op. 342 at 10 (1975).

44. *See* MODEL RULES OF PROFESSIONAL CONDUCT Rule 1.11, comment (1983).

45. ABA Formal Op. 90-357 at 13.

Model Rule 3.7 provides that if the testimony will be prejudicial to the client, the lawyer must withdraw.[46] Similarly, the lawyer must withdraw if it becomes necessary to testify for the client.[47] Most states prohibit Of Counsel from accepting employment where the likelihood of being called as a witness exists.

When the lawyer-witness must withdraw from representing a client because of a conflict, the firm must also withdraw from representation. The Model Code prohibits the lawyer's firm from serving as advocate if a member of the firm will be required to act as a witness on behalf of the client or if the lawyer's testimony will likely be prejudicial to the client.[48] The Model Rules provide for imputed disqualification of the firm where a member of the firm is precluded from representing a client by virtue of a conflict resulting from the combination of roles.[49] Whether the combination of roles involves an improper conflict is determined by the general conflict-of-interests rule,[50] which prohibits a lawyer from repre-

---

46. Rule 3.7 of the MODEL RULES OF PROFESSIONAL CONDUCT (1983) provides:

> (a) A lawyer shall not act as advocate at a trial in which the lawyer is likely to be a necessary witness except where:
> (1) the testimony relates to an uncontested issue;
> (2) the testimony relates to the nature and value of legal services rendered in the case; or
> (3) disqualification of the lawyer would work substantial hardship on the client.

A comparison with the Model Code was as follows: "DR 5-102(A) prohibited a lawyer or the lawyer's firm from representing a client if the lawyer 'learns or it is obvious that he or a lawyer in his firm ought to be called as a witness on behalf of his client.' DR 5-102(B) provided that a lawyer, and the lawyer's firm, may continue representation 'if the lawyer learns or it is obvious that he or a lawyer in his firm may be called as a witness other than on behalf of the client . . . until it is apparent that his testimony is or may be prejudicial to his client.'" DR 5-101(B) permitted a lawyer to testify while representing a client under certain circumstances.

47. *See* MODEL CODE OF PROFESSIONAL RESPONSIBILITY DR 5-102(A) and DR 5-101(B)(1)-(3) (1969, amended 1980).

48. *See* MODEL CODE OF PROFESSIONAL RESPONSIBILITY DR 5-101(B), 5-102(A), 5-102(B), and accompanying comments.

49. *See* MODEL RULES OF PROFESSIONAL CONDUCT Rule 3.7 (1983), *supra* note 46.

50. *See* MODEL RULES OF PROFESSIONAL CONDUCT Rule 1.7 (1983).

senting a client with interests adverse to those of another client, and the rule that prohibits a lawyer from representing a client with interests adverse to those of a former client.[51] For example, the lawyer's representation is improper where the testimony of the lawyer will substantially conflict with that of the client.

When the lawyer-witness is disqualified, the lawyer's firm is also disqualified. The few state bar ethics panels that have addressed the issue in the Of Counsel context have imposed imputed disqualification under the reasoning found in the Model Code or the Model Rules.[52] One state bar ethics panel has held that a firm is not automatically disqualified from representing an Of Counsel's client, even if the lawyer is called as a witness in an action by the opposing party.[53]

Summary

If one lawyer is disqualified because of a conflict, all affiliated lawyers are also disqualified. This rule is the result of a presumption: A disqualified lawyer is presumed to have conveyed confidential information to all lawyers with whom the lawyer is or has been affiliated. If the conflict arises between clients represented by lawyers currently affiliated in the same firm, the presumption is irrebuttable. But if the conflict arises between clients of lawyers who were once affiliated, some courts apply a rebuttable presumption. To rebut the presumption, the firm must show by clear and convincing evidence that the confidential information was not and is not likely to be disclosed.

Imputed disqualification frequently arises in the Of Counsel context. Of Counsel often move between firms; in some cases, Of Counsel are simultaneously affiliated with different firms. Where the conflict arises because Of Counsel and the affiliated firm are simultaneously representing clients with adverse interests, Of Counsel and the firm must both withdraw.

---

51. *See* MODEL RULES OF PROFESSIONAL CONDUCT Rule 1.9 (1983).

52. Michigan State Bar Ethics Opinion CI-1071 (undated); Texas State Bar Ethics Opinion 445 (1987).

53. Maryland State Bar Ethics Opinion 87-37 (1987) (if Of Counsel is named as a witness in litigation brought against the lawyer's principal client, the firm would still be permitted to represent the client).

Where Of Counsel is representing a client with interests adverse to those of a client of a former firm, many courts allow Of Counsel's present firm to rebut the presumption. For a successful rebuttal, Of Counsel must show by clear and convincing evidence that the confidential information was not shared. This includes evidence in the form of testimony, affidavits, or oral or documentary evidence of effective screening procedures.

Checklist

Is Of Counsel's Present Firm Vicariously Disqualified?

1. Does the conflict arise between clients of lawyers presently affiliated? If so, there is an irrebuttable presumption that confidences were disclosed.
2. Does the conflict arise between clients of lawyers who were at one time affiliated? If so, is the presumption rebuttable?
3. If the presumption is rebuttable, is there clear and convincing evidence that confidences were not disclosed? Were effective screening procedures in place at the time Of Counsel joined the firm? At the time the conflict first arose? Are institutional screening procedures currently in place?
4. How effective are the screening procedures? Is there restricted access to the client's file? Is there a physical separation between Of Counsel and the rest of the firm? Does Of Counsel practice in a different city or office of the firm? How large is the firm?

CHAPTER IX

Advertising the Of Counsel Relationship

In Formal Opinion 330, the committee considered whether the designation "Of Counsel" could be used on letterheads, professional announcement cards, and office shingles. Consideration was necessary, the committee wrote, because:

> [T]he Code of Professional Responsibility uses the term "Of Counsel" only in DR 2-102(A)(4) relating to letterheads, yet the problems concerning "Of Counsel" arise in connection with other professional notices.

Formal Opinion 330 held that where an Of Counsel relationship existed, that fact could be shown on professional announcement cards and shingles.[1] The committee also considered whether DR 2-102(A)(6) (a provision that was subsequently deleted from the Model Code) authorized use of the term in law lists or legal directories. Subdivision 6 had stated that data published in a law list

1. Formal Opinion 330 held that use of the term "Of Counsel" was permissible on professional announcement cards because of the language contained in DR 2-102(A)(2), which permits professional announcement cards to state "changed associations . . . or similar matters. . . ." The committee wrote, "The change of a lawyer's status to 'Of Counsel' or the addition to the firm's ranks of a lawyer whose status factually will be 'Of Counsel' falls within the quoted language and is permissible." ABA Comm. on Ethics and Professional Responsibility, Formal Op. 330 (1972). Moreover, the committee found that subdivision (3) of DR 2-102(A) contained general language that permitted a lawyer to use a shingle. *Id.*

or legal directory could only include the name of the lawyer, the lawyer's firm, and "names of professional associates." The fact that an Of Counsel relationship existed was not among the items of information that were expressly permitted to be published. Nevertheless, the committee construed the phrase "names of professional associates" to include lawyers who were Of Counsel.[2]

Unfortunately, Formal Opinion 330 failed to consider many other significant issues that arise by virtue of the Of Counsel relationship. The committee did not discuss whether the name of a lawyer who is Of Counsel may ethically be included in the firm name. Nor did the committee consider whether the out-of-state Of Counsel's jurisdictional limitations must be listed on professional announcement cards, letterheads, directories, and law lists. After Formal Opinion 330 was issued, the ABA Model Rules of Professional Conduct were developed to displace the ABA Model Code of Professional Responsibility. Constitutional law affecting lawyer advertising underwent a radical change. Some of these changes were reflected in the new Formal Opinion 90-357.

Because advertising plays a significant role in every Of Counsel relationship, this chapter considers the interrelationship of advertising and Of Counsel.

Lawyer Advertising and Solicitation

Canon 8 of the ABA Model Code of Professional Responsibility states, "Members of the public should be educated to recognize the existence of legal problems and the resultant need for legal services, and should be provided methods for intelligent selection of counsel."[3] This need has been met by lawyer referral programs and by lawyer advertising and solicitation of clients.

With the increased use of lawyer advertising and solicitation, disciplinary rules have developed. This has tended to hamper the lawyer's "duty to facilitate the process of intelligent selection of lawyers."[4] The disciplinary rules have limited lawyers' efforts to communicate to potential clients information useful in their decision about legal services. During the 1970s and 1980s, radical

---

2. ABA Formal Op. 330 at 71.

3. MODEL CODE OF PROFESSIONAL RESPONSIBILITY EC 8-3 (1969, amended 1981).

4. MODEL CODE OF PROFESSIONAL RESPONSIBILITY EC 2-1 (1969, amended 1981); *see also* MODEL CODE OF PROFESSIONAL RESPONSIBILITY EC 2-2 (1969, amended 1981).

changes in the rules, brought on by decisions of the United States Supreme Court, have resulted in an expansion of commercial advertising and other formal means of communication with potential clients.

History of Lawyer Advertising

The 1908 Canons of Professional Ethics contained provisions that, although not completely prohibitive, discouraged lawyer advertising. Canon 27 of the ABA Canons of Professional Ethics maintained that it was "unprofessional" for a lawyer to advertise or solicit professional employment. This canon prohibited most forms of advertising, whether in the form of "circulars, advertisements, or through touters."[5] But the same canon permitted professional cards, stating that the "publication or circulation of ordinary simple business cards, being a matter of personal taste or local custom, is not per se improper."[6]

The ban against lawyer advertising was justified in part on the ground that lawyer advertising and solicitation denigrated the profession and treated it as a business.[7] But as communities began to grow, the number of lawyers who began to ignore the 1908 ban also increased. The organized bar reacted by fighting back vigorously, issuing stern disciplinary rulings that solidified the organized bar's ban on overt lawyer advertising.[8]

By the late 1960s and early 1970s, developments in the law began to occur when lawyers and the Justice Department, on free expression and antitrust grounds, questioned the advertising ban.[9] The ban on lawyer advertising was first assaulted in 1975, in *Goldfarb v. Virginia State Bar*,[10] an antitrust case in which the plaintiff challenged a state bar's promulgation and enforcement of minimum fee schedules. Though the *Goldfarb* case applied to restrictions on fees, the rationale of *Goldfarb* was quickly applied to

---

5. CANONS OF PROFESSIONAL ETHICS Canon 27 (1908). For the original wording of the 1908 Canons of Professional Ethics, see ABA OPINIONS OF THE COMMITTEE ON PROFESSIONAL ETHICS WITH THE CANONS OF PROFESSIONAL ETHICS ANNOTATED AND CANONS OF JUDICIAL ETHICS ANNOTATED 75 (Chicago: American Bar Foundation 1967).

6. *See* CANONS OF PROFESSIONAL ETHICS Canon 27 (1908).

7. *See* D. CALHOUN, PROFESSIONAL LIVES IN AMERICA 82 (1965).

8. *See* Lawpoll, 63 A.B.A. J. 1541 (1977).

9. C. WOLFRAM, MODERN LEGAL ETHICS, § 14.2, at 777 (1986).

10. 421 U.S. 773 (1975).

lawyer advertising. A second attack came in 1976, when the Justice Department commenced a suit against the American Bar Association under the Sherman Act in *United States v. American Bar Association.*[11] Shortly after the *Goldfarb* case was handed down, the ABA liberalized the Model Code's advertising rules.[12]

In *Virginia State Board of Pharmacy v. Virginia Citizens Consumer Council,*[13] the United States Supreme Court held that commercial speech is entitled to an intermediate level of constitutional protection. But the extension of this doctrine, and the radical liberalization of the Model Rules on lawyer advertising, was not to occur until 1977 when the Supreme Court rendered its now famous decision in *Bates v. Arizona Bar Association.*[14]

The Effect of the First Amendment on Lawyer Advertising

The controversy in *Bates* arose after two recent law school graduates decided to place an advertisement in a newspaper announcing their new legal clinic and stating the fees they would charge for certain routine services.[15] The Arizona Bar attacked the advertisement as a violation of the disciplinary rule prohibiting lawyer advertising. The Supreme Court, in a 5-4 decision, held that the disciplinary rule was an unconstitutional abridgement on free speech. The Court held that "blanket suppression of legal advertising does not violate the Sherman Act, but does abridge first amendment rights."[16]

The holding in *Bates* was actually quite narrow: A state may not prevent a truthful advertisement concerning the availability and terms of routine legal services. Many questions went unanswered in Bates. What was the constitutional status of lawyer advertising concerning services other than routine legal services? May a state prohibit in-person solicitation by a lawyer? What standards should a state follow in adopting new codes of ethics allowing lawyer advertising?

After the *Bates* decision, all states and the District of Columbia altered their ethics codes to allow lawyers to engage in some form

---

11. United States v. American Bar Ass'n Civil No. 76-1182 (D.D.C. 1976).

12. The August 1976 amendments were criticized in Justice Powell's opinion in *In re* R.M.J., 455 U.S. 191 (1982).

13. 425 U.S. 748 (1976).

14. 433 U.S. 350 (1977).

15. *Bates,* 433 U.S. 350 (1977).

16. *Id.* at 384.

of advertising. But, since the *Bates* court left open the question of which standards to follow, many ethics codes continued to prohibit the very kind of advertising the Court felt was most needed by the public.

In 1982, the Supreme Court further refined its analysis of First Amendment protection for lawyer advertising in *In re R.M.J.*[17] In this case, the Court provided states with a standard to follow when determining the constitutionality of their own rules concerning lawyer advertising. In *R.M.J.*, the Court reversed a Missouri court that had reprimanded a lawyer for publishing newspaper advertisements listing areas of practice and using language other than that allowed by the rules and for listing courts in which he was permitted to practice, even though such information was not among the information authorized by the rules. He was also reprimanded for sending professional announcement cards to persons other than those permitted by the rules.

In striking down the Missouri rules as unconstitutional, the Court utilized the four-part commercial speech test developed in *Central Hudson Gas & Electric Company v. Public Service Commission of New York.*[18] The Court asked whether: (1) the commercial speech in question was misleading or proposed a lawful activity; (2) there was a substantial governmental interest at stake; (3) the regulation directly advanced that governmental interest; and (4) the regulation was no more extensive than necessary to serve that interest. It held that the advertisement was not unlawful or misleading. It further determined that the state did not show that there was at stake a substantial state interest that justified an absolute ban. The Court stated:

> [W]hen the particular content or method of the advertising suggests that it is inherently misleading or when experience has proven that in fact such advertising is subject to abuse, the states may impose appropriate restrictions. Misleading advertising may be prohibited entirely. But the states may not place an absolute prohibition on certain types of potentially misleading information, e.g., a listing of areas of practice, if the information also may be presented in a way that is not deceptive.[19]

---

17. 455 U.S. 191 (1982).
18. 447 U.S. 557 (1980).
19. Note, *supra* note 17, at 203.

Though the *R.M.J.* decision established an analytical framework for states to use in implementing rules concerning lawyer advertising, the decision left unanswered questions regarding which state interests are so "substantial" that the state can regulate lawyer communications affecting those interests.

In *Zauderer v. Office of Disciplinary Counsel*,[20] the Court addressed the question of whether a state can regulate advertisements placed in newspapers targeted for a specific class of litigants. Zauderer, an Ohio attorney, placed several newspaper advertisements featuring drawings of intrauterine devices, accompanied by a headline asking, "Did You Use This IUD?"[21] The advertisement went on to state that Zauderer was available to handle lawsuits for individuals who were injured by using the device, and that no legal fees would be charged unless there was a recovery. The Ohio disciplinary panel's finding that Zauderer had violated a rule against false and misleading statements was affirmed by the Ohio Supreme Court.

The United States Supreme Court found that the Ohio prohibition on lawyer advertising targeted at particular clientele regarding specific legal problems was unconstitutional. In its analyses, the Supreme Court restated the rule that commercial speech is entitled to limited First Amendment protection. The Court reaffirmed the rule allowing states to regulate false and misleading advertising, advertising that promulgates illegal transactions, or even nondeceptive, truthful advertising if the state's interest is substantial, as long as the means directly advance that interest. But here the Court made it more difficult for the states to restrict the content of commercial speech that is not misleading, deceptive, or untruthful.

Since *Zauderer*, lawyers are generally permitted to solicit business through print media as long as the advertisements are truthful and nondeceptive, and do not propose involvement in an illegal transaction. No longer are the state's interests in dignity and decorum substantial enough to warrant an absolute ban on all advertising. The accepted view, as enunciated in *Bates* and followed in *Zauderer*, is that dissemination of information to the public is of primary importance. The holdings of *Zauderer* and *Bates* are narrowly limited to the facts of those cases, but since *Zauderer* there has been a steady increase in lawyer advertising.[22]

---

20. 471 U.S. 626 (1985).

21. *Id.*

22. Kaspar, *Attorney and Client—Constitutional Law—Attorney Advertising: The Expanding Horizons of Permissible Conduct*, 62 N.D. L. REV. 575, 588 (1986).

The *Zauderer* decision was also significant in that it addressed both the problem of lawyer advertising and the problem of lawyer solicitation of legal business. Lawyer solicitation—the active seeking out of prospective clients—had previously been addressed by the Supreme Court in two companion cases, *In re Primus*[23] and *Ohralik v. Ohio State Bar Association.*[24] While *Bates* and *Zauderer* dealt with advertising through mass media, *Ohralik* and *In re Primus* involved the lawyer's in-person promotion of legal services. More important, the outcome of *Bates* and *Zauderer* rested on the rights of prospective clients to obtain information about available legal services, not on the rights of lawyers to express themselves. But these decisions made it unclear whether lawyers enjoyed the personal constitutional right of free expression.

In *Ohralik,* the client was a minor injured in an automobile accident, who, while visited by the lawyer in the hospital, was induced to sign an employment contract for the lawyer's services. The Court found the dangers of overreaching were too great not to allow the state to impose broad regulations on such behavior. On the other hand, the Court allowed First Amendment protection to the solicitation involved in *In re Primus.*[25] In that case, the lawyer targeted a mailing to a potential client. But in *Primus,* the client was poor, and the lawyer was offering the client free representation by the American Civil Liberties Union. The Court, noting that this was not "in-person solicitation for pecuniary gain,"[26] determined that this was a "form of political expression" entitled to First Amendment protection.[27] The lawyer's actions were therefore constitutionally protected, not as commercial, but as political, speech.

The outcome of both *Ohralik* and *In re Primus* made it clear that, in the view of the Court, states cannot absolutely prohibit all in-person solicitation where it is not for pecuniary gain. Even where the solicitation is for pecuniary gain, the state may not absolutely prohibit it. But such solicitation could be subject to stringent state regulations.

In the recent case of *Shapero v. Kentucky Bar Association,*[28] the Court ruled that states cannot categorically prohibit lawyers from soliciting business through truthful, nondeceptive direct mail tar-

23. 436 U.S. 412 (1978).
24. 436 U.S. 447 (1978).
25. 436 U.S. 412.
26. *Id.* at 422.
27. *Id.* at 428.
28. 486 U.S. 466 (1988).

geted to potential clients known to face particular legal problems. In *Shapero,* a Kentucky lawyer sought prior approval from that state's Attorney Advertising Commission of a letter that he proposed to send to potential clients who were about to have a foreclosure suit filed against them. The letter advised the client that "you may be about to lose your home," that "[f]ederal law may allow you to . . . ORDE[R] your creditor to STOP," that "you may call my office . . . for FREE information," and that "[i]t may surprise you what I may be able to do for you."[29] Although the letter was not found to be false or misleading, the commission failed to approve the letter, relying on a state supreme court rule that barred advertisements "precipitated by a specific event . . . involving or relating to the addressee . . . as distinct from the general public."[30] Although this rule was subsequently deleted by the state supreme court, the rule was replaced by Rule 7.3, which prohibited all targeted direct-mail solicitation by lawyers for pecuniary gain.[31]

The United States Supreme Court reversed the decision of the state supreme court. In so doing, the Court distinguished between in-person solicitation and targeted direct-mail solicitation. With targeted direct-mail solicitation, the Court wrote, there is a much lower risk of improper lawyer conduct through coercive tactics.[32] The recipients of such advertising are not faced with the presence of a trained advocate or the pressure of an immediate yes-or-no answer. They can simply put the letter aside, ignore it, or discard it. Moreover, any risks associated with a personalized letter can be minimized by requiring the lawyer to file the letter with a state agency having authority to supervise targeted mailings and penalize actual abuses. On remand, the Court directed the state court to consider whether the mailing was false or misleading by emphasizing trivial or uninformative facts, or by offering overblown assurances of client satisfaction.[33]

Current Ethics Rules Governing Lawyer Advertising

Against this developing constitutional background, the ABA amended both the Model Code and the Model Rules to include provisions governing the permissible content, format, and media

29. *Id.* at 469.
30. *Id.* at 469-70.
31. *Id.* at 470-71.
32. *Id.* at 475.
33. *Id.* at 479.

of lawyers' communications. Actually, even as the *Bates* decision was being prepared by the Supreme Court, the ABA was revising the Model Code's advertising rules.[34] The amended Model Code prohibits a lawyer from communicating any information that is false, fraudulent, misleading, deceptive, self-laudatory, or unfair.[35] The Model Rules, adopted by the ABA to replace the Model Code after the Supreme Court rendered its decision in *R.M.J.*, simply prohibit any "false or misleading communication about the lawyer or the lawyer's services."[36] Each state and the District of Columbia have also adopted rules that prohibit false, misleading, or deceptive communications.

The revised Model Code of Professional Responsibility adopts a "laundry list" approach to the rules on lawyer advertising.[37] DR 2-101(B) lists certain kinds of information that the lawyer may publish or broadcast.[38] But DR 2-101(C) forbids the lawyer from expanding

---

34. M. SCHWARTZ & R. WYDICK, PROBLEMS IN LEGAL ETHICS 71 (2d ed. West 1988).

35. *See* MODEL CODE OF PROFESSIONAL RESPONSIBILITY DR 2-101(A).

36. MODEL RULES OF PROFESSIONAL CONDUCT Rule 7.1.

37. *See* MODEL CODE OF PROFESSIONAL RESPONSIBILITY DR 2-101(B).

38. DR 2-101(B) of the *Model Code of Professional Responsibility* provides that the lawyer may advertise the following things:

- Name (including name of law firm and names of professional associates), addresses, and telephone numbers;
- One or more fields of law in which the lawyer or law firm practices, a statement that practice is limited to one or more fields of law, or a statement that the lawyer or law firm specializes in a particular field of law practice, to the extent authorized under DR 2-105;
- Date and place of birth;
- Date and place of admission to the bar of state and federal courts;
- Schools attended, with dates of graduation, degrees, and other scholastic distinctions;
- Public or quasi-public offices;
- Military service;
- Legal authorships;
- Legal teaching positions;
- Memberships, offices, and committee assignments in bar associations;
- Membership and offices in legal fraternities and legal societies;
- Technical and professional licenses;
- Memberships in scientific, technical, and professional associations and societies;
- Foreign language ability;
- Names and addresses of bank references;

the kind of information published without prior permission from the bar.[39] Model Rule 7.1, which prohibits false and misleading communications, governs all communications about a lawyer's services, including advertising permitted under Model Rule 7.2.[40] Under Model Rule 7.1, a communication is false and misleading if it contains a material misrepresentation of fact or law, is likely to create

---

- With their written consent, names of clients regularly represented;
- Prepaid or group legal services programs in which the lawyer participates;
- Whether credit cards or other credit arrangements are accepted;
- Office hours and telephone answering service hours;
- Fee for an initial consultation;
- Availability upon request of a written schedule of fees and/or an estimate of the fee to be charged for specific services;
- Contingent fee rates subject to DR 2-106(C), provided that the statement discloses whether percentages are computed before or after deduction of costs;
- Range of fees for services, provided that the statement discloses (in print size equivalent to the largest print used in setting forth the fee information) that the specific fee within the range that will be charged will vary depending upon the particular matter to be handled for each client and that the client is entitled without obligation to an estimate of the fee within the range likely to be charged;
- Hourly rate, provided that the statement discloses (in print size at least equivalent to the largest print used in setting forth the fee information) that the total fee charged will depend upon the number of hours that must be devoted to the particular matter to be handled for each client and that the client is entitled without obligation to an estimate of the fee likely to be charged;
- Fixed fees for specific legal services, the description of which would not be misunderstood or be deceptive, provided that the statement discloses (in print size at least equivalent to the largest print used in setting forth the fee information) that the quoted fee will be available only to clients whose matters fall into the services described and that the client is entitled without obligation to a specific estimate of the fee likely to be charged.

39. MODEL CODE OF PROFESSIONAL RESPONSIBILITY DR 2-101(C).

40. *Model Rules of Professional Conduct* provides:

(a) Subject to the requirements of Rule 7.1, a lawyer may advertise services through public media, such as a telephone directory, legal directory, newspaper or other periodical, outdoor, radio or television, or through written communication not involving solicitation as defined in Rule 7.3.

an unjustified expectation about results the lawyer can achieve, or compares the lawyer's services with other lawyers' services, unless the comparison can be factually substantiated.[41]

Current Ethics Rules Governing Solicitation

The use of general advertising to transmit information about a lawyer's services to a prospective client is viewed differently from the direct solicitation of prospective clients. While advertising makes it possible to inform clients about the need for legal services, direct solicitation causes a potential risk of undue influence, intimidation, and overreaching.[42]

The methods of solicitation are varied. A lawyer might attempt to persuade a client known to need legal services by using a direct, personal approach. Other forms of solicitation can be indirect, although its impact is similar to the face-to-face approach. Indirect solicitations can be effected through the mail, brochures, telephone, television, radio, a third party, or a computer-generated facsimile sheet. It is here that constitutional questions, such as the one addressed in *Shapero,* often arise. The 1969 Model Code attempted to regulate solicitation by prohibiting lawyers from recommending either themselves or another lawyer to a person who has not sought advice regarding the employment of a lawyer.[43] It also prohibited lawyers from giving people unsolicited advice to obtain legal services.[44]

(b) A copy or recording of an advertisement or written communication shall be kept for two years after its last dissemination along with a record of when and where it was used.

(c) A lawyer shall not give anything of value to a person for recommending the lawyer's services, except that a lawyer may pay the reasonable cost of advertising or written communication permitted by this rule and may pay the usual charges or a not-for-profit lawyer referral service or other legal service organization.

(d) Any communication made pursuant to this rule shall include the name of at least one lawyer responsible for its content.

41. *See* Model Rules of Professional Conduct Rule 7.1(a)-(c).

42. *See* Model Rules of Professional Conduct Rule 7.3, comment [1](1983).

43. Model Code of Professional Responsibility DR 2-103 (1969, amended 1980).

44. Model Code of Professional Responsibility DR 2-104(A) (1969, amended 1980).

The Model Rules broadly prohibit in-person solicitation, including solicitation through the mail, telephone, or telegraph:

> A lawyer may not solicit professional employment from a prospective client with whom the lawyer has no family or prior professional relationship, by mail, in-person or otherwise, when a significant motive for the lawyer's doing so is the lawyer's pecuniary gain. The term "solicit" includes contact in person, by telephone, telegraph, by letter or other writing, or by other communication directed to a specific recipient, but does not include letters addressed or advertising circulars distributed generally to persons not known to need legal services of the kind provided by the lawyer in a particular matter, but who are so situated that they might in general find such services useful.[45]

In the past, it was not clear whether mail directed toward a particular recipient should be referred to as advertising, and subjected to minimal restrictions, or as solicitation, and subjected to greater restrictions. Before Shapero, the answer depended upon the practicing lawyer's state, the content of the mailing, and the identity of the addressees.[46] After *Shapero,* it is still unclear how to classify this form of client contact. But the Supreme Court stripped some of the restrictions on this form of client contact, thereby permitting, for the first time, contact through direct mail with a potential client for pecuniary gain. Other forms of indirect client contact have not yet been addressed by the Court. Nor has the Court addressed the question of whether a "prospective client," as that term is used in the Model Rules, includes only nonlawyers.

Both the Model Code and the Model Rules permit lawyers to solicit legal business from other lawyers.[47] The Model Code only prohibits lawyers from soliciting a "layperson." The Model Rules prohibit lawyers from soliciting "a prospective client." Often, a prospective client is a layperson, but in some circumstances the prospective client is a lawyer. For example, a general counsel of a corporation might be targeted for solicitation by outside lawyers hoping to represent the corporation in various matters. The solicitation might be direct face-to-face contact, or it might be indirect (as by telephone or mailings). The Model Rules provision could be

---

45. MODEL RULES OF PROFESSIONAL CONDUCT Rule 7.3 (1983).

46. William C. Becker, Shapero—*Direct Mail Clarified,* 22 AKRON L. REV. 199 (1988).

47. MODEL CODE OF PROFESSIONAL RESPONSIBILITY DR 2-103; MODEL RULES OF PROFESSIONAL CONDUCT Rule 7.3.

interpreted as restricting lawyers from soliciting these general counsel, since the general counsel is seen as a representative of the corporation.

The outcome of *Shapero* necessarily eliminates the categorical prohibition on targeted mail contained in Model Rule 7.3 and indicated by the words "by mail" and "by letter or other writing, or by other communication directed to a specific recipient." It is unclear how other forms of solicitation (telephone, telegraph, television, and radio) to persons in need of legal services (whether these persons be laypersons only or laypersons and lawyers) will fare under the rule of *Shapero*. But there is no doubt that *Shapero* will be a touchstone for future changes in the rules of lawyer solicitation.[48]

Advertising and Soliciting the Of Counsel Relationship

Meticulous rules governing use of the Of Counsel designation in public communications have developed among the states. Although the Model Code regarded letterheads as involving a solicitation issue, rather than an advertising issue,[49] the rules that have developed generally follow a liberal approach to lawyer communication advocated by the Model Rules. Most forms of communication may be made as long as they are not false and misleading.

DR 2-102(A)(4) provides the type of information that can be included on the lawyer's letterhead, and further states that "[a] lawyer may be designated 'Of Counsel' on a letterhead if he has a continuing relationship with a lawyer or law firm, other than as partner or associate."[50]

The Model Rules provide that a lawyer's letterhead is a form of public communication and is subject to the Model Rule 7.1 stipulation that it not be false and misleading. But even as a form of solicitation targeted to a person known to be in need of legal services, communication contained on letterheads cannot be categorically

48. For an analysis of the rule of *Shapero*, and the forms of in-person solicitation that may now be permissible, see Note, *Professional Responsibility:* Shapero v. Kentucky Bar Association: *Guideline for a Constitutional Lawyer Solicitation Rule—Does* Shapero *Open the Door to In-Person Solicitation?* 42 OKLA. L. REV. 341 (1989).

49. As a solicitation issue, the letterhead rule, DR 2-102(A)(4), governs and clearly prohibits some forms of description. However, if the issue is approached as one of advertising, then the rule of advertising, DR 2-101(B)(12), governs and allows most forms of description regarding a lawyer's background. *See* WOLFRAM, MODERN LEGAL ETHICS, *supra* note 9, § 14.2 at 785.

50. MODEL CODE OF PROFESSIONAL RESPONSIBILITY DR 2-102(A)(4).

prohibited unless it is false and misleading.[51] What this means in terms of the Of Counsel relationship is that the lawyer cannot be designated as Of Counsel on the law firm's letterhead, business cards, advertising, and related communications unless there is a "close, regular, personal" relationship.[52] As long as there is an actual Of Counsel relationship, that fact can be included on all written communications by the lawyer, and by the law firm regarding the firm's services.[53]

For example, can Of Counsel's name be included in the firm's name? What information about Of Counsel's experience can be included on letterheads, professional announcement cards, and firm brochures? Must an out-of-state Of Counsel list jurisdictional limitations on the firm's letterhead?

Of Counsel's Name in the Firm Name

It is clear from DR 2-102(B)[54] that a firm may use or continue to use the name or names of one or more retired members of the firm. But, when the retired partner continues in an Of Counsel relationship, does inclusion of the retired member's name in the firm name imply the existence of a partnership or shareholder status that in fact does not exist? The law firm's ability to use the retired partner's name is governed by Model Rule 7.1 and 7.5, which state in pertinent part:

> Rule 7.1(a). A lawyer may, on the lawyer's own behalf, on behalf of a partner or associate, or on behalf of any other lawyer affiliated with the lawyer or the lawyer's law firm, use or participate in the use of any form of public communication that is not false, fraudulent, misleading, or deceptive. . . .

---

51. *Shapero*, 486 U.S. at 466.

52. ABA Formal Op. 90-357 (1990).

53. MODEL CODE OF PROFESSIONAL RESPONSIBILITY DR 2-102(A)(4); MODEL RULES OF PROFESSIONAL CONDUCT Rules 7.1, 7.2, 7.5.

54. Disciplinary Rule 2-102(B) states in part that:

> [a] lawyer in private practice shall not practice under a trade name, a name that is misleading as to the identity of the lawyer or lawyers practicing under such name, or a firm name containing names other than those of one or more of the lawyers in the firm, except that . . . a firm may use as, or continue to include in, its name the name or names of one or more deceased or retired members of the firm or of a predecessor firm in a continuing line of succession.

Code of Professional Responsibility, DR 2-102(B).

Rule 7.5(a). A lawyer shall not use a firm name, letterhead, or other professional designation that violates Rule 7.1. . . .

(d) Lawyers may state or imply that they practice in a partnership or other organization only when that is the fact.

In general, the rules require that lawyers be honest and clear in the representations they make to the public regarding the nature of their practice. Where a named partner of a law firm retires, but remains associated with the firm as Of Counsel, the firm may continue to utilize the partner's name in the firm name, provided that (i) the firm name retained has been long established and well recognized; (ii) the retiring partner maintains an Of Counsel relationship with the firm that is close, regular, and frequent; and (iii) the retiring partner's Of Counsel status is clearly designated in the law firm's letterhead, signs, advertising, and the like. For example, in Opinion RI-90, the Michigan State Bar Standing Committee on Professional and Judicial Ethics allowed a law firm to retain the name of a named shareholder after he had withdrawn from the firm and the active practice of law, where he remained associated with the firm in an Of Counsel status. The Committee found that the firm name had been long established and well recognized and communications about the lawyer's status would clearly indicate that he was retired.

In some cases, partnerships may even retain in their firm name the name of the retired partner who remains active practicing in a related firm located in another jurisdiction. One such case involved a New York law firm whose name consisted of three partners, one of whom resided in Washington, D.C. The District of Columbia partner, motivated by tax considerations, wanted to retire from the New York firm, become Of Counsel to the firm, and become a partner in a newly-formed partnership in Washington, D.C. The Washington, D.C., law firm would consist of all of the partners of the New York law firm and retain the same firm name designated by its District of Columbia rather than New York location. Before opening the District of Columbia office, the law firm asked the ethics committee whether it was permissible to form a second law firm while retaining the retiring partner's name in both.[55] Citing

55. Formal Opinion No. 1995-9, The Association of the Bar of the City of New York, Committee on Professional and Judicial Ethics (May 31, 1995).

DR 2-102(B), the New York City Ethics Committee noted that a lawyer may not practice under a firm name that is misleading about the identity of the lawyers practicing under the name. The committee further noted that the proposed arrangement was a departure from the usual principle that inclusion in a partnership's name of a partner who is not "deceased" and who, although nominally "retired," is still practicing law elsewhere, is likely to violate DR 2-102(B) because the firm title may be misleading. However, after considering the scenario presented, the committee concluded that the proposed name would not be misleading for several reasons. First, the committee held that naming the Washington, D.C., law firm with the three partners' names was accurate, since all three named partners would be members of the firm. Second, the committee concluded that the New York law firm should be able to keep the retiring partner's name, even though he would no longer be a partner of that firm, since the retiring partner would remain as Of Counsel to the New York law firm. In the committee's opinion, there was no requirement that a firm's name consist exclusively of partners; a partner's continuing Of Counsel relationship with the firm is enough. Here, the committee made clear that as long as the retiring partner continued to maintain a close, regular, personal relationship with the New York law firm, the New York law firm could continue to include him in its name.

Listing Out-of-State Of Counsel on Letterhead

The rules among the states differ also with regard to whether the name of a nonresident Of Counsel may be included on the firm's letterhead. As a general matter, as long as a lawyer's relationship with an out-of-state law firm is close and ongoing and involves frequent contact for the purpose of providing consultation and advice, the lawyer may be designated as Of Counsel on the law firm's letterhead, business cards, advertisements, and related communications. For example, in Opinion 522, the New Jersey Supreme Court Committee on Attorney Advertising, the Committee denied a New Jersey firm's request to list a Pennsylvania law firm on its letterhead as Of Counsel because the relationship between the firms was one of each firm referring legal matters to the other. The Committee held that listing the Pennsylvania firm as Of Counsel would be misleading by indicating that the out-of-state firm had some relationship with the New Jersey firm, which was not the case. The Committee could see "no valid reason for attorneys to include on their letterheads referral attorneys or firms . . . to whom they refer legal matters."[56]

Assuming the relationship is close, continuing, and regular, most jurisdictions allow the law firm to list on its letterhead names of out-of-state Of Counsel, even though the Of Counsel lawyers are not licensed to practice in that jurisdiction.[57] But, in most of these same jurisdictions, the letterhead must state the Of Counsel's jurisdictional limitations.[58] Some jurisdictions prohibit the letterhead from including the name of an out-of-state Of Counsel who is not licensed to practice in that jurisdiction,[59] Although Formal Opinion 330 did not address the issue, the Committee in 90-357 stated:

> An additional ethical consequence of the relationship implied by the term "of counsel" is that in any listing, on a letterhead, shingle, bar listing or professional card, which shows the of counsel lawyer's name, any pertinent jurisdictional limitations on the lawyer's entitlement to practice must be indicated.[60] (Citations omitted.)

Listing Areas of Specialization on Letterhead

There is little divergence of opinion on whether Of Counsel's areas of specialization may be included on the letterhead. Most jurisdictions hold that, if only particular services or areas of law are subject to the Of Counsel relationship, the letterhead may contain more descriptive language to explain the true nature of the Of Counsel relationship.[61] For example, Arizona allows the letterhead of a firm to list a lawyer as "Of Counsel for litigation purposes only" where

---

56. *Id.*

57. Alabama State Ethics Opinion 86-86 (1986); Iowa State Ethics Opinion 85-6 (1986); Michigan State Ethics Opinion CI-749 (1982).

58. Alabama State Ethics Opinion 86-86 (1986); Iowa State Ethics Opinion 85-6 (1986).

59. New York City Ethics Opinion 81-72 (undated).

60. ABA Formal Op. 90-357 at 13.

61. Arizona State Ethics Opinion 87-24 (1987); Michigan State Ethics Opinion CI-749 (1982) (letterhead may include designations of areas of expertise, but designations must not be false, deceptive, or misleading); New York City Ethics Opinion 81-54 (undated) (Of Counsel's areas of specialization may be listed); Suffolk County Ethics Opinion 88-1 (undated) (a lawyer may list the name of another lawyer who is not a partner or associate as Of Counsel for tax matters, as long as the lawyers have an actual and continuing relationship).

there is a substantial and continuing relationship.[62] In Philadelphia, a lawyer may be designated as "Tax Counsel" on the letterhead of two separate firms, provided both associations meet the requirements of an Of Counsel relationship.[63]

In some states, the phrase "Of Counsel" may be modified slightly to reflect accurately the true nature of the Of Counsel relationship. The phrase "Special Counsel" can be used on the firm's letterhead where the Of Counsel has been employed by the firm for a number of years as an associate and has acquired a high standing within the firm and the legal community.[64] Adding the word "Special" to "Counsel" is not a problem since it does not modify the word "Counsel" in a misleading way.[65]

Summary

As a type of commercial speech, lawyer advertising is protected under the First Amendment of the Constitution. As such, lawyer advertising is afforded an intermediate level of protection; advertising that is truthful and nondeceptive cannot be absolutely prohibited. Yet, even though states may not impose absolute prohibitions on all lawyer advertising, states may reasonably regulate the time, place, or manner of advertising as long as the regulations do not suppress or regulate the actual content of the advertising. States may absolutely prohibit false or misleading advertising or advertising that contemplates an illegal transaction. Thus, state regulations may require a warning or disclaimer on the advertisement, or ask that the lawyer forward a copy of the proposed advertisement to the appropriate state agency for approval before circulation.

Unlike advertising, in-person solicitation for pecuniary gain is not on a par with truthful advertising. The potential for overreaching and undue influence by the lawyer over the recipient "over-

---

62. Arizona State Ethics Opinion 82-6 (1982).

63. Philadelphia Ethics Opinion 86-143 (1986).

64. New York City Ethics Opinion 81-92 (undated). In the view of the New York City Ethics Committee, the mere fact that the Of Counsel had been an associate for several years, and would be compensated on the same basis as he was as an associate, was of no consequence. *But see* Minnesota Informal Ethics Opinion 12 (undated) (a law firm may not list a lawyer as Of Counsel on its letterhead; lawyer's role is similar to that of an associate).

65. New York City Ethics Opinion 81-92 (undated).

whelmed" by legal troubles requires that states be given the discretion to ban categorically all in-person solicitation for pecuniary gain. On the other hand, solicitation for pecuniary gain through targeted mailings cannot be categorically prohibited, although it can be subjected to stringent state regulations. The recipient of targeted mail advertising is not subject to the coercive personal presence of a trained advocate. The recipient can simply put the letter aside until later or completely ignore it. Any risk associated with targeted solicitation letters can be minimized by scrutiny by the reviewing agency.

Both the Model Code and the Model Rules now contain provisions that generally prohibit lawyer advertising only when the communication is false, fraudulent, or misleading. One form or another of these rules has been adopted by each state.

As forms of communication, the firm name, letterhead, and professional business card of a lawyer are subject to the general rules on lawyer advertising. Although the Model Code's rules on firm names, letterheads, and professional cards contain some restrictive aspects, the Model Rules have adopted a generally relaxed attitude and prohibit use of these forms of communication only when the content of the information conveyed is false or misleading. As long as there is an actual Of Counsel relationship, the lawyer or law firm can convey that fact in all communications. In some states, the phrase may be modified to reflect the lawyer's particular skills or areas of expertise. In most jurisdictions, a nonresident Of Counsel must list his or her jurisdictional limitations on the firm's letterhead.

Checklist

Is There an Actual Of Counsel Relationship?

1. If so, that fact may be included on all firm letterheads, professional announcement cards, shingles, law lists, and legal directories.

Is Of Counsel an Out-of-State Lawyer?

1. Are Of Counsel's jurisdictional limitations listed on the firm letterhead? Must Of Counsel be licensed to practice in the jurisdiction in which the firm is located before he or she may be listed on the firm's letterhead?

CHAPTER X

Uses of the Of Counsel Agreement

In this chapter we consider the uses of various forms of the Of Counsel agreement. The form of the agreement is a function of (1) the business objectives of the parties; (2) the nature of the relationship; and (3) the form of business organization. The interplay of these parameters is illustrated by examples in the Appendices.[1]

The Retired Partner

Many lawyers are not overly keen on retiring completely from the practice of law. Despite the lure of golf, hunting, fishing, or some other activity having no relation to the practice of law, few activities have the intellectual challenge—and joy—that law practice affords. Yet, continuing the high level of stress to which lawyers do become accustomed may not be in the best interest of the lawyer's physical and mental well-being. There are, of course, workaholics who have no desire to change their pattern of living or to engage in some activity other than law practice. Some lawyers, particularly those in small law firms with weak retirement programs, may feel that they cannot afford to retire because they will have insufficient income to maintain the standard of living to which they have become accustomed.

But most lawyers want some form of activity related to the practice of law, with a substantial amount of free time to do those

1. *See generally*, *infra*, pp. 203, *et seq.*

things that they have been unable to do during their active years. For the lawyer who has retired, or is planning to retire, the Of Counsel agreement offers a solution to some of those retirement problems, and provides the firm with an opportunity to take advantage of the experience of a senior member of the bar.

If a lawyer has practiced with a firm large enough to establish some form of pension planning, and there is a general notion—if not an express contract—that members of the firm will retire upon reaching a certain age, the Of Counsel agreement becomes the principal vehicle for establishing a relationship between a retired lawyer and that lawyer's former law firm.

Although it would be possible to incorporate the Of Counsel agreement into a pension plan, or even into the general partnership agreement, the best practice is to have a wholly separate agreement dealing solely with the Of Counsel relationship.

In Formal Opinion 90-357,[2] the ABA Standing Committee on Ethics and Professional Responsibility eliminated the earlier requirement that Of Counsel be compensated only for the legal work performed. A retired partner may now draw a pension or other retirement benefit, and still share in the firm's profits. As a result, the parties are free to agree upon such compensation arrangements as are mutually satisfactory.

At the outset, the Of Counsel agreement should make it clear that Of Counsel is neither a partner nor an associate of the firm. The name of an Of Counsel who is a retired partner may be included in the firm name. But the partnership should give careful consideration about whether this is in the best interest of the firm as a whole. To avoid liability as an implied partner, Of Counsel status should be clearly communicated in the firm letterhead, professional announcement cards, shingles, directories, and law lists.

Terms of the Agreement

As the parties draft the various terms of the Of Counsel agreement, they should foresee as many problems as possible, and draft a detailed agreement to meet their precise needs. Typical of some of the problems with which the drafters must contend are:

- *Compensation:* In 90-357, the Ethics Committee stated that it took no position on the manner in which Of Counsel should

2. *See supra* Chapters 3 through 5.

be compensated. This is a matter of contract between the parties. The parties may use a flat hourly rate, a percentage of gross receipts for business that originates with Of Counsel, a percentage of net income after deducting expenses related to such business, a drawing account, a draw plus a splitting of fees on matters Of Counsel brings to the firm, or any one of many combinations or variations of these approaches.

- *Perquisites:* The Of Counsel agreement should spell out in precise detail those items of expense (for example, car allowance, health insurance, malpractice insurance, bar association dues, travel and entertainment expenses, group term insurance, contributions to 401(k) plans, and so on) to be borne by the firm rather than by the individual lawyer.
- *Protection of Trade Secrets:* A law firm may wish to protect itself against the personal use or disclosure of trade secrets by Of Counsel. Alternatively, the Of Counsel agreement may incorporate this type of clause by reference to the general partnership agreement.
- *Malpractice Insurance:* Before entering into an Of Counsel agreement, a retiring partner should be certain that proper arrangements have been made for malpractice insurance. Since a lawyer's potential liability as Of Counsel is much less, the premium for coverage of Of Counsel's omissions and errors will be less than that for a member of a firm.[3] The Of Counsel agreement should provide that the law firm will make certain that Of Counsel has the necessary coverage.[4]
- *Other Fringe Benefits:* In addition to coverage for malpractice insurance, Of Counsel agreements often provide for payment by the law firm of Of Counsel's professional dues and licensing, reimbursement of business expenses, health insurance, and the like. If the parties desire an independent contractor relationship, they should specifically provide that Of Counsel should be treated as an employee for these purposes. The drafter should avoid using this rubric with refer-

3. The insurer for the law firm of one of the authors provides coverage for him as Of Counsel at no additional expense to the firm.

4. If the parties desire an independent contractor relationship, they should insert a clause detailing that, solely for purpose of the malpractice insurance coverage, Of Counsel should be treated as an employee.

ence to too many such characteristics if Of Counsel wishes to retain the independent contractor status.

- *Duties:* The description of Of Counsel's duties and responsibilities relating to the firm, clients, and other parties will present some of the most difficult drafting problems surrounding the Of Counsel agreement. Contracts will vary greatly depending upon what the parties are seeking to accomplish. In the case of the retired partner, the parties may wish to articulate with precision the extent and manner in which Of Counsel will cut back on former duties as a partner. For example, they may agree that Of Counsel need no longer be required to take an active role in the litigation conducted by the firm. Or there may be a reduction in the number of hours that Of Counsel will typically be expected to be on the premises of the firm. Or there may be some indication of Of Counsel's retaining a more active role in serving some clients rather than others. However the duties of Of Counsel are outlined, there must be some consonant relationship between these duties and the compensation and perquisites that Of Counsel may be expected to enjoy.

Independent Contractor v. Employer-Employee Relationship

Although there may be some situations in which an employer-employee relationship will be indicated, drafters usually find that the relationship of independent contractor is most beneficial for both Of Counsel and the firm. In drafting the agreement, the drafter must sail between the Scylla of the employer-employee relationship and the Charybdis of partnership. For some purposes, such as malpractice insurance, employee benefits, health insurance, and the like, the parties may wish to treat Of Counsel as an employee. At the same time, the parties must be careful about assigning duties to Of Counsel that would seem managerial, giving the semblance of power to make decisions for the firm. An absence of care in this drafting may cause the firm or Of Counsel to suffer some unnecessary vicarious liability.[5]

Tax Advantages of the Independent Contractor Status

As an independent contractor, the retiree may take business deductions "above the line" (that is, prior to determining adjusted gross

5. *See*, generally, Chapter 6, *supra*.

income), on Schedule C of Form 1040. The Of Counsel then will have the option of itemizing nonbusiness deductions or taking the standard deduction. This eliminates the two-percent floor on miscellaneous business deductions applicable to employees, since these amounts will be shown as part of the cost of doing business on the Schedule C.

The retired partner will have to pay a 12.4 percent tax on the first $68,400 of earnings for purposes of the social security taxes (FICA and FUTA), and 2.9 percent on all earnings for Medicare.[6] Since the independent contractor is self-employed, one-half of these amounts will be deductible, and will place Of Counsel on a par with an employee, at which one-half of these taxes are paid by the employer. A self-employed person with $100,000 of earnings would pay net social security and Medicare taxes of $5,690.80:

	Tax Rate	Taxable Amount	Amount of Tax
Social Security	12.4%	$68,400	$8,481.60
Medicare	2.9%	100,000	2,900.00
			$11,381.60
Less: 50% of social security and Medicare taxes			5,690.80
Net tax due			$5,690.80

The law firm also gains substantial tax advantages from the independent contractor relationship. It retains the use of the money that it would otherwise be required to withhold for the income tax payable by the lawyer who is classified as an employee. It files an information return, Form 1099, on which it reports the lawyer's earnings. Of Counsel files the Form 1040, including Schedule C, on which business income is reported. The independent contractor

6. These figures are current as of 1998. The maximum amount of earnings subject to social security taxes will increase from the present level of $68,400 in the future as the national average wage rises. The maximum for Medicare was $135,000 in 1993; for subsequent years, there is no limit.

also files a Schedule SE, which determines the taxes payable for social security and Medicare.

The Internal Revenue Service has required some Of Counsel who are practicing as independent contractors to answer elaborate questionnaires designed to elicit factual data with reference to the extent to which one party has "control" over the other.[7] If the common law element of control is present, the relationship is that of employer-employee; if not, then the parties are independent contractors. To the extent that some of the following questions are answered in the affirmative, the relationship of the firm with the lawyer will be that of employer-employee, rather than independent contractor:

1. Must the lawyer comply with the firm's instructions regarding the work?
2. Does the lawyer receive training from or at the direction of the firm?
3. Does the lawyer provide services that are integrated into the firm's business?
4. Does the lawyer provide services that must be rendered personally?
5. May the lawyer hire, supervise, and pay assistants for the firm?
6. Does the lawyer have a continuing relationship with the firm?
7. Must the lawyer follow set hours of work?
8. Does the lawyer work full-time for the firm?
9. Does the lawyer work on the firm's premises?
10. Must the lawyer work in a sequence set by the firm?
11. Must the lawyer submit regular reports to the firm?
12. Does the lawyer receive regular amounts at set intervals?
13. Does the lawyer receive payments for business or traveling expenses?
14. Does the lawyer rely on the firm to furnish tools and materials?
15. Does the lawyer lack a major investment in the facilities used to perform the services?

7. The issue of control has been the subject of much litigation in the determination of the coverage of typical fidelity bond. *Cf.* Auchincloss v. United States Fidelity & Guar. Co., 190 A.D. 6, 179 N.Y.S. 454 (1st Dept. 1919) and its progeny.

16. Is the arrangement such that the lawyer cannot make a profit or suffer a loss from his or her services?
17. Does the lawyer work for one firm at a time?
18. Is the arrangement such that the lawyer does not offer his or her services to the general public?
19. May the lawyer be fired by the firm?
20. May the lawyer quit work at any time without incurring liability?

No single affirmative answer—or even several affirmative answers—is necessarily determinative of whether the firm is in fact in "control" of the lawyer. But the questions provide a guide for one drafting an Of Counsel agreement to insure that a particular contract between a lawyer and a law firm will be construed as establishing an independent contractor, rather than an employer-employee, relationship. The drafter of the agreement should make certain that more than half of the above questions will be answered in the negative. This should not be too difficult since there are only one or two questions (for instance, the sixth question, dealing with the continuing relationship) that require an affirmative answer to maintain the Of Counsel arrangement.

Financial Planning and Retirement

It is beyond the scope of this book to deal with Of Counsel's estate planning and financial problems.[8] Yet certain areas, such as social security and Medicare, are so important for the semiretired lawyer that an abbreviated treatment of these matters is warranted.

Social Security

In legal theory, there are two social security taxes: (1) Old-Age, Survivors, and Disability Insurance (OASDI); and (2) Hospital Insurance (HI). OASDI pays for the typical social security benefits, and HI pays for Part A of Medicare—that is, hospital benefits for those who are covered. These two separate payroll taxes are added together and withheld from employees' wages. Since 1990, the tax rate for OASDI has been 6.20 percent on a maximum taxable amount, which reached $68,400 in 1998.

---

8. *Cf.* THE LAWYER'S GUIDE TO RETIREMENT: STRATEGIES FOR ATTORNEYS AND THEIR FIRMS, (Bridewell ed., American Bar Association 2d ed. 1994), for more extensive treatment of the financial problems discussed herein.

Beginning in 1994, *all* earnings became subject to taxation for purposes of hospital insurance, even though the concept of a maximum taxable amount was retained for purposes of OASDI. The basic tax rate for hospital insurance for employees is 1.45 percent. Self-employed persons pay at a tax rate double that of employed persons—that is, 12.40 percent for OASDI, and 2.90 percent for HI, for a total of 15.30 percent. But the self-employed person is permitted to deduct from adjusted gross income one-half of this tax on the income tax return. The result is to equalize the tax effect on the self-employed person with that on the employee.

The annual earnings limitation for persons under 65 who are drawing social security for 1998 is $9,120. For beneficiaries aged 65 through 69, the limitation is $14,500. The Of Counsel who has reached age 70 is free to earn an unlimited amount without jeopardizing social security.

For persons reaching 65 in 1998, the delayed retirement credit (DRC) is 5.5 percent. This rate continues through 1999, and then increases by one-half percent for every two years until it reaches 8 percent in 2008. The DRC is an additional benefit for Of Counsel who choose to continue working past age 65. For example, one who was born in 1943 and continues working until 2013 would receive an additional 40 percent premium above normal retirement income at age 65.

Medicare

The benefits of Medicare hospital insurance (HI), or Medicare, Part A, are automatically provided a retiree entitled to social security. These benefits come with responsibility for certain deductibles and copayments. When admitted to a hospital, an insured pays an initial deductible of $764, but no more than the actual charges. After the first 60 days, the patient must pay $191 per day. After 90 days, there is the option of paying $382 per day for up to 60 "lifetime reserve" days. The "benefit period" ends 60 days after discharge.

Medicare, Part B, is a voluntary[9] program in which the insured pays $43.80 per month to receive a wide variety of health services. This premium is deducted each month from the beneficiary's social

9. Although voluntary, nearly every person under Medicare, Part A, will also be covered by Part B. Unless Part B is specifically rejected, it will be deemed to have been accepted.

security benefits. With a few exceptions,[10] the insured pays the first $100 of charges allowable by Medicare in a calendar year, plus 20 percent of the charges for medical services.

In addition to Medicare, Parts A and B, most Of Counsel buy Medicare supplementary, or "Medigap" insurance. Since 1992, Medigap policies have been limited to ten standard plans. The coverages in these plans vary, but all include Parts A and B coinsurance, coverage for 365 additional hospital days after Medicare benefits end, and the first three pints of blood each year. A lawyer retiring from a large firm, corporation or government, will normally have no difficulty obtaining such coverage at reasonable cost, but it is sometimes difficult for a solo or small-firm practitioner to do so.

Taxation of Social Security Benefits

A portion of the retiree's social security benefits (SSB) may be included in gross income after retirement. Benefits include any social security payments plus any amounts withheld for Part B Medicare. To place the burden of this tax on those best able to pay it, Congress adopted concepts of a "base amount" (BA) and "modified adjusted gross income" (MAGI), to provide a rule for taxing a portion of SSB. MAGI is defined as adjusted gross income plus tax-exempt interest, plus certain foreign-source income. The law requires the recipient of SSB to include in gross income the *lesser* of (1) one-half of the SSB, and (2) one-half of the MAGI, plus the SSB, minus BA. For most taxpayers, the amount included in gross income will be simply one-half of the excess of social security benefits over the base amount.

For 1998, the base amount for single persons (or married persons living apart for the entire year) is $25,000, and for married persons filing a joint return, $32,000. Single persons must pay an *additional* thirty-five percent (or a total of eighty-five percent) on all SSB above $34,000. Married persons filing a joint return will have to include an additional thirty-five percent on all SSB above $44,000.[11]

---

10. The insured does not have to pay the $100 deductible or the 20 percent coinsurance for (1) pneumococcal vaccine and flu shots; (2) certain outpatient clinical diagnostic laboratory tests (for instance, blood and urine tests—but not x-rays); and (3) home health services.

11. The original proposal of the Clinton administration would have instituted the eighty-five percent rate at the $25,000 and $32,000 thresholds, rather than the $34,000 and $44,000 thresholds.

Health Care Reform

In 1993, the Clinton administration failed to get through Congress its comprehensive health care reform program. But the administration's efforts had the effect of focusing the nation's attention on a number of major health problems that remain to be resolved:

- Guaranteed coverage for all Americans, including the 37 million[12] who lack health insurance.
- Protection of coverage, including portability, so that an employee would not lose coverage by being laid off, changing jobs, or developing chronic illnesses.
- Affordability of health insurance through "managed competition," wherein limits on health-care spending would be enforced by a National Health Board that would decide whether providers were charging too much.
- Payment by employers of 80 percent of the cost of health insurance for employees, with employees paying the remaining 20 percent, at an average cost of $1,800 a year for an individual, and $4,200 a year for a two-parent family.
- Avoidance of any additional taxes to finance health care, except for a tax on cigarettes of about 75 cents a pack.[13]
- Giving all Americans a greater choice of insurance plans at different levels of price and service, and encouraging consumers to make greater use of health maintenance organizations (HMOs) and preferred-provider organizations (PPOs) to reduce costs.
- Consumer relief from the present system of elaborate medical billing and insurance claim forms.
- Flexibility among the states insofar as the selection of health care plans, such as the single-payer system used in Canada.
- Financial relief for companies that spend large amounts on health care through provision of a maximum cost of 7.9 percent of payroll.
- Subsidization of health care premiums for small businesses that employ low-income workers, but with provision that such businesses pay at least 3.5 percent of payroll for health care.

---

12. The number is now (1997) placed at 40 million.

13. The additional cigarette tax was initially projected at $1.00 per pack. Later, the administration said that this was too much, and that the tax should be somewhere between 70 and 80 cents.

- New benefits for mental-health care, including coverage for thirty visits a year of psychotherapy.
- Subsidization of prescription drugs, so that members of lower-cost medical groups pay no more than $4 per prescription, while those in more expensive health plans pay 80 percent of cost, with a $250 annual deductible.
- Coverage for the elderly, including medical care at home in lieu of hospitalization, and 100 days a year of long-term care.

Coverages under the Clinton plan were, for the most part, similar to what is presently provided under Medicare and Medicare supplement insurance. Hospital stays, doctor visits, ambulance trips, lab tests, and pregnancy-related services are covered. Some items, such as prescription drugs, preventive dental care for children, and long-term care[14] for the elderly, have been added. Abortion remains a controversial issue when (and if) the subject is raised in Congress.

Items that are excluded are similar to those that are excludable under Medicare. These include private-duty nursing, cosmetic surgery, hearing aids, adult eyeglasses and contact lenses, in vitro fertilization procedures, and sex-change operations.

Despite the failure of the 1993 Clinton program, health care remains a major national problem. The Clinton administration may have failed because it tried to accomplish too much too soon. The Clinton plan would have promoted preventive care by providing coverage for such items as annual physicals and first baby visits, usually excluded from most health insurance policies. It also encouraged shifts from the traditional fee-for-service approach to health care to health maintenance and preferred-provider organizations (HMOs and PPOs). Once a year (typically, in November), consumers could reconsider their health care choices. A person may decide to join an HMO, and pay only $10 a visit for medical services. In so doing, an insured may lose the opportunity to select his or her own physician, but this may be offset by a lower cost for health insurance.

---

14. Of Counsel should consider the purchase of long-term care insurance to protect against illness that extends over a long period of time. The American Bar Association offers an excellent policy, underwritten by the New York Life Insurance Company. A lawyer should buy this insurance prior to retirement, since the premium increases very dramatically with advancing age.

If a health reform program should be attempted in some future Congress, it is sure to face opposition on several fronts. Some want a single-payer system to eliminate much of the administrative costs inherent in managed competition. Others favor the "pay or play" system, which would require employers to extend basic insurance to all their employees, or contribute to a public trust that would provide the entitlement instead. Most analysts believe that some form of managed competition will eventually prevail.

Every American will be able to get health insurance, either through the employer, or by combining with others in purchaser groups (Health Insurance Purchasing Cooperatives or Alliances) to spread the cost of the premium. The consumer, rather than the bureaucrat, will choose his or her own best plan. Competition to get the consumer's business will be promoted by the bidding of different health plans, which will state their prices and coverages during each annual enrollment period.

In other words, managed competition will operate effectively through the recognition of five basic principles:

- Every American should be able to obtain health insurance, either through the employer or by joining an Alliance.
- The consumer should have the opportunity to choose or shift health insurance at least once a year.
- Health insurance plans should publish prices of various medical services in advance, thereby bidding for the consumer's business.
- Emphasis should be placed on preventive care, with a gradual shift away from treatment toward more prevention.
- The quality of medical services should remain at a level high enough to guarantee consumer satisfaction.

These principles are reflected in the following legislative goals suggested by students of health care reform:

- Every individual should be a part of some health plan, so that the whole of society is served.
- Prices for medical services should be stated in advance.
- Individuals should have a choice of a variety of plans, whether based on fee-for-service, health maintenance, or preferred provider principles.
- Employers, employees, and nonemployees should have an income tax deduction for their health care costs.

- Health care legislation should contain an effective section for medical malpractice.
- Antitrust laws should be amended to allow for managed competition; any laws directed against managed competition should be repealed.
- Any state laws in conflict with federal health care reform should be preempted.
- Medicaid should be repealed; Medicare should be integrated into overall health care reform.

The enactment of legislation to bring about health care reform involves the most complex legislation that this nation has known since the New Deal. Although we see no move for health care reform on the immediate horizon, we remain sanguine that this problem will eventually be attacked by those in position to bring about change in our society. Meanwhile, the retired or retiring partner who becomes Of Counsel must make sure of protection by those means that are presently available.

The Part-Time Lawyer

In contrast with the retired or retiring partner is the younger lawyer who desires for some reason to practice law on a part-time basis. The reasons vary: a specialty that provides the law firm with particular expertise; service of only one client whose needs do not require a full-time lawyer; a desire to teach or finish a novel, while practicing law half-time; or a wish to spend more time at home with family. Whatever the reason, the Of Counsel arrangement provides a vehicle whereby the young lawyer can satisfy both the law firm's needs and personal ones.

Assume that you have established your reputation as an excellent matrimonial lawyer in Metropolis, a city of approximately seven hundred thousand persons. Metropolis is the largest city in your state, which is predominantly rural with a population of three and one-half million. The next largest city has a population of two hundred fifty thousand. Twenty-five hundred lawyers are engaged in the active practice in Metropolis. Of these, over eighty percent are either solo practitioners or are practicing in firms of no more than five attorneys. There are twelve law firms with fifty or more lawyers.

During the last twenty years, you have built an excellent matrimonial practice, and have acquired the reputation of being the leading matrimonial lawyer in Metropolis and your state. You are listed as an Adjunct Professor at the University's law school in Metropolis, where you teach a course in Domestic Relations one semester each year. You frequently appear as a lecturer in continuing legal education programs sponsored by the local and state bar associations. And you have long been active in the Family Law Section of the ABA.

The prestigious law firm of Wills, Ingersoll, Martin and Peters, P.S.C. (WIMPs) is one of the leading firms in Metropolis, with a long list of corporate clients whom they regularly service in all aspects of commercial and corporate law, trusts and estates, taxation and the like. But WIMPs has never developed a matrimonial law practice.

Recently, Josiah Martin, managing partner[15] at WIMPs, invited you to lunch to discuss the possibility of your joining their firm on such terms as the two of you might find mutually agreeable. Martin explained that the firm needs to develop the area of matrimonial practice, and they need someone like you who is experienced and knowledgeable in the field.

Not all of Martin's partners are happy with the idea of having a matrimonial lawyer walking the halls of their prestigious firm. Martin's grandfather, who founded the firm, once remarked, "I'll never let some darn divorce lawyer inside this firm." But times have changed, and even some of Martin's partners have been divorced. "I hear that there's a lot of money in matrimonial practice these days," Martin observes.

Martin is worried that some of his partners may be reluctant to have you come into the firm as a partner. "A lawyer like that should start at the bottom, like everyone else," I. Grumble Alot, a former senior associate who recently made partner, has stated to the Recruitment Committee. Others are willing to accept you as a partner, as long as a portion of the net profit attributable to the

---

15. WIMPs is organized as a professional service corporation (P.S.C.). Technically speaking, it has *no* partners. But the principal stockholders of WIMPs, all of whom are lawyers, refer to themselves as partners, and to Josiah Martin as their managing partner. In their corporate structure, Martin holds the title of President, and J. Cuthbert Wills serves as Chairman of the Board and chief executive officer. Ingersoll is Secretary of the corporation; and Peters, its Treasurer. As a practical matter, the firm is run by the Executive Committee, chaired by Wills and consisting of the four persons in the corporate name, plus three other senior partners.

business that you generate will be distributed among the partners at the end of the year.

In response to Martin, you indicate that you would like to come into the firm, but you want an opportunity to think about the possibility of becoming Of Counsel. The following are some of your thoughts about the Of Counsel opportunity available at WIMPs:

Formal Opinion 90-357 indicated that compensation arrangements between Of Counsel and the firm can be whatever the parties desire.[16] You wish to retain as much of your earnings from fees as possible, but you recognize that WIMPs is entitled to reimbursement for any costs expended by the firm on your behalf. What is the best arrangement to resolve these competing demands? Should WIMPs be entitled to share in any portion of your earnings? Should you seek to share in the firm's earnings? Should you base the amount you pay WIMPs for overhead on a percentage of your gross earnings? On a percentage of *their* gross earnings? Or, a flat fee, with payment for some direct costs, such as long distance telephone calls?

WIMPs will no doubt have different ideas about how you should be compensated. From the firm's perspective, it will want to know:

- How much is it costing us to expand our area of practice to include matrimonial law?
- Would it be more cost effective to avoid entry into the field, contrary to the opinion of the managing partner?
- Under the assumption that we will invite you to join as Of Counsel, what revenues will the firm receive as a result of your practice?
- What costs will accrue to the firm by reason of the addition of you as Of Counsel?

One of the advantages of practicing with a large firm is the opportunity to participate in what are often extensive fringe benefit programs. You will certainly want to take advantage of the firm's retirement and health care programs. Solely for these purposes, you will want the contract between you and WIMPs to treat you as an "employee." In all other respects, you will be an independent contractor. As a solo practitioner for the past forty years, you have tried, but not too successfully, to establish an effective retirement

---

16. *See* Chapter 5, *supra*, especially at pp. 77 *et seq.*

program. The demands placed upon you by virtue of raising a family have made it extremely difficult—and at times, impossible—to contribute to your own defined contribution plan,[17] funded through the American Bar Retirement Association (ABRA). You have begun to think more about retirement, and you want to take part in the excellent retirement program at WIMPs.

You also wish to participate in WIMPs' excellent health care program. While you presently have hospital and medical insurance coverage, the premium that you pay is higher than WIMPs would have to pay if you were under their policy. Moreover, the insurance coverage under their policy would be somewhat greater than the coverage under your own. WIMPs would pay for your complete coverage, as long as the insurer agrees to include you under the firm's policy.

WIMPs has a number of other fringe benefits, such as the payment of your bar association dues, membership in a downtown club, and the like, but these are not at all critical in making your decision whether you should join WIMPs as Of Counsel.

One of the most important matters to be considered in your new arrangement with WIMPs is who will have the responsibility for paying for your malpractice insurance. If you become Of Counsel to WIMPs, the firm will be vicariously liable for any of your errors or omissions, but you will not be responsible for those of the partners of WIMPs. As a result, the premium that WIMPs will have to pay for you to be included under their policy will not be as great as would be the case if you were a partner. This amount may, indeed, be even less than what you pay for malpractice insurance as a solo practitioner.

One of the reasons Josiah Martin is anxious for you to join WIMPs either as Of Counsel or as the equivalent of a junior partner is his belief not only that you will make it possible for the firm to develop a matrimonial practice, but that it will also cause some of the existing departments within the firm to grow. For example, Martin points out, divorce practice may well lead to the drafting of

17. Most pension plans for solo practitioners and small firms funded through ABRA are defined contribution (DCP), rather than defined benefit (DBP), plans. In a DCP, a lawyer periodically contributes a percentage of earnings on a tax-sheltered basis, and takes an annuity that becomes taxable upon retirement. A DBP functions in the same manner, except that the amount contributed to the plan is determined by the goal that is set to produce a particular benefit upon retirement.

antenuptial agreements in connection with second marriages, which in turn may lead to estate planning for persons who have remarried. This would give some additional strength to the estate planning department, which Martin believes has not been as aggressive as it should. Martin foresees many symbiotic relationships between your practice as a matrimonial lawyer and other departments within the firm.

About eight years ago, when he first became managing partner, Martin established a very thorough intake screening system to guarantee that WIMPs would not represent any client that might present a conflict of interest.[18] Neither you nor Martin want to be faced with problems of this sort. Accordingly, you agree to examine your respective client files closely for any potential conflicts that might arise by your becoming Of Counsel. Any doubts will be resolved in favor of the existence of a conflict. Both of you will then consult with your respective clients, make a full disclosure, and obtain any necessary waivers. Martin assures you that any future conflicts will be easily avoided because of the screening system that has served the firm so well.

Neither you nor WIMPs has ever engaged in extensive lawyer advertising.[19] On occasion, you have purchased a slightly larger space in the yellow pages of your local telephone directory, but you have even abandoned that during the past two years. WIMPs has never advertised and doubts that it will ever need to. You both agree that it is very important that all of your stationery, business cards, and the like make clear the nature of the relationship between you and the firm. (A major consideration for insisting on Of Counsel status when you join WIMPs is to avoid liability for a potential securities fraud allegedly committed by one of WIMPs' partners.)

With these considerations in mind, you and Martin worked out an Of Counsel agreement that was satisfactory to all concerned. *See* Appendix D.

Of Counsel as a Vehicle for Firm Organization

The 1980s and 1990s have seen many changes in the organizational structures of firms, and in the lives of the young men and women who have entered the profession. Today, many firms push the at-

18. *See generally* Chapters 7 and 8, *supra.*

19. *See generally* Chapter 9, *supra.*

tainment of high billable hours and a high bottom line, sometimes at the expense of service to the client. As the profession has become more competitive, downsizing has increased. Simultaneously, law firms are seeking to eliminate unwarranted discrimination to minorities and women. Recently, they have come to recognize the importance of flexible work schedules, particularly for working parents with family responsibilities. Some have developed child care centers to accommodate changing needs of families. Husbands who once spent weekends working in the office now assist at home caring for the family.

In this environment, some law firms have adopted organizational structures that depart from the simple partner-associate arrangement of the past. These include the two-tiered partnership, various forms of employment (for instance, "permanent associates," "senior attorneys," "staff attorneys," and the like), reduced-hours arrangements, leaves, and sabbaticals. These arrangements serve a variety of professional, financial, family, or psychological needs.

One such structure is the law firm organized around a single lawyer who uses the Of Counsel agreement as the basis for the structure of the firm. Each lawyer with whom the principal works is the principal's (or the firm's) Of Counsel. Each of the contracting lawyers has a written contract with the principal of the firm. The resulting firm organization provides certain advantages not readily obtainable through traditional forms of organization.

The leader of the firm is typically a senior member of the Bar, in whom all have great confidence. The leader has had many years of practice, is highly respected, and is noted for thoroughness and integrity. Lawyers in the community are proud to be associated with such a colleague. Young lawyers find that such an association enhances their own skills as well as their reputation. In technical ways, the position of these lawyers is different from that of their counterparts who are associates or junior partners in the typical major law firm. For example:

- *Employment status:* The associate is an employee; Of Counsel may be an employee or an independent contractor, depending upon the contract with the principal.
- *Compensation:* The associate is on salary; Of Counsel will be compensated in accordance with the contract devised, which may include some fixed income, a percentage of gross receipts, a percentage of net earnings, or a mix of these various arrangements.

- *Malpractice insurance:* The firm's insurance would normally cover the associate; Of Counsel may be self-insured or have coverage through the principal.
- *Professional liability:* The principal will be liable for the errors and omissions of the associate or Of Counsel, but the associate or Of Counsel will not be responsible for the tortious wrongs and contract violations of the principal.
- *Overhead:* The associate is not responsible for any portion of the firm's overhead expense; Of Counsel will make an appropriate arrangement by contract to give such recognition to contributions to overhead as the parties deem appropriate.
- *Taxes:* Income taxes will be withheld by the firm on the associate's income, who will be treated as an employee. As long as Of Counsel has a contractual arrangement with the firm wherein he or she is treated as an independent contractor and not as an employee, Of Counsel will report gross income and business deductions on Schedule C of Form 1040. The firm will file Form 1099 with respect to any payments made to Of Counsel because of the contract with the firm.

Some years ago, *Barrister,* the magazine of the ABA's Young Lawyers Division, published an article that stated that a law firm of fourteen lawyers provided the optimum job satisfaction for a young lawyer. Such a firm would have adequate resources for a successful law practice, but would not be so large that is would cause the stress that sometimes characterizes the large law firm. The following paradigm illustrates how a lawyer might develop a law firm through the use of a series of Of Counsel agreements:

Lawyer, age 50, is a general practitioner in the City of Metropolis. His practice continues to grow, so that he finds it necessary to seek outside help. Lawyer's success has long been attributed to his persuasive powers in front of a jury. He acquired a reputation for an ability to obtain substantial verdicts in personal injury matters. He also achieved some success in criminal defense work, although he did not enjoy this aspect of the practice as much as tort litigation. As his practice expanded, he found it necessary to add personnel to his firm to develop practice in areas of the law with which he was less familiar. One by one, he added a young tax lawyer, a divorce lawyer, a commercial litigator, and an estate planner.

At the time that these lawyers executed their respective Of Counsel agreements with Lawyer, they were not so well known that they could attract a substantial number of clients. But each was so expert in his or her field that Lawyer's firm soon developed a reputation for total thoroughness and industry.

Lawyer has given each Of Counsel a free rein within his or her respective area, as long as the contracting lawyer carries out his or her responsibilities. He used a variety of devices, depending upon the particular needs of the individual. The tax lawyer, for example, was given a leave of absence to gain an LL.M. degree in Taxation. Since his return to the firm, the firm's tax practice continues to grow.

The divorce lawyer is a single parent with two children (now aged 15 and 12). Following her divorce, she joined Lawyer's firm when she was thirty-five years old. She had entered law school at age 27, after a successful, but financially unrewarding, career in accounting. Upon graduating from law school, she joined a large law firm, where she remained for three years. The firm indicated that she would probably become an income partner, but that it was unlikely she would ever become an equity partner. Suspecting the existence of a glass ceiling, she left to join Lawyer. While her children were growing, she worked at home much of the time. She is now beginning to do more work at the office, as her two children become better able to care for themselves.

The commercial litigator is a single white male with an arrogant attitude that is useful in dealing with adversaries, but less valuable in dealing with clients. He likes to work at night, and drive around in his Porsche during the day, seeing clients. Lawyer recognizes his natural talents as a litigator, but wants to see him in the office more often, where he would be more readily available for consultation.

The estate planner is a hard-working former trust officer from a local bank. A studious type, he enjoys the work in the probate court, as well as the planning and drafting of trust and estate documents. Lawyer worries that he may not be as effective with clients as he is with the law books.

Each Of Counsel has an agreement with Lawyer. No two of these contracts are the same: Some allow for the payment of a fixed amount of overhead expense to Lawyer each month; others provide for the retention of a percentage of gross income by each Of Counsel, and the payment of another percentage to the firm in lieu of overhead. Each year, Lawyer renegotiates Of Counsel agreements with each lawyer.

The firm organized around a series of Of Counsel agreements is not appropriate in some practice situations. The lawyer who is highly respected and also an able leader may not be available to provide the necessary central focal point for the firm's organization. Some might feel that it would not have the cohesiveness of more traditional firm organization. This, however, is a function of the extent to which those executing the agreements have faith in the leader of the firm.

While consideration of the Of Counsel agreement as a vehicle for firm organization is not indicated in every law practice, for those in which a high degree of flexibility in practice arrangements is desired, the arrangement might well prove to be the most appropriate.

* * *

The above illustrations are a few of the possible situations in which contracting parties may find it desirable to use an Of Counsel agreement. There will obviously be substantial differences among these agreements, depending upon the objectives sought to be achieved. In the next chapter, we shall deal with the next step: the planning and drafting of the Of Counsel agreement.

CHAPTER 📖 XI

Planning and Drafting the Of Counsel Agreement

Lawyer codes impose few restrictions on the formation of a law partnership.[1] The agreement need not be in writing;[2] in fact, just under half of existing law partnerships have no written agreement.[3] The same is true for Of Counsel and their agreements.[4] But in view

1. One limitation, however, applies to partnership agreements: The agreement may not contain a restrictive covenant limiting the right of any partner to practice law after withdrawing from the partnership, except as a condition to payment of retirement benefits. *See* MODEL CODE OF PROFESSIONAL RESPONSIBILITY DR 2-108(A) (1969, amended 1980); MODEL RULES OF PROFESSIONAL CONDUCT Rule 5.6(A) (1983); ABA Comm. on Ethics and Professional Responsibility, Formal Op. 300 (1961). For example, an agreement that requires forfeiture of financial benefits if the withdrawing lawyer practices law within a particular locale would violate the rule and would be unenforceable as against public policy, the rationale being that such an agreement limits the public's ability to choose counsel freely. The only exception to such an agreement is any restriction incident to provisions concerning retirement benefits earned for past service with the firm.

2. It might be argued that the Of Counsel agreement also need not be in writing. But the law of partnership is well developed through both statutory and case law, while the law with respect to Of Counsel is still developing. The parties are therefore able, by contract, to shape their relationship by articulating their rights and duties in relation to one another, as well as with respect to third parties.

3. M. ALTMAN & R. WEIL, HOW TO MANAGE YOUR LAW OFFICE, § 8.01 (Matthew Bender 1988) (hereinafter, ALTMAN & WEIL).

4. A recent survey of Louisville-area Of Counsel lawyers showed that about half did not have written Of Counsel agreements.

of the wide variety of situations in which Of Counsel are used today, it would be unwise to leave any of these arrangements to oral agreements or the general understanding of the parties. This chapter explores the parameters of such agreements, so that you may develop an Of Counsel agreement that will satisfy the needs of all those entering into the relationship.

Planning the Of Counsel Agreement

The parties must first consider what they hope to accomplish by entering into an Of Counsel agreement. A retiring partner, for example, often seeks to remain active without the burdens of a heavy practice to which he or she may be accustomed. If the firm has a well-established pension program, financial matters are normally secondary to other considerations.[5]

The law firm's objectives will normally be quite different from those of Of Counsel. What will be the incremental cost to the firm for placing a retiring partner in Of Counsel status? Will this cost be justified by the potential services Of Counsel may render, such as advice and counsel, instruction for younger lawyers, review of the work of partners and associates, and so on?

Is the lawyer's desire for Of Counsel status for a reason other than retirement? For example, is an arrangement sought that will allow more time for pursuits other than the practice of law? Or, is the lawyer a specialist looking for an association with a firm that will make it possible to pursue that specialty more effectively? Or, is the Of Counsel position a way to demonstrate an ability as a practicing lawyer, and possibly joining the firm as a partner at a later date?

For each of these possibilities, the firm must consider its own needs, and determine if these are in accord with the objectives of the putative Of Counsel. As a matter of form, the parties may find helpful the insertion of a preamble in the contractual agreement in which they state their goals. For example:

> WHEREAS, John P. Doe ("Doe"), presently a partner in Jones, Smith & Doe, is planning to retire at the end of the present fis-

---

5. The Of Counsel agreement should not be tied to the firm's pension program, or *vice versa.* Of Counsel agreements will vary in their terms from one partner to another, depending upon individual needs. But pension programs must be administered so that each retiring partner is treated fairly and equitably with respect to all those who have retired or will be retiring.

> cal year, June 30, 1998, and desires to remain actively involved with the firm; and
>
> WHEREAS, Jones, Smith & Doe (the "firm") desires that the said Doe remain active within the firm by being available for consultation and advice, and perform other related duties; NOW THEREFORE . . .

Essential Terms of the Of Counsel Agreement

While a written agreement may not solve all potential problems, lawyers will more likely feel bound by the terms of an Of Counsel agreement when it has been put down in writing and signed by both parties. The document may be a formal contractual agreement or a simple contract letter. In either event, the parties should not fail to consider the interests of third persons, since their rights will be affected by the agreement. Appendixes A through G present several Of Counsel agreements, based on different factual situations.

Title and Status

Fundamental to the drafting of an Of Counsel agreement is whether the parties desire a relationship more akin to that of employer-employee or independent contractor. For example, the parties may wish to establish an independent-contractor relationship for purposes of control, but an employer-employee relationship for purposes of compensation. If the drafter's primary concern is to allow Of Counsel as much independence as possible, the language of the agreement should reflect the parties' intention to create an independent-contractor relationship. If the parties then desire that Of Counsel participate in the firm's programs for malpractice and health insurance, these matters should be qualified by a phrase such as, "Solely for the purposes of the firm's health insurance [or, malpractice] insurance program, [Of Counsel] shall be treated as an employee."

The title and status of Of Counsel should be succinctly stated in the agreement. The independent-contractor relationship may be simply stated:

> [B]oth [the firm] and [Of Counsel] desire that [Of Counsel] establish a continuing affiliation with [the firm] as an independent contractor rather than as a partner or associate.[6]

6. ALTMAN & WEIL, *supra* note 3.

The parties' intention to create an employer-employee relationship can likewise be easily set out, as in the following provision:

> [Of Counsel] shall have the title of "Of Counsel" to the Firm. Notwithstanding the foregoing, [Of Counsel] shall be neither a partner nor a special partner of the Firm but shall be considered an employee of the Firm.[7]

Once the parties have stated their desired title and status, the remaining provisions of the agreement should be consistent. For example, in a case in which the firm was organized as a professional service corporation, the parties stated their intention to create an independent-contractor relationship. The remaining provisions were consistent with this intention: Of Counsel was not required to perform any specified number of hours of service to the corporation, and he was compensated on an hourly rate for services he actually rendered to clients of the firm.[8]

In another agreement, the parties set forth their desire to establish an employer-employee relationship. But they inserted provisions that were inconsistent with this relationship. The contract provided that Of Counsel would "have all of the duties and responsibilities as if he were a partner of the firm" and would be entitled to compensation "as if he were a partner of the firm."[9] While such an agreement accomplished the objective of giving Of Counsel the title and status he desired, it may also have subjected him to potential vicarious liability as a partner.

In some agreements, the parties state their desire to create an Of Counsel relationship, but also express their hope to enter into a different relationship when the Of Counsel agreement terminates. This frequently occurs where Of Counsel is taken in on a temporary basis or as a "probationary partner." In one such agreement, a provision expressed the parties' intention to enter into such an arrangement by stating:

> This agreement will be for a term of ______ months commencing on _______ and ending on _______ (the "Term"). It is [our] expectation that a mutual decision regarding [your] becoming

7. Appendix A at § 2.
8. Appendix D at §§ 1, 4, and 5.
9. Appendix A at §§ 4.1 and 5.

an Equity Partner in the Firm will be made at or prior to the conclusion of the Term.[10]

Duties

Since the Of Counsel relationship contemplates a working relationship with the firm or other lawyer, an essential component of the Of Counsel agreement is the specific delineation of Of Counsel's duties. As the court pointed out in *Mutual of Omaha Insurance Co. v. Chadwell*,[11] an Of Counsel agreement that contains no express provisions for the actual rendering of services is of dubious value. In the *Chadwell* decision, the law firm had merely agreed to pay Of Counsel for his "long and outstanding service to the firm."[12] When Of Counsel's widow tried to collect on the firm's accidental death policy, the insurance company successfully argued that the husband was not a covered employee. His estate was therefore ineligible for employee benefits. Failing to define his expected duties while continuing to provide him with a fixed compensation meant that his status was nothing more than that of a retired partner receiving retirement benefits.

Of Counsel's duties vary with each agreement. Much depends upon what the parties are seeking to accomplish. For example, one firm used an experienced senior lawyer primarily for the professional development of the firm's younger lawyers. This firm specifically provided that Of Counsel should:

(a) assist the Corporation in its continuing legal education program for its members and associates;
(b) review litigation files for the purpose of consulting on and recommending trial preparation, pleadings, strategy, and settlement;
(c) assist attorneys responsible for litigation files in pretrial discovery, motions, briefs, and trial;
(d) in his discretion, and with the agreement of the Corporation, assume responsibility for conducting discovery, motions, and trials, appellate proceedings, and related matters; and

10. Appendix B at § 1.
11. 426 F. Supp. 550, 552 (N.D. Ill. 1977).
12. *Id.* at 552.

(e) engage in other activities relating to firm development and client development for the Corporation.[13]

Other arrangements may set forth the duties expected of Of Counsel in more general terms. For example, one agreement contained this provision:

> As Of Counsel, he shall perform in the name of [the firm] such professional services as may be required by [the firm's] clients. [Of Counsel] shall foster the professional practice of [the firm] through the development of new clients and sources of business in a manner consistent with law and the applicable canons of professional ethics.[14]

Many Of Counsel agreements contain provisions that set a minimum number of hours that Of Counsel must bill to the clients of the firm. In one such agreement, the firm and Of Counsel agreed that, during a one-year period, he would "be required to bill to clients of the Firm a minimum of 1500 hours."[15] Another agreement provided that the Of Counsel arrangement "includes [Of Counsel's] full-time efforts."[16] Provisions such as these are not typical of most Of Counsel agreements. They are more analogous to provisions that would be found in an agreement between a law firm and an associate. Yet, if the parties desire to provide for a minimum number of hours in their agreement, they should be careful to agree only to the number of hours that Of Counsel is certain to work. A minimum of 1,500 billable hours per year might be excessive for a senior lawyer who wants to wind down his or her law practice.[17]

Some agreements contain exclusive-services provisions that preclude Of Counsel from performing services outside the firm. A typical provision might be one that prohibits Of Counsel from performing "professional services to any person, firm, corporation, or other entity for compensation or engage in any activity competitive with or adverse to [the firm's] practice during the term of this

---

13. Appendix D at ¶ 3, p. 218.

14. ALTMAN & WEIL, *supra* note 3.

15. Appendix A at § 4.4.

16. Appendix C, § 2.

17. In 1988, the annual billable hours for an associate averaged just over 1,800. For a partner in that same year, the average annual billable hours were 1,731. *See* Thomas F. Gibbons, *Law Practice in 2001*, 76 A.B.A. J. 68, 71 (Jan. 1990).

Agreement."[18] Or the agreement might restrict Of Counsel from accepting any position outside the firm without first giving written notice.[19]

Compensation

A key consideration in the agreement is the manner of compensation selected by the parties. Formal Opinion 330 did not explicitly restrict the methods of compensation in the Of Counsel arrangement,[20] but it implied that Of Counsel should be compensated only for work actually performed.[21] Formal Opinion 90-357 swept these restrictions aside by making it clear that "it is not relevant to the permissibility of use of 'of counsel' what the compensation arrangements are." For example, Of Counsel may draw a salary or a salary plus a share of the profits. If Of Counsel is a retired partner, compensation may include payments from the firm's retirement plan. In some cases, Of Counsel may receive no compensation, or even pay a portion of the firm's overhead.

Some commentators insist that Of Counsel should be compensated *only* for work actually and currently performed for the firm.[22] This is essential if the parties desire to treat Of Counsel as an independent contractor. But if they wish to establish an employer-employee relationship, they may deliberately choose to compensate Of Counsel with a fixed salary, whether weekly, monthly, or yearly. Difficult problems may arise if the parties wish to draft an agreement that will combine some features typical of the independent contractor (for instance, compensation directly related to the work performed) with those of an employee (for instance, a fixed salary, advance money, or annual bonuses). But if this is their desire, the basic philosophy of freedom of contract that characterizes 90-357 gives them the power to so provide.

A common method of compensation is for Of Counsel to receive a division of gross receipts for each case that he or she works on. In a typical arrangement, the parties may agree to divide Of

---

18. ALTMAN & WEIL, *supra* note 3.

19. Appendix A at § 4.10.

20. *See* Chapters 2 and 4.

21. *See* Chapter 2.

22. *Of Counsel: Revisited,* at 35 (Remarks of Don Jackson at the Annual Meeting of the American Bar Association, Senior Lawyers Division) (Aug. 8, 1988).

Counsel's gross receipts on a fifty-fifty basis after first reducing those receipts by allocable overhead. One such agreement provided:

> [The firm] shall pay [Of Counsel] annually fifty percent (50%) of the amount by which [Of Counsel's] gross receipts in each calendar year for professional services rendered by [Of Counsel] exceed the Overhead Cost.
>
> In addition to the compensation paid to [Of Counsel] under [the above paragraph], [the firm] shall pay [Of Counsel] fifty percent (50%) of [the firm's] gross receipts in each calendar year for professional services rendered by [Of Counsel] to [the firm's] clients, except that if [Of Counsel's] gross receipts under [the above paragraph] in any calendar year are less than the Overhead Cost, [the firm] shall be obligated to pay [Of Counsel] only that portion of this compensation under this paragraph which exceeds the amount of the deficit.[23]

Where Of Counsel anticipates using the firm's support services, the parties may vary the proportions. One such agreement illustrates the varying proportions that may be included in the agreement:

> With respect to work performed by us or our associates, clerks, or paralegals for your clients, or new matters referred to us from your existing clients or from new business generated by you, we shall be allocated from gross receipts of fees as collected eighty-two and one-half percent (82 1/2%), and you shall retain seventeen and one-half percent (17 1/2%). With respect to matters generated by you and where work is performed by you, one hundred percent (100%) of the sums collected shall be held for the benefit of your account.[24]

Another method is to compensate Of Counsel at an hourly rate. An example of this kind of arrangement appears in the following provision:

> The corporation shall pay [Of Counsel] as fees for his services at an hourly rate equal to eighty percent (80%) of the rate that his time is charged to any particular client or matter.[25]

---

23. ALTMAN & WEIL, *supra* note 3.
24. Appendix C at ¶ 4 (paraphrased).
25. Appendix D at ¶ 5.

These methods are commonly found where Of Counsel is analogous to an independent contractor, since the compensation is clearly related to the work actually done.

Where the parties have an employer-employee relationship, it is common to compensate Of Counsel on a flat rate per week or month. The flat rate may sometimes be coupled with an annual or semiannual bonus. The following provision is typical:

> [Of Counsel's] base compensation shall be __________ Dollars ($_________) per month ($__________ annualized), payable semimonthly. . . . In addition to [Of Counsel's] base compensation, [Of Counsel] shall receive an amount equal to ten percent (10%) of [his] Aggregate Source Collections, as defined below, in excess of $50,000. . . . Aggregate Source Collections shall be the sum of Source Collections for all clients. This additional compensation shall be computed semiannually and paid to [Of Counsel] on or before______________ . . . .[26]

Still another possibility is to provide support services to Of Counsel at no cost.

The parties should consider any restrictions on compensation imposed by their state bar. Some states prohibit fee splitting with Of Counsel where it is not directly related to the work actually performed.[27] Other states allow Of Counsel to share fees with the firm or other lawyer without regard to services performed. Drafters should check the ethics opinions of the state in which Of Counsel and firm are located to determine whether their proposed compensation arrangement complies with the state's requirements.

EFFECT OF PENSION PLAN PAYMENTS

Formal Opinion 90-357 removed the implication within Formal Opinion 330 that a retired partner whose sole income from the firm is the partner's pension or other retirement benefits could not be considered to be Of Counsel.[28] Informal Opinion 710 had a similar implication. Read strictly, Formal Opinion 330 required that any compensation received by Of Counsel must be directly related to work actually and currently performed. By contrast, payments received by the retired partner from a pension or other retirement

---

26. Appendix B at § 2.
27. *See* Chapter 2.
28. *See* Chapter 2.

plan are deemed to be compensation for past, rather than present, services.

In many law partnerships, the partnership agreement provides that the partnership will purchase a retiring partner's interest upon retirement or withdrawal from the firm.[29] These agreements typically provide for a payout period of five to ten years, with the total amount being based on a percentage of the firm's earnings.[30] The retired partner essentially becomes a creditor of the firm and has a vested interest in the firm's continued prosperity.[31] Out of concern that the firm remain prosperous, the retired partner may choose to remain active in the firm by becoming Of Counsel.[32] But now the lawyer has two simultaneous relationships with the firm: as a creditor of the firm and in association with the firm as Of Counsel.

Formal Opinion 90-357 has specifically eliminated any implication of impropriety in this arrangement. Despite this, the parties should spell out the distinction between these two relationships. This might be done within the Of Counsel agreement, or the parties might prefer to execute two separate contracts to further define their respective obligations under each agreement. In one contract, the firm would recognize its obligation to disburse to the retiring partner payments over a period of time.[33] The second contract would acknowledge the parties' desire to enter into a new relationship wherein the lawyer's status is recognized as Of Counsel.[34] Separating the two relationships protects Of Counsel from claims of vicarious liability by litigious clients.[35]

Overhead

Since most firms provide Of Counsel with an office, secretarial service, desk, telephone, and other support services, agreements be-

29. Corinne Maskaleris, *"Of Counsel"—Defined,* at 21 (compilation from transcript of *Of Counsel: Revisited,* a program presented by the Senior Lawyers Division of the American Bar association at the annual meeting, Aug. 6, 1988) (available from Senior Lawyers Division, ABA).

30. *Id.*

31. *Id.*

32. *Id.*

33. *Id.*

34. *Id.*

35. *Id.* at 22.

tween the parties should provide for overhead expenses. In an independent-contractor relationship, provisions should be made for Of Counsel to reimburse the firm for a fair share of the overhead costs.

A variety of arrangements can be used. In one arrangement, the firm charged Of Counsel a flat rate per month:

> [The firm] will charge [Of Counsel] $8,667 at the beginning of each month as [Of Counsel's] share of expenses for that month. This will be a charge against fees received by you. This $8,667 charge will include your share of all office costs, including rent, secretarial, telephone, equipment use, library, reception, accounting, word processing, office supplies, messenger services, postage, Bar dues, parking, health, life, disability and E&O insurance in accordance with [the firm's] current office practice.[36]

Or, the parties may agree to a flat rate per year:

> "Overhead Cost" means $20,000 for [this] calendar year and the amount mutually agreed by the parties for each calendar year thereafter. If this Agreement is terminated during a calendar year, Overhead Cost shall be prorated to the date of termination based on the number of months this Agreement is in effect.[37]

Where overhead is set at a flat amount per year (for instance, twenty thousand dollars), the parties usually agree to prorate the overhead costs and deduct the prorated amounts from Of Counsel's weekly or monthly compensation.

In other arrangements, the firm might deduct a certain percentage, such as 25 to 50 percent, from Of Counsel's gross receipts as a fair share of overhead. If the parties use a percentage as the basis for calculating Of Counsel's compensation, they must make it clear whether the percentage is to be based on Of Counsel's gross or net earnings. Whether the parties agree to a fixed percentage or a flat amount, the method for computing overhead expenses should be clearly spelled out in the Of Counsel agreement.

---

36. *See* Appendix C, § 5.

37. ALTMAN & WEIL, *supra* note 3.

Fringe Benefits

Malpractice insurance is essential for any person practicing law, whether as a solo practitioner, a member of a law firm, or Of Counsel. A malpractice policy usually provides coverage for all principals of the firm, as well as all employees, including lawyer associates, legal assistants, secretaries, and other staff. Whether Of Counsel is an independent contractor or employee, both parties must make sure that Of Counsel is covered by the firm's malpractice policy. With the increase in the cost of single coverage, protection under the firm's malpractice insurance group policy is an important fringe benefit for any lawyer. This benefit should be clearly set out in the Of Counsel agreement. The usual provision is that the insurance will be carried and paid for by the law firm.[38] In some cases, the firm may reimburse Of Counsel for obtaining a separate malpractice insurance policy. But this approach would cost more overall. A better practice is for the firm to purchase a policy that includes Of Counsel along with all lawyers in the firm. Of Counsel may then reimburse the firm for his or her portion of the coverage, if the partners so desire.

Most insurance carriers will cover Of Counsel lawyers, even though they are not in an employer-employee relationship with the firm. A few agreements provide for Of Counsel to reimburse the firm for any additional expenses incurred by including Of Counsel in the firm's policy. Other agreements provide malpractice insurance coverage for Of Counsel at the firm's expense regardless of the legal nature of the relationship—whether employee or independent contractor—with the firm. In the typical agreement, coverage is provided as a fringe benefit:

> In addition, the Firm will afford and pay for malpractice insurance coverage for [Of Counsel] on the same basis, if at all, as such insurance protection is afforded to Equity Partners. . . .[39]

Some agreements also include a provision for indemnification:

> The Firm shall provide errors and omissions insurance on behalf of the Firm and [Of Counsel] in the same manner as if [Of Counsel] were a partner or associate of the Firm. The Firm ac-

---

38. The cost to the firm for the additional malpractice insurance coverage for Of Counsel is normally substantially below that for a partner or principal, since the insurer's risk is much less.

39. Appendix B at § 4 (footnotes omitted).

> knowledges and agrees that that [Of Counsel] is an employee for purposes of [the State Labor Code] that provides for indemnification of employees. [Of Counsel] agrees to cooperate with the Firm [for liability of the Firm] arising out of or in any way connected with his activities on behalf of the Firm and further agrees to make himself available for purposes of the defense of any action.[40]

Where Of Counsel is covered by the firm's policy, the scope of the coverage should be the same as it is for other members of the firm. Of Counsel should keep in mind that the policy will apply only to acts committed in performing duties within the scope of his or her contract. If Of Counsel also maintains an independent or solo practice, or practices with another firm as Of Counsel or in some other capacity, separate coverage should be obtained for torts committed in those other practices.

Other fringe benefits typically include the firm's payment of professional dues and licensing, reimbursement for business expenses, and coverage under the firm's group health insurance plan. The accepted practice is for the firm to pay for Of Counsel's licensing dues; this will not jeopardize Of Counsel's independent status.

But the same is not true if the firm pays Of Counsel's business and travel expenses or coverage under medical and other health insurance programs. The common law considers workers to be employees if the person or firm for whom they perform services agrees to pay the workers' expenses and other benefits. Most health insurance programs require that all covered persons be full-time employees of the firm, working a minimum number of hours per week, typically thirty hours. This requirement alone may defeat Of Counsel's status as an independent contractor. But the independent-contractor status is preserved if the firm agrees to include Of Counsel under the firm coverage at the individual's own expense. One such agreement provided:

> If [Of Counsel] so elects, he will be covered under the Firm's medical, disability, life, and other insurance plans *at his own expense,* as is the case for the Firm's Equity and Contract Partners.[41]

Where Of Counsel is analogous to an employee, these benefits are provided to Of Counsel at the firm's expense:

---

40. *See* Appendix A at § 6.
41. Appendix B at § 4 (emphasis supplied).

[Of Counsel] shall participate in and shall receive benefits under all formal and informal employee benefit plans, understandings, arrangements, or programs now or hereafter generally made available to the Firm's associates and their families, including, but not limited to, any group health, life, dental, disability, or other insurance, or any pension or profit-sharing plans or arrangements, or any other type of benefit.[42]

Right to Terminate

Most Of Counsel agreements include a termination clause giving each party the right to terminate for any reason upon prior written notice, after a specified number of days. In addition, most agreements contain provisions for automatic termination upon Of Counsel's death, disability, or disqualification from the practice of law, or the dissolution or insolvency of the firm.

Summary

Planning the Of Counsel relationship requires careful coordination of both parties' expectations. A carefully worded written agreement should give due regard to the duties expected of Of Counsel, as well as compensation, overhead, fringe benefits, and right to terminate. By careful drafting, the parties may incorporate into their agreement the best features of various relationships. Appendixes A through G provide several different forms for typical Of Counsel agreements.

Checklist

Title and Status

1. Do the parties desire Of Counsel to be an independent contractor or an employee? Does the agreement clearly state their intentions?

Duties

1. Does the agreement describe the duties expected of Of Counsel? Does Of Counsel assist in the firm's continuing legal education programs? Does Of Counsel review briefs

---

42. Appendix A at § 7.

and memoranda? Is Of Counsel available for consultation and advice to the firm and its clients?

Compensation

1. Does the agreement provide for fee splitting between Of Counsel and the firm without regard to the services performed by Of Counsel? If so, does that comply with state ethics rules?
2. If an independent-contractor relationship is desired, does the agreement provide that compensation shall be directly proportional to the services performed?
3. If Of Counsel is a retired partner, is he or she entitled to payments from the firm's pension or other retirement plan? If so, does the agreement establish these two separate relationships of creditor and Of Counsel?

Overhead

1. If an independent-contractor relationship is desired, does the agreement provide that Of Counsel should reimburse the firm or other lawyer for overhead expenses?
2. If Of Counsel is to reimburse the firm or other lawyer for overhead, is the method of reimbursement clearly spelled out in the agreement?

Fringe Benefits

1. Is Of Counsel covered by the firm's malpractice policy? If so, has the policy been analyzed to determine the extent of coverage?
2. If an independent-contractor relationship is desired, does the agreement provide for the reimbursement of Of Counsel's expenses, such as payment for business and travel expenses, professional dues, licensing, and health insurance?
3. If the firm provides Of Counsel with health insurance, does Of Counsel satisfy the policy requirements for coverage?

Right to Terminate

Does the agreement give each party the right to terminate the agreement after a specified number of days?

APPENDIX A

Employment Agreement

by and between John Q. Lawyer and XYZ, a Partnership
[Employee and Partnership Employer]

Employment Agreement
This Agreement is entered into as of this ______________________ day of ____, 19/20___, by and between JOHN Q. LAWYER ("Lawyer"), an individual, and XYZ, a general partnership, with reference to the following facts:

Recitals

A. Lawyer is an attorney licensed to practice law in the State of Anystate;[1]

B. The firm of XYZ (the "Firm") is a partnership composed of attorneys licensed to practice law in the State of Anystate and various other states pursuant to a written agreement as of ____________________________ ________________, 19/20___ (the "Partnership Agreement"); and

C. The Firm desires to engage the services of Lawyer in order to gain Lawyer's experience, skills, background, and knowledge, and Lawyer desires to render such services on the terms and conditions hereinafter set forth.

In consideration of the agreements, covenants, and conditions herein contained, the Firm and Lawyer hereby agree as follows:

---

1. Some states require Of Counsel to be licensed to practice in the same state where the firm is located. *See* Chapter 3.

1. Term of Agreement
Subject to the provisions and conditions of this Agreement, the term of this Agreement shall be from ______________________________, 19/20___, to ______________________________, 19/20___.

2. Title and Status
Lawyer shall be engaged to perform legal services for and on behalf of the Firm. Lawyer shall have the title of "Of Counsel" to the Firm. Notwithstanding the foregoing, Lawyer shall be neither a partner nor a special partner of the Firm but shall be considered an employee of the Firm.[2] In that capacity, Lawyer shall have no right or authority to attend any partnership meeting except by invitation of the Firm or to vote at any meeting of the partners of the Firm.

3. Provisions of Partnership Agreement
For purposes of this Agreement, references are made to various provisions of the Partnership Agreement. Lawyer hereby acknowledges that he has received a copy of the Partnership Agreement as of ____________________________, 19/20___, and of all Amendments, including the most recent Amendments thereto, and that he has read the Partnership Agreement and the Amendments thereto and is familiar with the provisions of the Partnership Agreement and the Amendments thereto. Lawyer agrees to be bound by those provisions of the Partnership Agreement referred to in this Agreement, as they now exist and as they may be amended from time to time. Lawyer further agrees to be bound by any substantially similar provision of the Partnership Agreement covering the same subject matter as the provisions of the Partnership Agreement referenced herein, as may be adopted by the Firm from time to time. The Firm shall provide Lawyer with copies of all amendments to the Partnership Agreement that may be adopted from time to time. Any reference herein to the Partnership Agreement shall be deemed to be a reference to the Agreement as it now exists and as it may be amended from time to time.

4. Duties of Lawyer
4.1 Lawyer shall perform legal services on behalf of the Firm and, except as otherwise provided herein, shall, with respect to the rendering of legal services, have all of the duties and responsibilities as if he were a partner of the Firm[3] as provided in Article ______________________________ of the Partnership Agreement. Lawyer further agrees to be bound by all rules and policies that apply to attorneys of the Firm, as established and as

2. Formal Opinion 330 precludes Of Counsel's status from being like that of a partner. *See* Chapters 2, 4, and 5.

3. Including this type of provision may expose Of Counsel to partnership liability. *See* Chapters 4 and 9.

amended from time to time by the Executive Committee of the Firm or any similar governing body of the Firm.

4.2 Lawyer shall perform his services at the offices of the Firm located in City of Anytown, State of Anystate (the "Anystate office"), and at such other place or places as are necessary or convenient to the performance of his duties.[4] Lawyer shall be furnished with a private office in the Firm's Anystate office and such secretarial assistance, facilities, amenities, and services, including paid motor vehicle parking, as are now or may hereinafter be furnished to attorneys in the Anystate office.[5]

4.3 Clients for whom Lawyer renders legal services on behalf of the Firm shall be billed at hourly rates established by the Firm and otherwise in the manner that other clients of the Firm are billed.

4.4 During the period from ______________________________, 19/20___, through ______________________________, 19/20___, ______________________________ shall be required to bill to clients of the Firm a minimum of 1500 hours.[6] If Lawyer fails to record at least 1500 hours of billable time in such year, his compensation for such year shall be reduced by multiplying the aggregate number of units deemed held by Lawyer pursuant to Paragraph 5 of this Agreement by a fraction, the numerator of which shall be the number of full billable hours actually recorded by Firm during 19/20___ and the denominator of which shall be 1500. The product of such multiplication shall be rounded to the nearest tenth and shall be used to calculate Lawyer's compensation for the calendar year ending ______________________________, 19/20___. Lawyer acknowledges that the provisions of this Paragraph 4.4 shall apply whether or not the Firm has established minimum hours for the partners of the Firm for any particular fiscal year.

4.5 In accordance with the provisions of the Partnership Agreement and except as otherwise provided in this Agreement, Lawyer covenants that during the term of this Agreement he will not perform legal services for any other person or entity. Lawyer further agrees that any clients introduced to the Firm by him or any clients for which he performs legal services during the term of this Agreement shall be and become clients of the Firm.

4.6 Lawyer agrees that all legal fees earned and received by him in the conduct and practice of law, including, but not limited to, all sums, whether paid to Lawyer or to the Firm, received as an executor, administrator, guardian, trustee, appraiser, director, or officer of a corporation; royalties from the sale of books, magazine articles, and pamphlets con-

---

4. Requiring work to be performed on the employer's premises may indicate an employer-employee relationship. *See* Chapter 4.

5. *See* Chapter 4.

6. Requiring Of Counsel to work full-time may indicate an employer-employee relationship. *See* Chapter 4.

cerning subjects related to the practice of law; salaries, fees, and honoraria from speeches and teaching engagements concerning subjects related to the practice of law, and expense allowances in connection with speeches and teaching engagements, less the amount of expenses actually incurred by Lawyer, shall be income of the Firm.

4.7 No salaries, commissions, fees, gratuities, or other things of value with a fair market value exceeding one thousand ($1,000) dollars shall be accepted, directly or indirectly, by Lawyer personally from any client of the Firm or any officer, director, or principal thereof, unless with the express consent of the Firm, and the fair value of any such item received with such consent, though retained by Lawyer, shall be treated for accounting purposes a compensation to the Firm and shall be charged against Lawyer's compensation. The Executive Committee of the Firm may authorize, however, any exception to any provision of Paragraph 4.1, and this Paragraph 4.7 shall not apply to any benefits or compensation received by Lawyer from the ABC Company for services rendered prior to the date of this Agreement. The Firm hereby acknowledges that Lawyer will continue to receive a salary and benefits from the ABC Company through ______________________________, 19/20___, and a retirement allowance thereafter, but that no services will be performed therefor after ________________________________, 19/20___.

4.8 In all matters affecting the Firm's practice of law, Lawyer shall maintain a standard of professional conduct that shall in all respects conform with the standards of the Canons of Ethics of the Bar Associations of the State of Anystate, as such Canons may be applicable to him or the Firm, and such additional generally acceptable standards as may be required by the Executive Committee of the Firm.

4.9 Lawyer agrees to devote his full working time[7] and attention to the Firm's business and practice and exert his best efforts for the successful conduct, operation, and management of the Firm. It is, however, specifically understood that Lawyer may have, and may continue to have and further acquire, financial and business interests and investments, and Lawyer shall be entitled to devote such time and attention to those financial and business interests and investments as will in no way interfere with the full-time practice of law, and such conduct shall not be considered a breach on his part of the requirement of this Agreement with respect to the time and attention to be devoted to the business and practice of the Firm.

4.10 Lawyer shall not, after the date hereof, accept a position as an officer or director of a corporation or similar entity, a trustee of a trust, a general partner of a partnership or any other position involving management or control of an entity (hereinafter collectively called a "Position") without first giving at least fourteen (14) days' prior written notice to the

---

7. *See* Chapter 4.

Executive Committee of the Firm and his intention to accept a Position. The Executive Committee may, by written notice to Lawyer within fourteen (14) days of its receipt of the notice, prohibit Lawyer from accepting the Position if the Executive Committee determines that Lawyer's taking the Position would adversely affect the Firm. The provisions of this Paragraph 4.10 shall not apply to a Position held by Lawyer with an entity owned entirely by Lawyer and members of his extended family. For purposes of this paragraph, Lawyer's extended family shall include all persons to whom Lawyer or his spouse is related by blood or adoption up to the fourth (4th) degree of consanguinity. Nothing in this paragraph shall, however, be deemed to abrogate the provisions of Paragraph 4.6 of this Agreement.

4.11 Lawyer shall charge reasonably for all professional services rendered by him, following generally the policies of the Firm as to fees charged. Lawyer may serve professionally without charge to any member of his own family, any relative or any client entitled to such legal aid as may be permitted under the canons of professional ethics; and, with the consent of the Firm, may serve without charge or less than regular charge the organized bar, or any civic, educational, religious, or charitable organization or project.

4.12 Lawyer shall at all times duly and punctually pay and discharge his separate and private debts and engagements, whether present or future, and keep the Firm indemnified therefrom and from all actions, proceedings, costs, claims, and demands in respect thereof.

4.13 Lawyer agrees to be bound by the provisions of Section ____ of the Partnership Agreement, provided, however, that Lawyer may exercise any stock options that he received in his capacity as an employee of the Corporation or any subsidiary or affiliate thereof at any time. Lawyer agrees to notify the Executive Committee of the Firm at least three (3) business days prior to disposing of any stock acquired by virtue of the exercise of such options (the "stock"). Lawyer further agrees not to dispose of such stock at that time, if, within two (2) business days following receipt of such notice, the Executive Committee of the Firm notifies Lawyer that he may not dispose of such stock at that time and the Executive Committee of the Firm has a reasonable basis for doing so.

5. Compensation

In consideration of the services performed by Lawyer, the Firm shall pay to Lawyer an amount equal to the amount to which Lawyer would be entitled, pursuant to the provisions of the Article ________________________ of the Partnership Agreement, if he were a partner of the Firm,[8] except as provided in Paragraph 4.4 of this Agreement. Because Lawyer's compen-

8. *See* Chapters 4 and 5.

sation is dependent on the profitability of the Firm, Lawyer shall be entitled to receive the same information and reports regarding the finances of the Firm as if he were a partner of the Firm and shall have the same rights as a partner of the Firm to inspect the Firm's books and accounts, as provided in Section ________________________________ of the Partnership Agreement. The compensation provided hereunder shall be paid at the times and in the same manner as if Lawyer were a partner of the Firm; provided, however, that the Firm agrees, at Lawyer's request, to defer the income receivable by him from the Firm during 19/20___, until January 1, 19/20___.

6. Expenses
The Firm shall directly pay or shall fully reimburse Lawyer for all reasonable expenses that are customarily paid on behalf of, or reimbursed to, associates of the Firm.[9] The Firm shall provide errors and omissions insurance on behalf of the Firm and Lawyer in the same manner as if Lawyer were a partner or associate of the Firm.[10] The Firm acknowledges and agrees that Lawyer is an employee[11] for purposes of the law of the State of Anystate that provides for indemnification of employees. Lawyer agrees to cooperate with the Firm in the defense of any action against Lawyer or the Firm arising out of or in any way connected with his activities on behalf of the Firm and further agrees to make himself available for purposes of the defense of any such action.

7. Benefits
Lawyer shall participate in and shall receive benefits under all formal and informal employee benefit plans, understandings, arrangements, or programs now or hereafter generally made available to the Firm's associates and their families, including, but not limited to, any group health, life, dental, disability, or other insurance, or any pension or profit-sharing plans or arrangements, or any other type of benefit.[12]

8. Vacation
Lawyer shall be entitled to vacation time at the rate of fifteen (15) business days for each twelve (12) months of service. Lawyer shall also be entitled to all holidays observed by the Firm, its partners or employees.

---

9. *See* Chapter 4.

10. For a discussion of errors and omissions insurance coverage and its effect on Of Counsel status, *see* Chapter 5.

11. A blanket characterization as "employee" may not guarantee employee status, particularly where the agreement uses partnership traits.

12. For a discussion of employee benefits and Of Counsel's status, *see* Chapter 5.

9. Termination

This Agreement shall automatically terminate on ____________________, 19/20___, and shall remain in effect until such date unless terminated strictly in accordance with any of the following provisions:

9.1 The Firm may terminate this Agreement at any time upon thirty (30) days' prior written notice to Lawyer.

9.2 Lawyer may terminate this Agreement at any time upon thirty (30) days' prior written notice to any member of the Executive Committee of the Firm.[13]

9.3 This Agreement shall automatically terminate on the occurrence of any of the following events:

1. The death, disability, or incapacity of Lawyer.
2. The voluntary or involuntary dissolution of the Firm;
3. The bankruptcy or insolvency of the Firm.

10. Trade Secrets

10.1 For the purpose of this Agreement, "trade secrets" shall mean (a) any information that is used in the Firm's business and that derives independent economic value from not being generally known to the public or to persons who can obtain economic value from its development or use, and (b) the Firm's information encompassed in all client files, computer printouts, manuals, plans, proposals, marketing and sales plans, financial information, costs, pricing information, client lists, and all concepts or ideas on or reasonably related to the business of the Firm that have not been publicly released by duly authorized representatives of the Firm (except Lawyer's personal files and form files).

10.2 Lawyer agrees to regard and preserve as confidential information all trade secrets pertaining to the Firm's business that have been or may be obtained by Lawyer by reason of his services for the Firm. Lawyer further agrees that he shall not, without written authorization from the Executive Committee of the Firm, use for his own benefit or purposes or disclose to others, either during the term of this Agreement or thereafter, any trade secret or other confidential information connected with the business or other development of the Firm. Lawyer agrees that he shall not remove the Firm's documents, client files, computer printouts, manuals, plans, proposals, reports, studies, client lists, or other documents or things at all related to or connected with the Firm's trade secrets (except Lawyer's personal files and form files). Lawyer further agrees to be bound by Section ____ of the Partnership Agreement, regarding files of the Firm.

---

13. A termination clause is a common provision. *See* Chapter 5.

11. Integration Agreement
Except as otherwise provided in the Partnership Agreement, this Agreement contains the entire agreement between the parties and supersedes all prior oral and written agreements, understandings, commitments, and practices between the parties. No amendments to this Agreement, except as expressly provided herein to the contrary, may be made except by a writing signed by both parties.

12. No Waiver
No waiver by the Firm of any term, provision, or condition of this Agreement, whether by conduct or otherwise, in any one or more instances, shall be deemed to be or be construed as a further continuing waiver by the Firm of any such term, provision, or condition of the Agreement.

13. Partial Invalidity
In the event that any provision of this agreement shall be held to be unenforceable, invalid, or inoperative for any reason, the validity of the remainder of the terms and provisions of this Agreement shall not be affected thereby in any respect.

14. Arbitration

14.1 In case any disagreement, difference, or controversy shall arise between Lawyer, his heirs, executors, or administrators and the Firm with respect to any matter in relation to or arising out of or under this Agreement, whether as to the construction or operation thereof, or the respective rights and liabilities of the Firm or otherwise, and the parties to the controversy cannot mutually agree as to the resolution thereof, then such disagreement, difference, or controversy shall be determined by arbitration under the commercial arbitration rules of the American Arbitration Association.

14.2 The power hereby given to the arbitrators shall not terminate or be revoked by the death of Lawyer, and the arbitrators shall proceed with the arbitration notwithstanding such death. Any award made by a majority shall be final, binding, and conclusive upon all parties and those claiming under them. The arbitrators shall have no power to make any award inconsistent with or contrary to the terms and provisions of this Agreement. The costs and expenses of any arbitration shall be borne and paid as the arbitrators shall, by their award, direct.

14.3 The submission to arbitration in accordance with the requirements of this Section 14 of any and all agreements, differences, or controversies that may arise hereunder is made a condition precedent to the institution of any action at law or in equity with respect to the controversy involved, and no such action at law or equity shall be instituted by anyone until after an award has been made by the arbitrators and shall be restricted solely to the subject matter of the challenge of such award on the grounds and only in the manner permitted by law. Such action at law shall not be a trial *de novo* as to the merits but shall be restricted to a challenge of the award on such grounds as are permitted by law.

15. Notices

15.1 Any notice to the Firm required or permitted hereunder shall be given in writing to the Firm, either by personal service or by registered or certified mail, postage prepaid, duly addressed to the Firm c/o the Executive Committee of the Firm at its Anystate office, with a copy to the "Administrative Partner in Anytown." Any such notice to Lawyer shall be given in a like manner and, if mailed, shall be addressed to Lawyer at the last known address shown in the files of the Firm.

15.2 Any such notice to either party so deposited in the mail shall be deemed for all purposes of this Agreement to have been given forty-eight (48) hours after such deposit.

IN WITNESS WHEREOF, the parties hereby execute this Agreement, as of the date hereof.

DATED: ____________________________________

DATED: ____________________________________

APPENDIX 📖 B

Of Counsel Agreement

[Independent Contractor and Partnership]

This agreement is made on ____, 19/20___, by and between JOHN Q. LAWYER ("Lawyer"), an individual, and XYZ, a general partnership (the "Firm"), regarding a Contract Partner/Of Counsel[1] between Lawyer and the Firm.

1. This agreement will be for a term of ______________ months commencing on ____ and ending on ____ (the "Term"). It is the Firm's expectation that a mutual decision regarding Lawyer becoming an Equity Partner in the Firm will be made at or prior to the conclusion of the Term.[2]

2. Lawyer's base compensation shall be ____________________ Dollars ($______________) per month ($__________________ annualized), payable semimonthly,[3] plus an automobile allowance of $______________ per month. In addition to ____'s base compensation, Lawyer shall receive an amount equal to ten percent (10%) of Lawyer's Aggregate Source Collections, as defined below, in excess of $50,000.00. Source Collections with respect to any client shall be the

---

1. *See* Chapter 5 for a discussion of setting out Of Counsel's title and status. The use of "Contract Partner/Of Counsel" in this contract creates an unnecessary ambiguity. It would be better practice to use the term "Of Counsel" to make it clear that an independent contractor relationship was intended.

2. *See* Chapter 4 for a discussion of probationary partners in the Of Counsel context.

3. *See* Chapters 2, 4, and 5 for a discussion of permissible methods for compensating Of Counsel.

product obtained by multiplying (i) the total fees and nonrefundable retainers collected by the Firm during the Term and for a period of thirty (30) days following the conclusion of the Term from that client by (ii) Lawyer's percentage share (between 0 percent and 100 percent) of source credit for that client, as mutually agreed to by you, the Intake Committee, and the Firm's Managing Partner. Aggregate Source Collections shall be the sum of Source Collections for all clients. This additional compensation shall be computed semiannually and paid to Lawyer on or before ______________________________________ (as to Aggregate Source Collections in excess of $50,000.00). For tax purposes only, Lawyer will be compensated as if he were an Equity Partner of the Firm.

3. Lawyer hereby agrees that he (like the Firm's Equity Partners) shall have no ownership interest in the work in process, accounts receivable, or goodwill of the Firm. Lawyer hereby agrees that if he leaves the Firm during or after expiration of the Term, he will use his best efforts thereafter to assist the Firm in collecting on the unpaid work in process and unpaid accounts receivable from those clients for which he was the original source or shared source attorney.

4. If Lawyer so elects, he will be covered under the Firm's medical, disability, life, and other insurance plans at his own expense,[4] as is the case for the Firm's Equity and Contract Partners. In addition, the Firm will afford and pay for malpractice insurance coverage for Lawyer on the same basis,[5] if at all, as such insurance protection is afforded to Equity Partners, and will pay for his parking and dues for the State Bar of Anystate and other bar association dues on the same basis as for Equity Partners.

5. In light of the Firm's desire that Lawyer actively develop and promote the Firm's financial institutions and business practice, Lawyer will be reimbursed for reasonable and documented business expenses in accordance with customary Firm procedures applicable to Equity and Contract Partners. Further, the Firm will pay the membership dues for such trade associations set forth on Schedule A hereto.[6]

6. As a Contract Partner/Of Counsel, Lawyer is not required to contribute capital to the Firm, nor will he have any formal voting rights at any Partnership meetings.[7] Otherwise, he will be welcome to participate in discussions and meetings of the Firm and of the Partnership, except as to

---

4. This kind of provision preserves Of Counsel's status as an independent contractor. *See* Chapter 5.

5. In this provision, Of Counsel chose to reimburse the Firm for inclusion in the firm's malpractice policy. This provision indicates an independent contractor relationship, rather than an employer-employee relationship. *See* Chapter 5.

6. *See* Chapter 4.

7. This provision would prevent Of Counsel from being characterized as a partner of the firm. *See* Chapter 4.

Partnership meetings or portions of meetings where only Equity Partners may participate. In addition, Lawyer will be given copies of periodic Firm financial information normally distributed to Contract Partners. Lawyer will not share in or be liable for any profits or losses of the Firm, including any malpractice liability not arising from his acts. He will be designated as the billing attorney on clients for whom he is the source attorney, subject to the approval of his Department Head and the Firm's Managing Partner.

7. Section ____ of the Firm's Partnership Agreement, a copy of which section is attached hereto and incorporated herein, shall be applicable to this Contract Partner/Of Counsel arrangement.

8. Lawyer may assign his rights and delegate his duties under this agreement to a professional corporation of which he is the sole shareholder and employee. In accordance with the foregoing, the parties hereby execute this Agreement as of the date set forth below.

DATED: ____

DATED: ____

APPENDIX C

Of Counsel Agreement

[Independent Contractor and Partnership]

This Contract, made on ________________________________, 19/20___, between JOHN Q. LAWYER ("Lawyer"), an individual, and XYZ (the "Firm"), establishes the parties' agreement that Lawyer will become associated with the Firm on an "Of Counsel" basis in the practice of law.[1]

1. This relationship will commence as of ______________________, 19/20___, and will continue indefinitely thereafter, with either party having the right for any reason, on thirty (30) days' written notice, to terminate the relationship.[2]

2. As of the commencement date, all legal services performed by Lawyer will be on behalf of the Firm. This arrangement includes Lawyer's full-time efforts and precludes legal services (including teaching and serving on a board of directors) being rendered for a fee to any party outside of this arrangement.[3] All fees will be billed through the Firm and collected by the Firm, with the exception of one preexisting relationship that Lawyer has with ABC Company. Lawyer agrees to use the Firm's basic accounting systems and billing systems to permit effective coordination

---

1. While this provision indicates the parties' intention to create an Of Counsel relationship, it does not establish whether Of Counsel's status will be analogous to that of an independent contractor or that of an employee. *See* Chapter 5.

2. *See* Chapters 4 and 5 for a discussion of the parties' right to terminate and common termination clauses.

3. This provision tends to indicate that the Of Counsel relationship is analogous to an employer-employee relationship. *See* Chapter 4.

with the Firm's office procedures. Lawyer shall have full judgment as to billing of matters for clients that Lawyer brings to the Firm, including arbitrarily discounting or writing off fees, and the manner in which bills are sent to clients. All funds collected will be deposited in the general account of the Firm. All fees billed by Lawyer shall be accounted for separately, and accrued to the mutual benefit of both parties pursuant to the terms of this Agreement. To the extent of funds held for the benefit of Lawyer in excess of allocated expenses, the same shall be distributed to Lawyer at such time and in such amounts as the Firm directs.

3. The Firm will include Lawyer at its expense in the Firm's E&O coverage effective with the commencement date of this relationship.[4] All costs required for Lawyer's clients will be advanced by the Firm, and all recovery of costs will accrue to the Firm. If any costs are not billed to and paid by Lawyer's clients, Lawyer will reimburse the firm for them.[5]

4. Lawyer has indicated that he anticipates over a period of time the need for partners, associates, clerks, or paralegals of the firm to assist with the performance of legal services to his clients from time to time.[6] Any associates, secretaries, and support personnel will be hired by the Firm, with input from Lawyer. With respect to work performed by the Firm or the Firm's associates, clerks, or paralegals for the clients of Lawyer, or new matters referred to the Firm from the existing clients of Lawyer or from new business generated by Lawyer, the Firm shall be allocated from gross receipts of fees (but not costs because of the agreement as set forth above), as collected eighty-two and one-half percent (82 1/2%), and Lawyer shall retain seventeen and one-half percent (17 1/2%). With respect to matters generated by Lawyer, one hundred percent (100%) of the sums collected shall be held for the benefit of Lawyer's account. From time to time, there may be matters where the Firm will want Lawyer to assist the Firm because of Lawyer's particular background and expertise. With respect to matters referred by the Firm to Lawyer, either with respect to existing clients or new clients or new business generated by the Firm in an area where Lawyer can provide special expertise or assistance, Lawyer shall retain eighty-two and one-half percent (82 1/2%) for his time expended, and the Firm shall retain seventeen and one-half percent (17 1/2%) of fees as collected. The parties appreciate that there may be times when it is difficult to determine the origination of the client or client matter and the Firm will work with Lawyer to make those allocations fairly.

5. The Firm will charge Lawyer the amount of $_______________ at the beginning of each month as his share of expenses for that month.

---

4. *See* Chapter 5 for a discussion of malpractice liability coverage for Of Counsel and its effect on his status.

5. *See* Chapters 4 and 5.

6. For a discussion of overhead expenses, *see* Chapter 4. *See also* Chapter 5 for a comparison of overhead expense provisions in the Of Counsel contract.

This will be a charge against fees received by Lawyer. This charge will include Lawyer's share of all office costs, including rent, secretarial, telephone, equipment use, library, reception, accounting, word processing, office supplies, messenger services, postage, Bar dues, parking, health, life, disability, and E&O insurance in accordance with the Firm's current office practice. It also includes the amount of $__________ per month ($__________ per year) reserve for promotional activities to be undertaken by Lawyer. This contemplates secretarial needs on the basis of up to one-half a full-time secretary with word processing and office overflow as backup.

6. Notwithstanding anything to the contrary above, expenses shall be as follows:

a. For the period from __________ through __________, $__________ each month plus __________ percent (_____%) of actual fees collected (in excess of the first $__________) for legal services performed after __________.

b. For the period from __________ through __________, $__________ per month plus __________ percent (_____%) for legal services performed after __________, but not to exceed $__________ per month, and with no accrual of the difference between $__________ and $__________ per month.

c. After __________, $__________ per month plus __________ percent (_____%) of actual fees collected (in excess of $__________) but not to exceed __________ per month, with the difference between $__________ and $__________ accruing and being carried forward on a month-to-month basis.

If this Agreement is terminated by either party, Lawyer shall have no personal obligation for any accumulated expenses, except with respect to __________ percent (_____%) of any uncollected receivables for legal services performed by Lawyer after date of termination.

By __________________________

By __________________________

DATED: __________________________

APPENDIX 📖 D

Of Counsel Agreement

[Independent Contractor and Professional Service Corporation]

This Agreement is made on ______________________________, 19/20___, between XYZ, P.C., a professional corporation ("Corporation") and JOHN Q. LAWYER ("Lawyer"), an individual ("Lawyer "). The parties mutually desire that Lawyer establish an "Of Counsel" relationship to the Corporation. Accordingly, the parties desire to set forth the terms and conditions by which that relationship shall be governed. Therefore, it is agreed between the parties as follows:

1. *Employment.* The Corporation shall retain and employ Lawyer as an independent contractor, not as an agent or employee, in an "Of Counsel" relationship to the Corporation.[1]

2. *Term.* The employment of Lawyer shall commence upon the date this Agreement is signed by both parties and shall continue until such time as either party terminates the Agreement by thirty (30) days' advance written notice to the other.[2]

3. *Duties.* During the term of this Agreement, Lawyer, subject to his availability and upon the request of the Corporation, shall: (a) assist the Corporation in its continuing legal education program for its members and associates; (b) review litigation files for the purpose of consulting on and recommending trial preparation, pleadings, strategy, and settlement; (c) assist attorneys responsible for litigation files in pretrial discovery, mo-

---

1. This provision clearly sets out the parties' intention as to Of Counsel's status. *See* Chapter 5.

2. *See* Chapters 4 and 5 for a discussion of the right to terminate and its effect on Of Counsel's status, as well as for common termination clauses.

tions, briefs, and trial; (d) in his discretion, and with the agreement of the Corporation, assume responsibility for conducting discovery, motions, and trials, appellate proceedings, and related matters; and (e) engage in other activities relating to firm development and client development for the Corporation.[3]

4. *Time Requirements.* Lawyer shall not be required to perform any specified number of hours of service to the Corporation.[4] However, he shall devote such time as may be necessary to handle and complete those matters which he undertakes for the Corporation or for which his services are engaged by clients of the Corporation, and otherwise discharge his duties as set forth in paragraph 3 of this Agreement.

5. *Compensation.* The Corporation shall pay Lawyer as fees for his services at an hourly rate equal to eighty percent (80%) of the rate that his time is charged to any particular client or matter.[5] Lawyer's time will be billed by the Corporation at the same rate as a senior shareholder's time is billed to a particular client or matter for similar services. With regard to any contingent fee matter or other matter for which it has been agreed with the client that billing will be at the conclusion of the matter, Lawyer's fees will be paid at such time as the matter is concluded. For the purposes of this Agreement, matters will be deemed "concluded" and fees determined to be due within thirty (30) days after a final bill has been submitted to the client or a binding settlement executed on behalf of the Corporation's client. However, except as to fees related to clients or matters that Lawyer originates and for which he is principally responsible, his fees shall not be contingent on payment of the bill or receipt of fees by the Corporation. With regard to time spent by Lawyer in connection with the Corporation's continuing legal education program, Lawyer will be paid at the rate of $____________________ per hour. As additional compensation, the Corporation shall:

A. Pay the dues for Lawyer's membership in the American Bar Association, the State Bar of Anystate, and the Anycounty Bar Association.[6]

B. Cover Lawyer under the Corporation's group health insurance plan and pay all premiums related thereto;[7]

C. Pay nonreimbursed expenses arising in connection with attendance at American Bar Association Committee meetings;

---

3. This provision clearly sets out the duties expected of Of Counsel. This is important, particularly where Of Counsel is a retired partner of the firm and is receiving compensation from a firm retirement plan. *See* Chapters 2, 3, and 5.

4. This provision preserves Of Counsel's status as an independent contractor, consistent with the parties' intentions. *See* Chapters 4 and 5.

5. This provision satisfies some states' requirement that Of Counsel be compensated only for work actually performed. *See* Chapters 2, 4, and 5.

6. *See* Chapter 5.

7. *See* Chapter 5.

D. Cover Lawyer under the Corporation's professional liability (*i.e.*, errors and omissions) insurance policy and pay all premiums related thereto;[8] and

E. The Corporation may, in its discretion, pay to Lawyer such bonuses at such times and in such amounts as it deems appropriate.

6. *Expenses.* The Corporation shall reimburse Lawyer for all reasonable out-of-pocket expenses (including automobile mileage) incurred or advanced by Lawyer in connection with any client matter or entertainment or business promotion expense.[9]

7. *Records.* Lawyer shall keep records of all time spent and expenses incurred in the same manner and in the same form as is prescribed for members and associates of the Corporation. Such time and expenses shall be submitted to the Corporation's office manager on at least a semi-monthly basis, that being on the fifteenth (15th) day and the last day of each month or if that day falls on a weekend or holiday, on the business day just preceding that date.

8. *Billing.* It shall be the obligation of the Corporation to prepare and mail all bills to clients to whom Lawyer renders service or expends costs in the manner and form generally utilized by the Corporation.[10] Lawyer shall receive a copy of all bills prepared by the Corporation for services rendered or costs advanced to clients originated by Lawyer for his review price bills being forwarded to the client.

9. *Payment.* All fees and reimbursement of expenses due Lawyer pursuant to Paragraphs 5 and 6 of this Agreement shall be paid by the Corporation to him on the fifteenth (15th) day of each month for all amounts determined to be due prior to the last day of the preceding month, and on the last day of each month for all amounts determined to be due prior to the fifteenth (15th) day of the same month.

10. *Taxes.* It shall be Lawyer's sole responsibility to pay such federal, state, and local taxes (including but not limited to income taxes and FICA taxes) as may be imposed or levied upon the income earned or derived by him under this Agreement.[11] It is expressly understood and agreed that the Corporation shall not withhold any such taxes from the compensation paid to Lawyer.

11. *Support.* The Corporation shall provide Lawyer with necessary and suitable office space, office supplies, office furniture, and dictating equipment.[12] In addition, the Corporation shall provide Lawyer with non-

---

8. *See* Chapter 5.

9. *See* Chapter 4.

10. For a discussion of integration of billing procedures and its effect on the status of Of Counsel, *see* Chapter 4.

11. *See* Chapter 4 for a comparison of amounts of social security taxes paid by employees and independent contractors.

12. *See* Chapters 4 and 5 for a discussion of overhead.

exclusive secretarial and clerical services. With regard to any client or matter originated by Lawyer, the Corporation will assign such attorneys and other personnel to assist Lawyer as may be necessary. The assignment of particular personnel to such matters shall be at the discretion of the Corporation, upon consultation with Lawyer, based upon the availability, qualifications, abilities, and experience of such attorneys or other personnel.

12. *Legal Directories.* During the term of this agreement, the Corporation shall, at its sole expense, cause Lawyer's name to be listed as "Of Counsel" on the Corporation's stationery, in the Martindale-Hubbell Directory, Anystate and Anycounty Bar directories, telephone directories, and in other listings or directories, in which the Corporation may from time to time list its name and the name of its members and associates of the Corporation.[13]

13. *Announcements and Cards.* The Corporation shall, at its sole expense, cause announcements of Lawyer's association with the Corporation to be printed and sent to such persons or organizations as the Corporation may designate. Further, the Corporation, at its sole expense, shall provide Lawyer with business cards indicating his association with the Corporation in the form and style generally utilized by the Corporation.

14. *Termination.* This Agreement may be terminated at the discretion of either party, with or without cause, upon the party wishing to terminate the Agreement and giving the other party at least thirty (30) days' advance written notice of the termination. If this Agreement is terminated, Lawyer shall be entitled to receive from the Corporation payment of all sums that may thereafter become due for services performed by during the term of this Agreement.[14]

15. *Death or Dissolution.* In the event of death during the term of this Agreement, all sums that are then payable to Lawyer or thereafter become payable to him for services rendered prior to his death, shall be paid to Lawyer's personal representative in accordance with this Agreement as though Lawyer were still alive. In the event of dissolution of the Corporation during the term of this Agreement, the Corporation shall pay all sums due or to become due to Lawyer under this Agreement pursuant to its plan for liquidation or dissolution.

16. *Binding Effect.* This Agreement shall be binding upon the heirs, personal representatives, administrators, executors, and assigns of each of the parties.

---

13. *See* Chapter 8 for a discussion of permissible methods of communicating the Of Counsel relationship. *See* Chapter 9 for a discussion of how failing to properly communicate the Of Counsel relationship affects Of Counsel's liability.

14. *See* Chapters 4 and 5 for a discussion of the parties' right to terminate the agreement and common termination clauses.

17. *Partial Invalidity.* It is expressly understood and agreed by the parties that should any paragraph or any provision or portion of this Agreement be held invalid, illegal, or void, then and in such event, any paragraph, provision, or portion so held to be invalid, illegal, or void shall be deleted from this Agreement, and this Agreement shall be read as though such invalid, illegal, or void paragraph, provision, or portion was never included herein, and the remainder of such Agreement excluding such invalid, illegal, or void paragraph, provision, or portion shall nevertheless subsist and continue with force and effect.

18. *Governing Law.* This Agreement shall be construed in accordance with the laws of the State of Anystate.

19. *Modification of Agreement.* No modification or amendment of this Agreement shall be binding unless executed in writing by all parties. No waiver of any provision of this Agreement shall be deemed a waiver of any other provision, nor shall any waiver constitute a continuing waiver.

20. *Effect of Headings.* The subject headings of the paragraphs and subparagraphs of this Agreement are included for purposes of convenience only, and shall not affect the construction or interpretation of any of the provisions of this Agreement. Executed the date first appearing above.

______________________________________, P.C.

By: ______________________________________

Title:______________________________________

ATTEST:

______________________________________, Secretary

APPENDIX E

Of Counsel Agreement

[Independent Contractor and Partnership]

THIS AGREEMENT made this ________________________________ day of _____________________, 19/20___, by and between JOHN Q. LAWYER ("Lawyer"), an individual licensed to practice in the state of Anystate,[1] and X, Y & Z ("XYZ"), a partnership engaged in the practice of law in Anytown, Anystate;

WITNESSETH, THAT WHEREAS XYZ desires to establish a continuing affiliation with Lawyer as Of Counsel, as an independent contractor, rather than as partner or associate;[2]

NOW THEREFORE, in consideration of the mutual covenants and obligations hereinafter set forth, the parties agree as follows:

1. Term

This Agreement shall commence on __________________, 19/20___, and continue in force until terminated pursuant to this Agreement. Either party may terminate this Agreement by giving the other sixty (60) days' written notice at any time after one year from the date of this Agreement. This Agreement shall terminate immediately if Lawyer is disqualified from the practice of law in the state of Anystate.

---

1. Some states require that Of Counsel be licensed to practice law in the same state as the affiliated firm or other lawyer. *See* Chapter 3.

2. Formal Opinion 330 precludes the Of Counsel relationship from being like that of a partner or associate. *See* Chapters 2 and 4; *see also* Chapter 5 for methods of clearly setting out the status of Of Counsel as an employee or independent contractor.

2. Definitions

(a) "Overhead Costs"[3] means twenty (20) percent of Gross Receipts for the calendar year 19/20___, and the amount to which the parties mutually agree for each calendar year thereafter.

(b) "Gross Receipts" means all moneys received by XYZ from clients for professional services rendered by Lawyer and any additional moneys received by XYZ from clients for which Lawyer is the attorney who originated the business.

(c) "Expenses" means any amounts incurred by Lawyer or XYZ in connection with professional services rendered by Lawyer or any other attorney of XYZ to Lawyer clients.

3. Duties[4]

During the term of this Agreement, Lawyer shall perform professional services on behalf of XYZ and not for any other individual or entity.[5] Both Lawyer and XYZ will work toward the development of new clients and sources of business in a manner consistent with law and the Model Rules of Professional Conduct of the American Bar Association.

4. Compensation[6]

XYZ shall compensate Lawyer for all services rendered in the following manner:

(a) XYZ shall pay Lawyer fifty percent (50%) of all gross receipts received by XYZ for professional services rendered by Lawyer, payable monthly. The fifty percent (50%) of gross receipts retained by XYZ shall include Lawyer's share of Overhead Costs.

(b) In addition to the amounts received as income under 4(a) of this Agreement, XYZ shall pay Lawyer an additional ten percent (10%) of gross receipts received from XYZ in each calendar year from clients for which Lawyer is the attorney who originated the business.

(c) XYZ shall reimburse Lawyer for all reasonable expenses incurred in connection with the rendering of professional services.

(d) XYZ shall pay all professional dues, premiums for malpractice insurance,[7] and expenses incurred by Lawyer in connection with attending any and all professional seminars. Lawyer may be entitled to partici-

---

3. *See* Chapters 4 and 5 for a discussion of overhead and a comparison of methods of overhead expense provisions in the Of Counsel contract.

4. Provisions describing Of Counsel's expected duties are important, particularly where Of Counsel is a retired partner also receiving compensation from the firm's retirement plan. *See* Chapters 3 and 5.

5. An exclusive services provision tends to indicate a relationship akin to that of an employee. *See* Chapters 4 and 5.

6. *See* Chapters 2, 4, and 5 for a discussion of permissible methods of compensation.

7. *See* Chapter 5 for a discussion of professional malpractice insurance.

pate in any group health insurance plan provided he pays his share of the premium for such insurance.

(e) At the end of each calendar month, XYZ shall pay Lawyer seventy percent (70%) of the estimated Gross Receipts less Overhead Costs allocable to Lawyer.

(f) Within thirty (30) days after the end of each calendar month, XYZ shall furnish an accounting to Lawyer showing Gross Receipts and Overhead Costs allocable to Lawyer. XYZ shall pay Lawyer the remaining thirty percent (30%) of any compensation due Lawyer for professional services rendered by Lawyer in the previous calendar month.

(g) Within thirty days at the end of each calendar year, XYZ shall furnish Lawyer a complete accounting of all Gross Receipts and Overhead Costs allocable to Lawyer. XYZ shall pay Lawyer any balance of compensation to which he may be entitled by virtue of the annual accounting. Lawyer shall pay XYZ any amount which he has been paid in excess of the amount to which he is entitled.

(h) Within one calendar quarter following the termination of this Agreement or until Lawyer's compensation has been fully paid, whichever period is less, XYZ shall furnish Lawyer a complete accounting of all Gross Receipts and Overhead Costs allocable to Lawyer. XYZ shall pay Lawyer any balance of compensation to which he may be entitled by virtue of the final accounting. Lawyer shall pay XYZ any amount which he has been paid in excess of the amount to which he is entitled. Within the same period, XYZ and Lawyer shall arrange for the payment of any future amounts to which Lawyer may become entitled.

5. Billing

XYZ shall be responsible for billing clients for all professional services rendered by Lawyer. Payments received by XYZ shall be deposited in the firm's bank account.

6. Facilities and Services[8]

XYZ shall provide such facilities, office space, equipment, furniture, supplies, and services necessary to the performance of Lawyer's duties under this Agreement. XYZ shall furnish stationery with letterhead showing Lawyer's Of Counsel status and shall amend its directory listings to include Lawyer as Of Counsel.

7. Indemnification

Lawyer agrees to indemnify XYZ for any liability suffered by XYZ, its partners, employees, or agents arising from his acts or failure to act that is not covered by XYZ's professional indemnity insurance. This does not ap-

---

8. *See* Chapters 4 and 5 for a discussion of provisions that require Of Counsel to perform work on the premises of the employer and a discussion of overhead expenses.

ply to a deductible or self-insured retention on a liability that is otherwise covered by XYZ's professional indemnity insurance. XYZ agrees to indemnify Lawyer for any liability which he may suffer arising from the acts or failure to act of XYZ's partners, employees, or agents, which is not covered by XYZ's indemnity insurance. This does not apply to a deductible or self-insured retention on a liability which is otherwise covered by XYZ's professional indemnity insurance.

8. Governing Law
This Agreement shall be interpreted, construed, and governed according to the laws of the State of Anystate.

9. Integration
This Agreement contains the complete understanding of the parties and shall be binding upon their respective successors, heirs, or assigns.

10. Assignability
This Agreement is personal and the rights and obligations thereunder are not assignable.

11. Disclosure of Information
Following the termination of this Agreement, in the absence of authorization, neither party shall disclose to or use for the benefit of any person, partnership, corporation or other entity, any files, trade secrets, or other confidential information obtained by either party during the term of this Agreement.

IN WITNESS WHEREOF, XYZ has caused this Agreement to be signed by its duly authorized partner, and Lawyer has executed this Agreement in the state of Anystate on the day and year first above written.

____

X, Y & Z

____

JOHN Q. LAWYER

APPENDIX F

Of Counsel Agreement

[Letterhead of Law Firm][1]

[Month, Day, Year]

John J. Doe, Esq.
1000 Broadway
Major City, ZZ 00000

Dear John:

As you will retire as a partner of our firm at the end of this fiscal year, the firm invites you to remain associated with us as Of Counsel, under the following terms.

1. *Title.* Your title will be "Of Counsel." The firm will be permitted to list your name in that capacity, as it deems fit, on letterheads, brochures, professional listings (such as Martindale-Hubbell), and other promotional materials.

2. *Status; Health and Life Insurance Coverage.* Your status will be that of an independent contractor, but we shall nevertheless take such steps as may be necessary to assure that you are eligible to remain, and remain, a member of the group covered by the firm's health and life insurance policy. In this connection, you will have the opportunity to purchase from the firm's health and life insurance carrier such coverage as the carrier offers at group rates, and at your own expense. If the firm, rather than you, is

1. Taken from Appendix C to *Law Partnership: Its Rights and Responsibilities,* by George H. Cain, American Bar Association, 1996. That publication also contains a discussion of the case law interpreting noncompetition clauses in Of Counsel and law partnership agreements.

billed by the carrier, then the firm, in turn, will bill you for the amount that shall be reimbursable to the firm.

3. *Duties of the Firm.* In addition to offering the insurance coverage aforementioned, the firm will provide you with an office in the firm's ______________ [location] facility, equivalent in size to an associate's office, as long as you make minimal use thereof. The firm will also provide secretarial assistance, limited to (a) handling of correspondence related to professional organizations of which you may be a member, (b) forwarding of mail to you, and (c) responding to telephone calls made to you. You will also have access to all the firm's office services (telephone, computer online service, facsimile, photocopy, and so forth). The firm will pay or reimburse you for the use of parking facilities in the building where your office is located. The firm will pay or reimburse you for the dues of the American Bar Association, the [state] Bar Association, and the [local] Bar Association. Reimbursement, if any, of your expenses for attendance at meetings of such organizations will require the firm's approval before you incur such expenses. You are invited to attend meetings of the partnership. Upon your request to the secretary of the Executive Committee, you will receive copies of agenda materials for such meetings.

4. *Compensation.* You will receive no compensation from the firm for your service as Of Counsel. In consideration of the provision of services mentioned in paragraph 3, above, you agree to assist the firm, to a reasonable degree, with client development efforts upon request by the firm, but not to exceed the expenditure by you of more than five hours per month. Should you incur any out-of-pocket expenditures for such activity (such as, for example, expenses for client entertainment or meals), you will be reimbursed by the firm therefor.

5. *Retirement Benefit; No Competition.* During your service as Of Counsel, the firm will pay to you the retirement benefit provided for Retired Partners under the firm's partnership agreement. As long as the firm is paying such benefit to you, you will refrain from the active practice of law. "Active practice of law" means the provision of legal service or advice to clients, whether or not for compensation; however, it does not include serving as an arbitrator or mediator in your personal capacity and not as a representative of this firm (and off its premises), nor writing articles or making addresses to professional organizations. Should the firm request that you perform any legal services, by way of providing advice to other lawyers of the firm or to clients of the firm, the firm will first agree with you upon an appropriate method and amount of compensation, and will undertake to provide and pay for legal malpractice insurance for you. Except as stated in the preceding sentence, and except to the extent otherwise required by provisions of the partnership agreement, the firm will not provide you with any legal malpractice insurance.

6. *Arbitration.* Any dispute between us arising out of this agreement shall be settled by arbitration in the city of ____________________, state of

__________, according to the commercial arbitration rules of the American Arbitration Association, before a single arbitrator who shall be a partner in a law firm with at least seven (7) partners, and who shall have been a member of the bar of the state of __________ for at least thirty (30) years. Judgment upon any arbitration award may be entered and enforced in any court of competent jurisdiction. Notwithstanding the foregoing, either party to this agreement, by notice to the American Arbitration Association, may insist that the arbitration be conducted by three arbitrators and that the arbitrators be selected as prescribed in the partnership agreement.

7. *Term.* This agreement shall extend for a period of one (1) year from the date hereof, but shall be renewable from year to year for additional periods of one (1) year, upon your application to the Executive Committee of the firm, submitted at least sixty (60) days before the anniversary date hereof. The Executive Committee shall act upon the application within thirty (30) days after its receipt; but failing such action, this agreement shall be renewed on the same terms for the further period of one (1) year from the date hereof.

If the foregoing is satisfactory, please sign and return one counterpart of this letter to me to evidence our agreement. We look forward to your acceptance and to a continuation of our long and pleasant relationship.

Sincerely,

JONES & SMITH

By ______________________________
A Partner

APPENDIX 🕮 G

Of Counsel Agreement

[Letterhead of Law Firm]

[Month, Day, Year]

John J. Doe, Esq.
1000 Broadway
Major City, ZZ 00000

Dear John:

We are delighted that we have reached an understanding with you with regard to your affiliation with Law Firm XY&Z (the "Firm"). This letter will confirm in writing our understanding regarding your relationship with the Firm, and supersedes any other arrangement, whether or not reduced to writing, you may have had with this Firm. This letter also sets forth the terms of our offer.

Commencing on [month, day, year], you will have an Of Counsel position in the Firm. As Of Counsel, you will be expected to perform legal services on business generated by you and by other members of the Firm and to meet a commitment of a minimum of 1800 billable hours and 100 non-billable business development hours per fiscal year. You will be assigned to the Labor and Employment Practice Group. Your practice and activities will be under the direct supervision of Mr. John J. Smith, Esq.

Election to Partnership is accomplished by vote of the Partners, once each year, based upon recommendations of the Firm's Executive Committee. Based on existing Firm policy, you will considered for election to Partnership for the Firm's fiscal year beginning [month, day, year,], or at such time as the Executive Committee considers it appropriate. Since at least at the outset, virtually all your practice will be devoted to [special client], the work you perform to increase the amount of [special client] business received by the Firm and to maintain the existing [special client] business will be taken into account and given great value in the process of your evaluation for Partner.

Following one year of employment, you may enter the Firm's Profit Sharing Plan on the next entry date of April 1 or October 1, provided you work over 1000 hours. If you become a Partner, you would then be required to contribute 10% of Partner compensation to the Firm's Profit Sharing Plan. Those mandatory contributions would be withheld from your Partner compensation as paid.

You also will be eligible to make salary deferral contributions to the Firm's 401(k) Plan, at the first plan entry date following your first year anniversary (subject to the Plan's provision).

The Firm will expect you to devote all of your time and effort to the practice of law with XY&Z, and all legal fees or other forms of compensation related to your professional services, from whatever source, shall be the income of the Firm.

Our Firm has a commitment to civic and pro bono activities, and reasonable amounts of time devoted to bar association, civic affairs, and so forth are consistent with your practice with the Firm.

You will be compensated an annualized rate of [salary figure] payable semimonthly. You will receive the following benefits:

1. Aggregate annual reimbursement of up to $1,000.00 for dues for country clubs, downtown luncheon clubs, athletic clubs, and other civic and social organizations that you may be interested in pursuing;
2. Comprehensive hospitalization and major medical insurance (Firm pays single premium only, effective on the 91st day of employment, but family coverage is available; Cafeteria Plan with "premium conversion" available for health insurance family premiums);
3. $150,000 group term life insurance, effective one month from date of hire;
4. Long-term disability insurance, effective date of hire;
5. $150,000 group term accidental death and dismemberment insurance, effective one month from date of hire;
6. Two weeks paid vacation annually;
7. Dues for American, [state], and [local] Bar Associations and similar preapproved professional associations;
8. Bar exam and bar review classes as necessary to take the [state] bar exam;
9. Continuing legal education, including tuition, travel, and other costs of attending preapproved specialized seminars;
10. Professional liability insurance;
11. Up to 90 days paid disability leave.

The Firm does not offer employment on a fixed term basis, and any representations in this letter or during our meetings with you should not be construed as a proposed contract for any fixed term. Either you or the Firm has the right to terminate our association for any reason.

The Firm will review your performance from time to time in the Firm's discretion, with the expectation that a formal review will be made approximately annually. Your rate of compensation may be adjusted, either up or down, in connection with any such review. The Firm reserves the right to adjust the formal review schedule based upon its fiscal year, interim evaluations, and scheduling of other professional personnel reviews.

You have disclosed to us any potential claims against you for any act or omission in the conduct of any business conducted by you in your professional capacity as a lawyer. You agree to and do hereby indemnify and hold this Firm and its present and future partners harmless from any responsibility or liability to contribute money to any judgment based on or settlement of any such claim (whether so disclosed or not). You understand that this Firm will not apply to our professional liability carrier for prior acts coverage for you, and therefore, any professional liability coverage for any claim arising from any act or omission in the conduct of any business conducted by you in your professional capacity as a lawyer prior to your joining this Firm as Of Counsel must be purchased by you individually. You will, of course, be covered by the Firm's professional liability insurance policy for any act or omission in your professional capacity occurring after the date you become Of Counsel.

We trust that this letter sets forth our mutual understandings with respect to your affiliation with our Firm as Of Counsel. If there are any questions regarding our arrangement, please contact me. Assuming this letter is satisfactory, please indicate your acceptance by signing and returning to me the enclosed copy of this letter. We certainly look forward to your joining us in the practice of law and to our mutual development of your practice.

Sincerely,

XY&Z Law Firm

By: Z, Managing Partner

APPENDIX H

Formal Opinion 330 (August 1972)

The relationship indicated by term "Of Counsel" is a close, continuing, personal relationship between an individual lawyer and a law firm or lawyer, and the relationship is one that is not that of a partner, associate, or outside consultant. A law firm may not be "Of Counsel" to another lawyer or law firm. While a lawyer conceivably could be "Of Counsel" to two law firms or lawyers, one cannot simultaneously have more than a maximum of two "Of Counsel" relationships. The term "Of Counsel" may be used if it correctly describes the existing relationship, on letterheads and professional announcement cards and in law lists and directories.

Code of Professional Responsibility; DR 2-102(A)(1), (2), (3), (4) and (6); DR 2-1-2(C) and (D); EC 2-13.

This Committee has been requested to reconsider Informal Opinions 1173 (February 19, 1971) and 1189 (September 8, 1971), particularly with regard to whether professional corporations may be shown to be "Of Counsel" or "In Association With" another firm, lawyer, or professional corporation. The Committee has reconsidered those opinions and has determined that a Formal Opinion will be helpful in clarifying the matter. Clarification is in order because the Code of Professional Responsibility uses the term "Of Counsel" only in DR 2-102(A)(4) relating to letterheads, yet the problems concerning "Of Counsel" arise in connection with other professional notices.

Generally speaking, the Code regulates the conduct of lawyers without regard to whether a particular lawyer practices as a solo practitioner, a partner in a partnership, a member of a professional legal association, or as an associate of another. The provisions of the Code evidence a desire, however, that the particular relationship existing between or among lawyers be stated clearly so that the public will not be misled. *See* EC 2-13, *cf.* DR 2-102(C) and (D). EC 2-13 states:

> In order to avoid the possibility of misleading persons with whom he deals, a lawyer should be scrupulous in the representation of his professional status. He should not hold himself out as being a partner or associate of a law firm if he is not one in fact, and thus should not hold himself out as a partner or associate if he only shares offices with another lawyer.

Even though lawyers are thus admonished to be scrupulous in the representation of their professional status and relationships, terms such as "associate" and "Of Counsel" are not defined. The Ethical Considerations and Disciplinary Rules of the Code generally speak in terms of what a *lawyer* must or should do or not do. Occasionally reference is made to a *law firm,* which is said (in the Code's Definitions) to include a *professional legal corporation.* In some instances, reference is made to the *partners* or *associates* of a lawyer. Yet none of these status-indicating terms, other than "law firm" and "professional legal corporation," is defined in the Code. Accordingly, clarification is dependent upon a determination of the scope of "associate," "professional associates," and "Of Counsel" as these terms are used in DR 2-102(A)(1), (2), (4) and (6).

It has been said, "The word 'associate' has a variety of meanings. Principally through custom the word when used on letterheads of law firms has come to be regarded as describing those who are lawyer employees of the firm. Because the word has acquired this special significance in connection with the practice of law the use of the word to describe relationships other than that of employer-employee is likely to be misleading." *In re Sussman,* 241 Ore. 246, 405 P.2d 355 (1965). ABA Opinion 310 (1963) adds that "associates" may be used "to describe a situation in which the firm or the individual [lawyer] has other lawyers working for them or him who are not partners and who do not generally share in the responsibility and liability for the acts of the firm." *Also see* Opinion 219 (1941), holding that the use of "associates" negates the existence of a partnership in which they are partners.

The use of the term "Of Counsel" was considered in Informal Opinions 678 (1963), 710 (1964), and 1134 (1969). In Informal Opinion 678 it was said, "It is the impression of the members of this Committee that the term, 'Of Counsel,' shown on a firm's letterhead or shingle, is customarily used to indicate a former partner who is on a retirement or semi-retirement basis, or one who has retired from another partnership or the general private practice or from some public position, who remains available to the firm for consultation and advice, either generally or in a particular field." Opinion 678 concluded that it would be misleading to use "Of Counsel" where the relationship involved only an individual case.

Informal Opinion 710 permitted the name of a retiring judge to appear as "Of Counsel" to a firm that included his son, a former law partner. The opinion stated in part, "From your letter of inquiry we infer that you do not intend to become a partner in the new firm nor would you be an 'associate' inasmuch as you would not be an employee of the firm, although perhaps you would (1) share responsibility and liability with the firm in those cases in which you become 'Of Counsel' . . . or (2) be recompensed in those cases on an independent contractor basis, without sharing responsibility and liability with the firm."

Turning to Informal Opinion 1173, we find its basic holding to be consistent with the guidance gleaned from the authorities cited above. Informal Opinion 1173 correctly held that, under DR 2-102(A)(4), a Chicago law firm may not be shown as "Of Counsel" on the letterhead of a New York lawyer or law firm. It also held, and we reaffirm, that it would be improper to "permit a law firm ever to be designated 'Of Counsel,' in legal directories, [or] in shingles, letterheads or cards of another lawyer or law firm wherever located." DR 2-102(A)(4) states that "[a] lawyer may be designated 'Of Counsel' on a letterhead if he has a continuing relationship with a lawyer or law firm, other than as partner or associate." Without necessarily adopting the descriptive language in Informal Opinion 678, we recognize that DR 2-102(A)(4) uses "Of Counsel" in a manner not inconsistent with earlier usage and that the term relates to an individual lawyer. Thus the term cannot be used with regard to a law firm, whether it be a partnership or professional legal corporation.

Informal Opinion 1173 also held that "it is not proper . . . for any lawyer or law firm to be designated 'Of Counsel' to more than one lawyer or law firm. . . ." Upon reconsideration, we recognize that, while it would be highly unusual for a lawyer to be able to maintain simultaneously with two law firms the close, personal relationship indicated by the term "Of Counsel," it may not be impossible, however, for one to maintain such a relationship with more than two law firms. This conclusion requires a restatement of the nature of the relationship that is indicated by the description "Of Counsel."

The lawyer who is described as being "Of Counsel" to another lawyer or law firm must have a continuing (or semipermanent) relationship with that lawyer or firm, and not a relationship better described as a forwarder-receiver of legal business; *see* DR 2-102(A)(4), and *cf.* DR 2-107(A). His relationship with that lawyer or firm must not be that of partner (or fellow member of a professional legal corporation) nor that of an employee; *see* DR 2-102(A)(4). His relationship with the lawyer or law firm must be a close, regular, personal relationship like, for example, the relationship of a retired or semi-retired former partner, who remains available to the firm for consulting and advice, or a retired public official who regularly and locally is available to the firm for consultation and advice; *see* Informal Opinion 678. While it would be misleading to refer to a lawyer who shares in the profits and losses and general responsibility of a firm as being "Of Counsel," the lawyer who is "Of Counsel" may be compensated on a basis of consultation fees; *see* Informal Opinion 710. He is compensated as a *sui generis* member of that law office, however, and not as an outside consultant. Generally speaking, the close, personal relationship indicated by the term "Of Counsel" contemplates either that the lawyer practice in the offices of the lawyer or law firm to which he is "Of Counsel" or that his relationship, for example by virtue of past partnership of a retired partner that has led to continuing close association, be so close that he is in regular and frequent, if not daily, contact with the office of the lawyer or firm; *see* Informal Opinion 1134. The term obviously does not apply to the relationship which is merely that of a forwarder and receiver of legal business. In short, the individual lawyer who properly may be shown to be "Of Counsel" to a lawyer or law firm is a member or component part of that law office, but his status is not that of a partner or an employee (nor that of a controlling member of a professional legal corporation).

Given this view of the relationship indicated by the term "Of Counsel," it follows that one lawyer possibly could have the requisite relationship with two firms simultaneously, for example, one with which he practiced for many years before his retirement and another at a location to which he has moved after retirement. It has been recognized that a lawyer may be a member of two law firms (*see* New York State Opinion 231); and there is no per se prohibition against one's being "Of Counsel" to two law firms, even though this would seem impossible if the lawyer were currently a partner in any other firm, and even though it may be difficult for the lawyers to avoid other ethical problems such as the problem of differing interests; *see* DR 5-105(D); *cf.* Informal Opinion 710. To the extent that one lawyer does in fact have the requisite relationships properly designated "Of Counsel" to more than one lawyer or law firm simultaneously, Informal Opinion 1189 is modified.

Informal Opinion 1189 considered the question whether the designation "Of Counsel" may be used in connection with directories, law lists, shingles, and cards. The problem was created because the term "Of Counsel" was used only in regard to letterheads, subdivision (4) of DR 2-102(A).

Where a relationship exists which may be described accurately as an "Of Counsel" relationship, we hold that the relationship may be designated on a professional announcement card (see subd. 2), on a shingle (subd. 3), and in a law list or legal directory (subd. 6).

Little difficulty is encountered with regard to professional announcement cards, for subdivision 2 of DR 2-102(A) permits the use of a card stating "changed associations . . . or similar matters. . . ." The change of a lawyer's status to "Of Counsel," or the addition to the firm's ranks of a lawyer whose status factually will be "Of Counsel," falls within the quoted language and is permissible.

Subdivision 3 of DR 2-102(A) in general language permits a lawyer or law firm to use a shingle. Neither this subdivision nor the statements of underlying policy in the Ethical Considerations indicate any reason to prohibit the use of the term "Of Counsel" to indicate the status of an affiliated lawyer if the term accurately indicates the true relationship of the lawyers.

Proper interpretation of subdivision 6 of DR 2-102(A) is more difficult. That provision states in detail what may appear in a listing in a reputable law list or legal directory. In part, subdivision 6 states, "The published data may include only the following: name, including name of law firm and names of professional associates. . . ." "Of Counsel" is not listed among the permitted items of information. It is our opinion, however, that "professional associates" as used in subdivision 6 is intended to refer not only to "associates" but also to the affiliated lawyer who is more accurately described as being "Of Counsel."

Although we held that a listing in a law directory may properly show, if the statement describes the professional status accurately, that a lawyer is "Of Counsel" to the lawyer or law firm, we find nothing in the list of permissible data to support a view that the listing of a lawyer or law firm may include a reference to another lawyer or law firm that works, either occasionally or regularly, *in association with* the listed firm, or to whom or from whom legal business is occasionally or regularly referred. We believe that it is not permissible to include the statement in a listing that another lawyer or law firm is "New York Counsel," "In Association With," "Correspondent," and so forth. Thus, we construe "names of professional associates" to include only an individual lawyer whose status is accurately described either as that of partner in a firm, an employee of a lawyer or law firm, a member of a professional legal corporation, or one who is "Of Counsel." This much is reasonably necessary in order to make clear the professional status of the lawyers affiliated with an office; but to permit more under the guise of listing the "names of professional associates" would be to permit a degree of advertising not contemplated by DR 2-102(A)(6). Informal Opinion 1189 is modified to the extent it is inconsistent with the views here expressed.

APPENDIX I

Formal Opinion 90-357 (May 10, 1990)

Use of Designation "Of Counsel"; Withdrawal of Formal Opinion 330 (1972) and Informal Opinions 678 (1963), 710 (1964), 1134 (1969), 1173 (1971), 1189 (1971) and 1246 (1972)

The use of the title "of counsel," or variants of that title, in identifying the relationship of a lawyer or law firm with another lawyer or firm is permissible as long as the relationship between the two is a close, regular, personal relationship and the use of the title is not otherwise false or misleading.

In this opinion the Committee revisits the general subject of use of the title "of counsel." The subject was last comprehensively addressed by the Committee in Formal Opinion 330 (1972), and one or another aspect of the subject has also been addressed by the Committee in a number of informal opinions, both before and after Formal Opinion 330.[1] The reasons

1. Informal Opinion 678 (1963), Informal Opinion 710 (1964), Informal Opinion 1134 (1969), Informal Opinion 1173 (1971), Informal Opinion 1189 (1971), Informal Opinion 1246 (1972), Informal Opinion 1315 (1975), and Informal Opinion 84-1506 (1984). The present opinion supersedes both Formal Opinion 330 and the referenced informal opinions that preceded it, and those opinions are hereby withdrawn.

This opinion is based on the Model Rules of Professional Conduct and, to the extent indicated, the predecessor Model Code of Professional Responsibility of the American Bar Association. The laws, court rules, regulations, codes of professional responsibility, and opinions promulgated in the individual jurisdictions are controlling.

for considering yet again this much-visited subject are several. One is that there has been a proliferation of variants of the term "of counsel," and of arrangements that one or another such variant term has been used to designate, not all of which are addressed by the Committee's prior opinions. Another reason is that the Committee's prior opinions may be unjustifiably restrictive with regard to some relationships that are commonly designated by the term "of counsel." Finally, it is desirable to consider whether the supersession of the ABA Model Code of Professional Responsibility (1969, amended 1980) by the ABA Model Rules of Professional Conduct (1983, amended 1989) warrants any modification of the Committee's previously announced views, all of which had reference solely to the Model Code or to its predecessor, the Canons of Professional Ethics.

To address the last question first, it is the Committee's conclusion that there have been no changes involved in the transition from Model Code to Model Rules that have any substantive effect on the use of the term "of counsel." The Model Code included a specific reference to the title "of counsel" in DR 2-102(A)(4), relating to letterheads, and the term does not appear in the Model Rules; but there is no substantive significance to this difference. Moreover, the textual basis in both the Model Rules and the Model Code for determining whether particular uses of the title are or are not ethically permissible is in substance the same—a prohibition against misleading representations—although the particular provisions embodying this prohibition are different in form. Model Rule 7.5(a) provides, in part, that "[a] lawyer shall not use a firm name, letterhead or other professional designation that violates Rule 7.1"; and the latter Rule states in part that "[a] lawyer shall not make a false or misleading communication about the lawyer or the lawyer's services." Similarly, DR 2-101(A) of the Model Code provides that "[a] lawyer in private practice shall not practice under a . . . name that is misleading, deceptive . . . or unfair statement or claim"; DR 2-102(B) provides that "[a] lawyer in private practice shall not practice under a . . . name that is misleading as to the identity of the lawyer or lawyers practicing under such name"; and EC 2-13 states that "[i]n order to avoid the possibility of misleading persons with whom he deals, a lawyer should be scrupulous in the representation of his professional status." The essence of the ethical requirement under both the Model Rules and the Model Code is avoidance of misrepresentations as to the lawyer's status, and the relationship between lawyer and firm.

Of present concern are the representations implied by the use of the title "of counsel" on letterheads, law lists, professional cards, notices, office signs and the like: that is, its use in circumstances where there is a holding out to the world at large about some general and continuing relationship between the lawyers and law firms in question. A different use of the same term occurs when a lawyer (or firm) is designated as of counsel in filings in a particular case: in such circumstances, there is no general holding out as to a continuing relationship, or as to a relationship that applies to anything but the individual case.[2]

The issues that have been addressed in the Committee's previous opinions and that will be revisited here are, generally speaking, of two kinds, relating respectively to defining the relationship among lawyers and firms that the title "of counsel" is properly understood to evoke, and to identifying the resulting ethical implications of and limitations on its use.

As to the meaning of the title, it is appropriate to note preliminarily that, although "of counsel" appears to be the most frequently used among the various titles employing the term "counsel" it is by no means the only use of that term to indicate a relationship between a lawyer and a law firm. Other such titles include the single word "counsel" and the terms "special counsel," "tax [or other specialty] counsel" and "senior counsel."[3] It is the Committee's view that, whatever the connotative differences evoked by these variants of the title "counsel," they all share the central, and defining, characteristic of the relationship that is denoted by the term "of counsel," and so should all be understood to be covered by the present opinion. That core characteristic properly denoted by the title "counsel" is, as stated in Formal Opinion 330, a "close, regular, personal relationship"; but a relationship which is neither that of a partner (or its equivalent, a principal of a professional corporation), with the shared liability and/or managerial responsibility implied by that term; nor, on the other hand, the status ordinarily conveyed by the term "associate," which is to say a junior non-partner lawyer, regularly employed by the firm.[4]

This core characteristic of the title "counsel" is shared by several kinds of relationships that in other respects vary in significant ways. There appear to be four principal patterns of such relationships, all of which in the Committee's view are properly referred to by the title "of counsel" (or one of its variants). Perhaps the most common of such relationships is that of a part-time practitioner who practices law in association with a firm,

---

2. The distinction between use of the term "counsel" on the filings in a particular case on the one hand, and in general announcements implying a continuing relationship on the other, is significant because, as discussed below, its use in the latter connection is improper when it rests on no more than collaboration in a single case. *See* note 7 below and accompanying text.

3. This opinion does not endeavor to address other terms of similar import that do not include the word counsel, such as "consultant," "consulting attorney," and "corresponding attorney."

4. Formal Opinion 330 relied in part on one passage in the Model Code that comes close to providing a definition of the term, DR 2-102(A)(4), which provides in part that "A lawyer may be designated 'Of Counsel' on a letterhead if he has a continuing relationship with a lawyer or law firm, other than as a partner or associate."

but on a basis different from that of the mainstream lawyers in the firm. Such part-time practitioners are sometimes lawyers who have decided to change from a full-time practice, either with that firm or with another, to a part-time one, or sometimes lawyers who have changed careers entirely, as for example former judges or government officials. A second common use of the term is to designate a retired partner of the firm who, although not actively practicing law, nonetheless remains associated with the firm and available for occasional consultation. A third use of the term is to designate a lawyer who is, in effect, a probationary partner-to-be: usually a lawyer brought into the firm laterally with the expectation of becoming partner after a relatively short period of time. A fourth, relatively recent, use of the term is to designate a permanent status in between those of partner and associate—akin to the category just described, but having the quality of tenure, or something close to it, and lacking that of an expectation of likely promotion to full partner status.[5]

In the Committee's view, the "of counsel" designation, or one of its variants, is appropriately applied to any of the four kinds of relationships just described. Prior opinions of the Committee may, however, be read as finding the term inapplicable to one or more of these relationships. For example, Formal Opinion 330 states that the relationship implied by "of counsel" would not be that of an employee of the firm, yet both the third and the fourth of the relationships identified in the preceding paragraph involve, as a technical matter, the status of an employee. Insofar as Formal Opinion 330 may be read to conclude that neither the probationary partner model nor the permanent between-partner-and-associate model are permissibly designated of counsel, that conclusion is disavowed. Additionally, Formal Opinion 330 may be read as limiting the permissible use of the term "of counsel" by retired partners of a firm, because of possible implications from language in that opinion that an of counsel lawyer must be compensated for such legal work as the lawyer does, but only for that legal work—which, if strictly read, would exclude both a retired partner whose sole income from the firm is the partner's pension or other retirement benefit and counsel who share in some degree in the firm's profits. *See also* Informal Opinion 710. It is the Committee's view that, the other conditions just described having been met, it is not relevant to the permissibility of use of "of counsel" what the compensation arrangements are.[6] Similarly, some retired partners might be deemed to be excluded by the suggestion in Formal Opinion 330 that an of counsel's relationship to the firm must be "so close that he is in regular and frequent, if not daily, con-

5. Other terms sometimes used to designate this status are "senior attorney" and "principal attorney."

6. The Committee expresses no view, however, on whether an arrangement under which the of counsel lawyer shares in the profits of the firm may expose the lawyer to malpractice liability as a partner.

tact with the office of the lawyer or firm" (citing Informal Opinion 1134). Again, insofar as Formal Opinion 330 carries any implication that the contact must be so frequent as to verge on daily, the Committee now disavows it.

Nonetheless, the Committee remains of the view, as stated in earlier opinions, that it is not ethically permissible to use the term "of counsel" to designate the following professional relationships: a relationship involving only an individual case, *see* Informal Opinion 678, Formal Opinion 330;[7] a relationship of forwarder or receiver of legal business, *see* Formal Opinion 330; a relationship involving only occasional collaborative efforts among otherwise unrelated lawyers or firms, *see id.*; and the relationship of an outside consultant, *see id.*

The characteristic of continuing and frequent professional contact bears particular emphasis in the context of use of the variant of the term "of counsel" that indicates a field of concentration: "tax counsel," "antitrust counsel" and the like. Such terms, although in the Committee's view as permissible as other variants of the term "counsel," must like them be confined to relationships that in fact involve frequent and continuing contacts, and not merely an availability for occasional consultations.[8] There is, moreover, in the term designating a specialty, a clear representation that the of counsel lawyer in fact has a special expertise in the designated area; and, for the firm, that it also has, by reason of the of counsel relationship, that special expertise.[9] It bears emphasis also that the use of a title indicating a specialty counsel, like the other uses here discussed, involves mutual attribution of all disqualifications of both the lawyer and the firm—and not just attribution with respect to matters falling within the designated area of specialty.

The Committee's previous opinions have expressed the view that a lawyer cannot properly be of counsel simultaneously with multiple firms, because the necessary "close, regular, personal relationship" cannot exist on a plural basis. Thus, the Committee's initial view, expressed in Informal Opinion 1173, was that a lawyer could not be of counsel to more than a single firm; this was modified in Formal Opinion 330 to set a limit of two firms. On further consideration, the Committee finds the conclusion it

---

7. The reference is not to the appearance of a lawyer or firm on the court filings of a particular case, but rather to representation of an "of counsel" relationship on firm letterhead, professional cards, and the like on the basis of collaboration on a single case. *See* text at note 2 above.

8. The use of such terms may also be subject to ethical provisions of a particular jurisdiction limiting the use of terms designating specialization. *See* Model Rule 7.4(c).

9. As on other points mentioned in this opinion, the Committee expresses no view as to the malpractice liability implications of such representation of special expertise.

reached on this subject in Formal Opinion 330 to be a doubtful one. The proposition that it is not possible for a lawyer to have a "close, regular, personal relationship" with more than two lawyers or law firms is not a self-evident one. A lawyer can surely have a close, regular, personal relationship with more than two clients; and the Committee sees no reason why the same cannot be true with more than two law firms. There is, to be sure, some point at which the number of relationships would be too great for any of them to have the necessary qualities of closeness and regularity, and that number may not be much beyond two, but the controlling criterion is "close and regular" relationships, not a particular number. As a practical matter, nonetheless, there is a consideration that is likely to put a relatively low limit on the number of "of counsel" relationships that can be undertaken by a particular lawyer: this is the fact that, as more fully discussed below, the relationship clearly means that the lawyer is "associated" with each firm with which the lawyer is of counsel. In consequence there is attribution to the lawyer who is of counsel of all the disqualifications of each firm, and, correspondingly, attribution from the of counsel lawyer to each firm of each of those disqualifications. *See* Model Rule 1.10(a). In consequence, the effect of two or more firms sharing of counsel lawyer is to make them all effectively a single firm, for purposes of attribution of disqualifications.

The Committee has also previously held that a firm cannot be of counsel to another lawyer or law firm, *see* Informal Opinion 1173; Formal Opinion 330. The reasoning here was that the term connotes an individual rather than a firm. This may be still so as a matter of current usage;[10] but semantics aside, the Committee's prior opinions do not suggest, and the Committee does not now perceive, any reason that a firm should not be of counsel to another firm. Moreover, the Committee held in Formal Opinion 84-351 (1984) that two law firms could ethically present themselves as "affiliated" or "associated" with each other, and in Informal Opinion 1315 (1975), the Committee gave its approval to arrangements whereby two firms effectively became "of counsel" to each other by each designating a partner of the other firm as "of counsel" to itself. As with multiple of counsel relationships of a single lawyer, the relationships between firms addressed in Formal Opinion 84-351 and Informal Opinion 1315 would of course entail complete reciprocal attribution of the disqualifications of all lawyers in each firm.

A final issue regarding permissible use of the title "of counsel" is presented by the question whether the name of a lawyer who is of counsel may also be included in the name of the firm to which the lawyer is of counsel. This question may arise in two different sorts of circumstance, which in the Committee's view lead to two different results. The first is

---

10. It may be noted that firms are quite conventionally identified as of counsel to other lawyers or firms on the signature page of court filings.

where a name partner in a firm retires from active practice and, as is of course permissible, the firm retains the lawyer's name in the firm name, *see* Model Code DR 2-102(B), *cf.* Model Rule 7.5(a) and Comment; but the retired partner also assumes of counsel status of the sort that has been described above. The second is a situation where the affiliation is altogether new, and where although the lawyer lends his or her name to the firm, the lawyer is not undertaking the responsibilities of a partner or principal.

The issue raised by both of these circumstances is whether they entail implicit representations to the public that are misleading. The Committee believes that in the case of a new or recent firm affiliation there is no escaping an implication that a name in the new firm name implies that the lawyer is a partner in the firm, with fully shared responsibility for its work. On the other hand, the Committee also believes that there is not a similar misleading implication in the use of a retired partner's name in the firm name, while the same partner is of counsel, where the firm name is long-established and well-recognized.[11]

To turn from consideration of the circumstances where use of the titles under discussion is or is not proper and address the ethical implications of and limitations on their use, the most important implication has already been averted to. There can be no doubt that an of counsel lawyer (or firm) is "associated in" and has an "association with" the firm (or firms) to which the lawyer is of counsel, for purposes of both the general imputation of disqualification pursuant to Rule 1.10 of the Model Rules and the imputation of disqualifications resulting from former government service under Rules 1.11(a) and 1.12(c); and is a lawyer in the firm for the purposes of Rule 3.7(b), regarding the circumstances in which, when a lawyer is to be a witness in a proceeding, the lawyer's colleague may nonetheless represent the client in that proceeding. Similarly, the of counsel lawyer is "affiliated" with the firm and its individual lawyers for purposes of the general attribution of disqualifications under DR 5-105(D) of the Model Code. *See* Formal Opinion 330; Formal Opinion 84-351.

An additional ethical consequence of the relationship implied by the term "of counsel" is that in any listing, on a letterhead, shingle, bar listing or professional card, which shows the of counsel's lawyer's name, any pertinent jurisdictional limitations on the lawyer's entitlement to practice must be indicated. *See* Model Rule 7.5(d); Model Code DR 2-102(D).

---

11. The Committee does not express a view as to whether, when the retired partner's name remains included in the firm name, the retired partner may on that account be exposed to malpractice liability as if he or she were still a general partner.

TABLE OF CASES

Akerly v. Red Barn Sys., Inc., 551 F.2d 539 (3d Cir. 1977), 132n
American Casualty Co. v. Costello, 174 Mich. App. 1, 435 N.W.2d 760 (1989), 78n, 79n
Artromick International, Inc. v. Drustar, Inc., 134 F.R.D. 226, 231 (S.D. Ohio 1991), 123n
Atasi Corp. v. Seagate Technology, 847 F.2d 826, 829, 830, 831, 832 (Fed. Cir. 1988), 124n, 134, 137n
Atasi Corp. v. Seagate Technology, 847 F.2d 826 (Fed. Cir. 1986), 125–126
Auchincloss v. United States Fidelity & Guar. Co., 190 A.D. 6, 179 N.Y.S. 454 (1st Dept. 1919), 171n
Bankers Trust Company v. Cerrato, Sweeney, Cohn, Stahl & Vaccaro, 187 A.D. 2d 384, 590 N.Y.S. 2d 201, 202 (First Department 1992), 103, 103n
Bates v. Arizona Bar Association, 433 U.S. 350, 384 (1977), 61n, 150–151, 152, 153
Blackmon v. Hale, 1 Cal.3d 548, 463 P.2d 418, 83 Cal. Rptr. 194 (1970), 105n
Bockian, Esanu, Katsky, Korins & Siger, 124 Misc. 2d 607, 476 N.Y.S.2d 1009 (1984), 94
Bonavire v. Wampler, 770 F.2d 1010 (11th Cir. 1985), 107–108
Brown v. Gerstein, 17 Mass. App. 558, 460 N.E.2d 1043 (1984), 107
Central Hudson Gas & Electric Company v. Public Service Commission of New York, 447 U.S. 557 (1980), 151

City of Cleveland v. Cleveland Elec. Illuminating Co., 440 F. Supp. 193, 209 (N.D. Ohio 1976), *aff'd* 537 F.2d 1310 (6th Cir. 1977), *cert. denied* 435 U.S. 996 (1978), 132n

Cohen v. Lipsig, 92 A.D. 536, 459 N.Y.S.2d 98 (Second Department 1983), 105

Complaint of Maritima Aragua. S.A., 847 F. Supp. 1177, 1181 (S.D.N.Y. 1994), 139–141

Cottman v. Cottman, 56 Md. App. 413, 468 A.2d 161 (1983), 108n

DeVaux v. American Home Assurance Co., 387 Mass. 814, 444 N.E.2d 355 (1983), 94n

Duggins v. Guardianship of Washington, 632 So. 2d 420, 35 ALR5th 909 (Miss. 1993), 104, 108n

Emle Indus. v. Patentex, Inc., 478 F.2d 562 (2d Cir. 1973), 132n

EZ Paintr Corp. v. Padco, Inc., 746 F.2d 1459, 1462 (Fed. Cir. 1984), 136n

Fitzgibbon v. Carey, 70 Or. App. 127, 688 P.2d 1367 (1984), 103n

Floro v. Lawton, 187 Cal. App. 2d 657, 10 Cal. Rptr. 98 (2d Dist. 1960), 104n

Fund of Funds, Ltd. v. Arthur Andersen & Co., 567 F.2d 225 (2d Cir. 1977), 131n

Goldfarb v. Virginia State Bar, 421 U.S. 773 (1975), 149–150

Grennan v. Well Built Sales of Richmond County, Inc., 35 Misc.2d 905, 231 N.Y.S.2d 625 (1962), 102n

Haagen-Dazs Co., 639 F. Supp. at 287, 136n, 137n

Hart v. Commercial Bank, 957 F. Supp. 958 (E.D. Mich. 1997), 107n

Heathcoat v. Santa Fe International Corp., 532 F. Supp. 961 (E.D.Ark. 1982), 122

Hirsch v. Weisman, 189 A.D.2d 643, 592 N.Y.S. 2d 337, 338 (First Department 1993), 101–102, 102n

Homa v. Friendly Mobile Manor, Inc., 93 Md. App. 337, 612 A.2d 322, 325, 326, 327, 328, 329, 330, 331, 332, 334, 335 (1992), 95n, 95–100, 96n, 97n, 98n, 99n, 100n

Husted v. Gwin, 446 N.E. 2d 1361 (Ind. App. 1983), 105n

In re Loomis, 273 N.Y. 76, 6 N.E.2d 103 (1937), 102n

In re Muscillo's Estate, 159 N.Y.S.2d 253 (Sur. 1957), 102n

In re Primus, 436 U.S. 412 (1978), 153

In re R.M.J., 455 U.S. 191 (1982), 61n, 150n, 151–152, 155

In re Sussman, 241 Or. 246, 405 P.2d 355 (1965), 79n

In re ZB Surfside Co., 1994 Bankr. LEXIS 1852 (Bankr. S.D.N.Y. 1994), 121n

International Business Mach. Corp. v. Levin, 579 F.2d 271 (3d Cir. 1978), 131n

Jackson v. Jackson, 20 N.C. App. 406, 201 S.E.2d 772 (1974), 105n

Jenson v. Touche Ross & Co., 335 N.W.2d 720, 730, 731, 732 (Minn. 1983), 124n, 135–136
Kirschenbaum v. Rehfield, 539 So. 2d 12 (Fla. Dist. App. Ct. 1989), 94n
Kiser v. Bailey, 92 Misc.2d 435, 400 N.Y.S.2d 312 (1977), 102n
Kovacevic v. Fair Automotive Repair, Inc., 641 F. Supp. 237, 244 (N.D. Ill. 1986), 136n
LaSalle Nat'l Bank v. Lake County, 703 F.2d 252 (7th Cir. 1983), 125n, 136n
Levy v. Jacobs, 5 Misc.2d 994, 148 N.Y.S.2d 607 (1955), 102n
Livingston v. Cox, 6 Pa. 2d 360 (1847), 104n
Loyola Federal S. & L. Ass'n v. Trenchcraft, 17 Md. App. 646, 663, 303 A.2d 432 (1973), 99n
Mahoney v. Middlesex County Comm'rs, 144 Mass 459, 11 N.E. 689 (1887), 93n
Manoir-Electroalloys Corp. v. Amalloy Corp., 711 F. Supp. 188 (D.N.J. 1989), 123n
Marketti v. Fitzsimmons, 373 F. Supp. 637 (W.D. Wis. 1974), 132n
McGarity v. Craighill, Rendleman, Ingle & Blythe, 63 N.C. App. 106, 349 S.E.2d 311 (1986), 93n
McGarity v. Craighill, Rendleman, Ingle & Blythe, 83 N.C. App. 106, 349 S.E.2d 313, 94n
Missan v. Schoenfeld, 95 A.D.2d 198, 465 N.Y.S.2d 706 (Sept. 1, 1983), 78n
Model Bldg. & Loan Ass'n v. Reeves, 114 Misc. 137, 186 N.Y.S. 759 (N.Y. Sup. Ct.), *rev'd on other grounds,* 201 A.D. 329, 194 N.Y.S. 383 (First Department), *rev'd,* 236 N.Y. 331, 140 N.E. 715 (1921), 105n
Monon Corporation v. Townsend, Yosha, Cline & Price, et al., Case No. 49A02-9511-CV-675 (Ind. App. 1997), 9–12
Moore v. State Bar, 62 Cal. 2d 74, 396 P.2d 577, 41 Cal. Rptr. 161 (1964), 105n
Mustang Enterprises v. Plug-In Storage, Inc., 874 F. Supp. 881 (N.D. Ill. 1995), 138–139
Mutual of Omaha Insurance Co. v. Chadwell, 426 F. Supp. 550, 551, 552 (N.D. Ill. 1977), 45, 82, 82n, 191
Myers v. Aragona, 21 Md. App. 45, 318 A.2d 263 (1974), 108
Nemet v. Nemet, 112 A.D.2d 359, 491 N.Y.S2d 810, 811 (2d Dept.), 119n
Nemet v. Nemet, 112 A.D.2d 359, N.Y.S2d (2d Dept. 1985), *appeal dismissed,* 66 N.Y.2d 602 (1986), 114n
Nemours Found. v. Gilbane, Aetna, Fed. Ins., 632 F. Supp. 418, 429 (D. Del. 1986), 136n
Noble v. Sears Roebuck & Co., 33 Cal. App. 3d 654, 109 Cal. Rptr. 269 (1973), 94n

Novo Terapeutisk Laboratorium A/S v. Baxter Travenol Laboratories, Inc., 607 F.2d 186 (7th Cir. 1979), 132n
Ohralik v. Ohio State Bar Association, 436 U.S. 447 (1978), 153
Ortiz v. Barrett, 222 Va. 118, 278 S.E.2d 833 (1981), 103n
Panduit Corp. v. All States Plastic Mfg. Co., 744 F.2d 1564, 1580 (Fed. Cir. 1984), 132n
Peterson v. Harville, 445 F. Supp. 16 (D. Or. 1977); *aff'd* 623 F.2d 611 (9th Cir. 1980), 105n
P/T Ltd. II v. Friendly Mobile Manor, 79 Md. App. 227, 556 A.2d 694 (1989), 96n
Royal Bank & Trust Co. v. Weintraub, Gold & Alper, 68 N.Y.2d 124, 506 N.Y.S.2d 151, 497 N.E.2d 289 (1986), 110n
Schiessle v. Stephens, 717 F.2d 417 (7th Cir. 1983), 132n, 136n
Shapero v. Kentucky Bar Association, 486 U.S. 466, 469–71, 475, 479 (1988), 153–154, 157–159, 160n
Silver Chrysler Plymouth, Inc. v. Chrysler Motors Corp., 518 F.2d 751, 756–57 (2d Cir. 1975), 124n, 125n, 132n
Smith v. Whatcott, 757 F.2d 1098, 1101–02 (10th Cir. 1985), 136n
Staron v. Weinstein, 701 A.2d 1325, 1997 N.J. Super. LEXIS 440 (1997), 100–101
T.C. Theatre Corp. v. Warner Bros. Pictures, 113 F. Supp. 265 (S.D.N.Y. 1953), 132n
Tennent Shoe Co. v. Birdseye, 78 S.W. 1036 (Mo. App. 1904), 105n
Tormo v. Yormark, 398 F. Supp. 1158 (D.N.J. 1975), 104–105
Trittipo v. O'Brien (Ill. App., 1990), 47n
Trone v. Smith, 621 F.2d 994 (9th Cir. 1980), 124n
United States *ex rel.* Lord Elec. Co. v. Titan Pacific Constr. Corp., 637 F.Supp. 1556, 1559, 1560, 1565–66 (W.D. Wash. 1986), 124n, 132n, 133–134, 136n, 137
United States v. American Bar Association Civil No. 76-1182 (D.D.C. 1976), 150
Ventro v. Darlson, 468 So. 2d 463 (Fla. App. 4 Dist. 1985), 110n
Virginia State Board of Pharmacy v. Virginia Citizens Consumer Council, 425 U.S. 748 (1976), 150
Walker v. Stevens, 79 Ill. 193 (1875), 93n
Westinghouse Elec. Corp. v. Kerr-McGee Corp., 580 F.2d 1311 (7th Cir.), *cert. denied* 439 U.S. 955 (1978), 131n
Williams v. Burns, 463 F. Supp. 1278 (D. Colo. 1979), 105n
Young v. Bridwell, 20 Utah 2d 332, 437 P.2d 686 (1968), 93n
Zauderer v. Office of Disciplinary Counsel, 471 U.S. 626 (1985), 152–153

INDEX

ABRA (American Bar Retirement Association), 181
advertising, 17, 61–62, 147–148, 159–164
  effect of First Amendment on, 150–154
  ethics rules governing, 154–157
  ethics rules governing solicitation, 157–159
  Formal Opinion 330 on, 24
  history of, 149–150
  listing areas of specialization on letterhead, 163–164
  listing out-of-state Of Counsel on letterhead, 162–163
  Of Counsel's name in firm name, 160–162
  and solicitation, 148–149, 153
agency, 97–98
agreements. *See* Of Counsel agreement
Aisenstark, Avory, 8
American Bar Retirement Association (ABRA), 181
American Civil Liberties Union, 153
apparent authority doctrine, 80, 94
associate
  contrasted with Of Counsel, 79–80
  versus employee, 20–21
  permissibility of status, 20–24, 37
associated counsel, and malpractice, 103–105
Azrael, Mimi, 3

Bachmand & Lapointe, P.C., 138–139
Barnes & Thornburg, 9–12
benefit programs, 36–37, 168–169, 198–200
Blumenthal, Harry, 5
Boies, David, Jr., 5
Bondy, Thomas, 102
breach of contract, 93
breach of fiduciary duty, 93
Brill, Steven, 5
Brokerage & Management Corp., 140–141
business deductions, 84

Cain, George M., 4
Callimanopulos, Gregory, 139–141
Canons of Professional Ethics, 149
career changes, 4–5, 47–48
Chinese wall defense, 136–137
"close, continuing, personal" relationship (Formal Opinion 330), 19–20

"close, regular, personal" relationship (Formal Opinion 90-357), 31–37, 42
  compensation, 35–37
  firms Of Counsel to one another, 32–34
  required contact with the firm, 32
  specialty counsel, 34–35
compensation
  Formal Opinion 90-357, 35–37
  Formal Opinion 93-374, 35n
  Formal Opinion 330, 21–22
  in Of Counsel agreement, 167–168, 193–196
  Of Counsel as firm's organizational structure, 183
  outside consultant, 87–79
conflicts of interest, 113–114
  advancing inconsistent positions, 123
  disqualification of Of Counsel, 124–126
  duties of the lawyer, 114–115
  effect of Formal Opinion 90–357, 117–123
  under Model Rules, 115–117
  outside consultant, 87
  peripheral-representation exception, 124–126
  in simultaneous representation, 118–121
  in successive representation, 121–123
consultants. *See* outside consultant
contract, breach of, 93
contract, privity of, 93
contractual liability, 82–83, 94
control, 170–171
core characteristics, 30–38, 74
Cravath Swaine & Moore, 5

delayed retirement credit, 173
direct-mail solicitation, 154
discharge, right to, 86
disqualification. *See* conflicts of interest; imputed disqualification
duties, in Of Counsel agreement, 169, 191–193

elected officials, 15–16, 56–58, 141–143
e-mail, 109n
employee
  versus associate, 20–21
  versus independent contractor, 80–86
  permissibility of employee status, 37–38, 183
employment agreement, example of, 203–211
employment-at-will doctrine, 86
errors and omissions, 93, 198–199
estoppel, 107, 108–111
ethics rules
  governing advertising, 154–157
  governing solicitation, 157–159
expense-sharing arrangements, 59–60
express partnership, 77–79, 105–108

fidelity bond, 171n
fiduciary duty, breach of, 93
financial planning, 172–174
firm. *See* law firm
First Amendment, effect on lawyer advertising, 150–154
Formal Opinion 84-351, 138–139, 140
Formal Opinion 90-357, 27–28, 238–244
  compensation, 35–37
  and conflicts of interest, 117–123
  core characteristics of Of Counsel relationship, 30–38
    "close, regular, personal" relationship, 31–37, 42
    employee status is permissible, 37–38
    partner or associate status is not permissible, 37
  designations governed by, 28–29
  expense-sharing arrangements, 59–60
  impermissible relationships, 30
  law firm as Of Counsel, 39–40, 61–64
  law firms as Of Counsel to one another, 32–34

law professors, 58
liberalized rules governing Of Counsel relationships, 60–68
law firm as Of Counsel, 61–64
multiple Of Counsel relationships, 64–66
Of Counsel's name in firm's name, 66–68
multiple Of Counsel relationships, 38–39, 64–66
Of Counsel's name in firm name, 40, 66–68
out-of-state Of Counsel, 58–59
permissible relationships, 29–30, 43–51
part-time practitioner, 29, 47–48
permanent senior attorney, 29–30
probationary partner, 29, 48–49
retired partner, 29, 43–47
senior attorney, 49–51
prohibited relationships, 51–56
forwarder-receiver of legal business, 52
lawyer associated in single case, 51–52
occasional collaborator, 52–53
Of Counsel versus outside consultant, 53–56
public officials, 56–58
required contact with the firm, 32
specialty counsel, 34–35
Formal Opinion 330, 233–237
advertising, 24
"close, continuing, personal" relationship, 19–20
compensation, 21–22
defining Of Counsel, 18
law firms as Of Counsel, 23–24
multiple Of Counsel relationships, 22–23
"not a partner, associate, or outside consultant," 20–24
Formal Opinion 93-374, on compensation, 35n
Formal Opinion 94-388, on law firms as Of Counsel to one another, 33–34
forwarder-receiver relationship, 52
FranData Corp., 4
free speech, 150–154
Friendly Mobile Manor, Inc., 95–100
fringe benefits, 36–37, 168–169, 198–200

government officials and employees, 15–16, 56–58, 141–143

Hartog, Fay, 3–4
health care reform, 175–178
Hill, Steadman & Simpson, 138–139
holding out, 107
Homa, Leonard S., 95–100
Hospital Insurance (HI), 85n, 172–174

implied partnership, 77–79, 105–108
imputed disqualification, 113–114, 129
affiliated law firms, 138–141
former government employees, 141–143
and lawyer as witness, 143–145
presumption of shared confidences, 130–137
Chinese wall defense, 136–137
former affiliates: rebuttable presumption, 131–136
present affiliates: irrebuttable presumption, 130–131
rules governing, 129–130
income taxation. *See* taxation
indemnification, 198–199
independent contractor
versus employee, 80–86, 169–179
and malpractice, 94
and partnership, examples of agreement, 212–214, 215–217, 223–226
and professional service corporation, example of agreement, 218–222
tax advantages, 169–172
Informal Opinion 678, 14, 51, 54
Informal Opinion 710, 15
Informal Opinion 1134, 15, 57

Informal Opinion 1173, 61
Informal Opinions, defining Of Counsel, 13–18
irrebuttable presumption, 130–131

judges, mandatory retirement for, 5n. *See also* public officials

Kaplan, Howard, 7
Kolton, Jeff, 4

law firm
  imputed disqualification and affiliated law firms, 138–141
  as Of Counsel, 16, 23–24, 39–40, 61–64
  Of Counsel organizational structure, 182–186
  Of Counsel's name in firm name, 40, 66–68, 160–162
  as Of Counsel to one another, 32–34
  required contact with the firm, 32
law professors, 58
lawyer
  represented by another lawyer, 116
  as witness, 143–145
lawyer advertising. *See* advertising
legal malpractice. *See* malpractice
letterhead
  examples of, 227–229, 230–232
  listing out-of-state Of Counsel on, 162–163
  listing specialization areas on, 163–164
Levan, Schimel, Richman and Belman, P.A., 95–100
Lewis, Warren L., 4
Lewis & Trattner, 4
liability
  contractual, 82–83, 94
  professional liability, 184
  vicarious liability in tort, 93
LLEs (limited liability entities), 10n
long-term care insurance, 176n
Louis Buddy Yosha Professional Corporation, 110–111

Major League Baseball, 5
malpractice, 92–93
  associated counsel, 103–105
  express or implied partnership, 105–108
  independent contractors, 94
  lawyer represented by another lawyer, 116
  liability based on contractual arrangements, 94
  and Of Counsel relationship, 95–103
  partnership by estoppel, 108–111
  vicarious liability in tort, 93
malpractice insurance, 83, 168, 184
Maraven, 139–141
Mar Coral, 139–141
Medicare, 85n, 170, 172–174
Medigap insurance, 174
Michigan Standing Committee on Professional and Judicial Ethics, 120–121
misrepresentation, 75–79
Model Code of Professional Responsibility, 13–18, 27–28, 141, 155–157
Model Rules of Professional Conduct, 27–28, 113, 115–117, 130, 141–142, 158
Monon Corporation, 9–12, 110–111
multiple Of Counsel relationships, 16–17
  Formal Opinion 90-357, 38–39, 64–66
  Formal Opinion 330, 22–23

negligence, 93
New Jersey Supreme Court Committee on Attorney Advertising, 162–163
New York City Ethics Committee, 162

OASDI (Old-Age, Survivors, and Disability Insurance), 85n, 172–173
occasional collaborator, 52–53

Of Counsel, 1–2. *See also* Of Counsel agreement
  contrasted with associate, 79–80
  contrasted with outside consultant, 53–56, 86–89
  contrasted with partner, 75–79
  defining, 13–26
  as employee or independent contractor, 80–86
    contractual liability, 82–83
    income taxation, 84–85
    right to discharge, 86
    right to terminate, 86
    tort liability, 83
  versus other legal relationships, 73–75
  patterns of relationships, 2–12
    part-time lawyers, 2–4
    permanent status, 7–8
    probationary partner, 6–7
    retired partner, 6
    second careers, 4–5
Of Counsel agreement
  examples of, 212–232
    independent contractor and partnership, 212–214, 215–217, 223–226
    independent contractor and professional service corporation, 218–222
    letterhead of law firm, 227–229, 230–232
  financial planning and retirement, 172–174
  health care reform, 175–178
  independent contractor v. employer-employee relationship, 169–172
  part-time lawyer, 178–182
  and pension plan payments, 195–196
  planning, 188–189
  retired partner, 166–167
  tax advantages of independent contractor status, 169–172
  terms of, 167–169, 189–200
    compensation, 167–168, 193–196
    duties, 169, 191–193
    fringe benefits, 168–169, 198–200
    malpractice insurance, 168
    overhead, 196–197
    perquisites, 168
    protection of trade secrets, 168
    right to terminate, 200
    title and status, 189–191
  uses of, 166–186
  as vehicle for firm organization, 182–186
    compensation, 183
    employment status, 183
    malpractice insurance, 184
    overhead, 184
    professional liability, 184
    taxes, 184
office-sharing arrangements, 59–60
Old-Age, Survivors, and Disability Insurance (OASDI), 85n, 172–173
organizational structure of firm, 182–186
out-of-state Of Counsel, 58–59
out-of-state Of Counsel, listing on letterhead, 162–163
outside consultant, 21n, 86–89
  compensation, 87–89
  conflicts of interest, 87
  contrasted with Of Counsel, 53–56, 86–89
  permissibility of status, 20–24
outside counsel, and malpractice, 103–105
overhead, 59–60, 184, 196–197

partnership. *See also* retired partner
  contrasted with Of Counsel, 75–79
  implied, 77–79, 105–108
  and independent contractor, examples of agreement, 212–214, 215–217, 223–226
  permissibility of status, 20–24, 37
partnership by estoppel doctrine, 107, 108–111
part-time practitioner, 2–4
  Formal Opinion 90-357, 29, 47–48
  Of Counsel agreement, 178–182

Pascal Turner, Ltd. II, 95–100
Patterson, Belknap, Webb & Tyler, 7
payroll taxes, 172–173
pension programs, 188n, 195–196
peripheral-representation exception, 124–126
permanent Of Counsel status, 7–8
permanent senior attorney, 29–30
perquisites, 168
Plug-In Storage, Inc., 138–139
political officeholders, 15–16, 56–58, 141–143
Poole, William T., 95–100
presumption of shared confidences. *See* shared confidences
Price, Henry J., 9–12, 110–111
principal attorney. *See* senior attorney
privity of contract, 93
probationary partner, 6–7
  Formal Opinion 90-357, 29, 48–49
professional liability, 184
professional service corporation and independent contractor, example of
agreement, 218–222
professors of law, 58
public officials, 15–16, 56–58, 141–143

rebuttable presumption, 131–136
referrals, 52
respondeat superior doctrine, 80, 92, 93
Restatement of Agency, Second, 81
retired partner, 6
  Formal Opinion 90-357, 29, 43–47
  Of Counsel agreement, 166–167
retirement, mandatory, 5n
retirement planning, 172–174
revolving door, 141
Rossignol, Kenneth, 95–100

screening, 142–143
second careers, 4–5, 47–48
senior attorney, 7
  Formal Opinion 90-357, 29–30, 49–51
shared confidences, 130–137
  Chinese wall defense, 136–137
  former affiliates: rebuttable presumption, 131–136
  present affiliates: irrebuttable presumption, 130–131
Sherman Act, 150
single case, lawyer associated in, 51–52
social security taxes, 84–85, 170, 172–173
solicitation, 148–149, 153, 159–164. *See also* advertising
  by direct mail, 154
  ethics rules governing, 157–159
Special Counsel, 164
specialization areas, listing on letterhead, 163–164
specialty counsel, 34–35, 74
Staron, Elzbieta, 100–101
Staron, Mariuz, 100–101
status, in Of Counsel agreement, 189–191
Steinbrenner, George M., Jr., 5
substantial relationship test, 121–122, 135–136

taxation, 84–85
  advantages of independent contractor status, 169–172
  business deductions, 84
  and Of Counsel as organizational structure, 184
  payroll taxes, 172–173
  social security taxes, 84–85, 170, 172–173, 174
terminate, right to, 86, 200
Thelander, Robert C., 100–101
Time Warner, Inc., 5
title, in Of Counsel agreement, 189–191
tort liability, 83, 94
Townsend, Yosha, Cline & Price, 9–12, 110–111
Trade Resolve, 139–141
trade secrets, protection of, 168
Turning Points (Cain), 4–5

Uniform Partnership Act, 41n, 108

vicarious liability in tort, 93

Wabash National Corporation, 9–12
Watson Farley & Williams, 139–141
Weiner, John S., 95–100
Weinstein, Sheldon G., 100–101
Weisner, William W., 7
witness, lawyer as, 143–145
wrongful discharge, 86

Yosha, Louis Buddy, 9–12

Zuller & Bondy, 102

ABOUT THE AUTHORS

HAROLD G. WREN has been Of Counsel to the law firm of Voyles & Johnson, P.S.C., Louisville, Kentucky, since 1991. He holds his A.B. and LL.B. from Columbia, and his J.S.D. from Yale. He first practiced with Willkie Farr & Gallagher of New York, and then entered the academic world, where he was Dean of three law schools, and a teacher at four others. His books include *Creative Estate Planning* (1970) and *Tax Aspects of Marital Dissolution* (with Leon Gabinet) (2d ed. 1997). He is a past Chair of the Senior Lawyers Division of the American Bar Association.

BEVERLY J. GLASCOCK is a nurse attorney with the law firm of Dinsmore & Shohl, LLP, in Louisville, Kentucky, where her practice concentrates on medical malpractice defense and health care law. She advises clients in areas relating to risk management, medical record issues, hospital recordkeeping, and medical device regulations, and has spoken extensively to health care and hospital risk-management groups concerning medical records release and recordkeeping issues. Ms. Glascock is a graduate of Indiana University (1979) and the University of Louisville School of Law (magna cum laude, 1990).